THE NOTABLE
ELEMENTS OF SUCCESS

THE NOTABLE ELEMENTS OF SUCCESS

THE BEST POSSIBLE WAYS TO ENHANCE YOUR PURPOSE AND ENRICH YOUR LIFE

Charles Ajero

This book may be purchased in bulk for educational purposes; business profits; and sales, marketing, and promotion. It also may be purchased for personal development, practice-based training, and building important relationships. For information regarding special discounts for bulk purchases, please visit the book's eStore at www.CreateSpace.com/5643365.

Copyright © 2016 by Charles Ajero.
ISBN: 0997129301
ISBN 13: 9780997129304
Library of Congress Control Number: **2016901180**
Oakland, Ca

DEDICATION

This book is dedicated to remember and honor my father because everything that's worth seeking is worth remembering. Dr. Stephen Ajero was a compassionate father who believed in unity, peace, and love and died in the course of compassion, sympathy, and a labor of love, caring for others. As a result of this, I have seen the miraculous work of God working in me.

I also dedicate this book to the most powerful intuition within you—your power to know what reason cannot comprehend—and to all those who help you discover your true self and share and enjoy its magic and vital forces emancipating within you and clearing the way to life.

Most of all, I dedicate this to myself and God within me, and also in remembrance, love, and appreciation for my father, and my mother, Mrs. Comfort Ajero.

CONTENTS

ACKNOWLEDGMENTS

S triving to achieve an enduring life is a more valuable endeavor than living a life without purpose, meaning, and direction. It requires years of continuous development, struggle, and self-discipline to build and embody the essence of life and acquire the intellectual knowledge to achieve a lifetime of success and good relationships.

I am so grateful for the inspiration, passion, love, vitality, and wisdom of the passionate and inspiring thinkers and doers of our time who shaped the modern world of today, thereby encouraging capable young folks to continue the work to make a better world. These people hold the ultimate truth, which is that all men and women are created equal and endowed by their Creator with natural rights to live and enjoy more life and happiness and to achieve more success. They also hold the principal sources of all knowledge and the roots of all wisdom and understanding because they believe they are part and parcel of their Creator. So I believe too, and as a result, I am serving the same uniqueness to make the world a better place.

Therefore, I am grateful for all the people who are inspiring success and making the world a better place to live and breed more value. Most important, I am grateful for God for sustaining, encouraging, and maintaining my passion to do greater things in life and to continuously pursue greatness and excellence, and for helping me keep a mindful sense of gratitude. I am also grateful for God for his endless protection and guidance, for his divine providence and infinite wisdom, for bringing us desirable results, and for promoting our well-being and growing the future of awesomeness.

By this reckoning, and as a result of my own personal experience, I consider all the mindful work of God to be a symbolic truth, which of course I encourage every man and woman to believe and abide by because it enhances your mind and enriches your heart. This is one of the reasons I am expressing my desire, appreciation, and gratitude to the one and only God, who is and who will always be.

PREFACE

The world of business commerce has grown significantly bigger and better since organizations started using and believing in *The Notable Elements of Success.* Business is much better, stronger, bigger, and much more demanding. The way of doing business has changed dramatically and improved significantly. The world of commerce has been altered from an old-age pattern of thought into a new, transformational one. This has become the age of profitable innovation and the ultimate edge of consciousness with all of its profound understanding.

These profound changes in business concepts and paradigm shifts in belief systems have brought high profits in the marketplace, grown careers, and produced better results. So if you want to achieve your greatest potential and conquer your biggest fears, you must effectively use the knowledge-based innovation systems of *The Notable Elements of Success,* which governs the business results you seek. Remember, your business success lies in your mental power and strength of character, which are what feed real economic growth, expand economic opportunities that foster business success, and bring you a far more expansive economic vision that will enhance multiple lives.

INTRODUCTION

This book provides you the most comprehensive ingredients of success; the best possible ways to live a better life and achieve a greater future; and the very best ways to grow your business, increase profits, and build solid and lasting relationships. Allow me to illustrate how these valuable tools of success are connected and why they are critical components of success.

As you may already know, learning through creative intelligence is the very best thing you can do to better your life and greatly enhance your purpose. Experiencing life with the very best people, who are known as the capable folks, will help you eventually get the best out of each day. Therefore, capable folks are one of the most valuable components of success. They are the ones who shape the modern world with their self-conscious, intelligent minds, and self-motivational attitudes. They capture attention and produce multiple results. It's crucial to remember that without motivation, these people couldn't have achieved success and therefore would not be capable of performing and living better, so motivation is the driving force and the key to successful living.

When you are driven by motivation through a constructive mental direction, you can do wonders, perform better, and most important, increase your power and strength. So a constructive mental direction plays a critical role in life as well as in business success. Without a constructive mental direction, you cannot succeed in business because it shapes a brilliant business mind that serves all profitable innovation and supports the most dynamic life. A brilliant business mind is the key to success in life and in business.

However, you need appreciable value to continuously grow in business and increase in power. Appreciable value plays a crucial role in life as well as in business and eventually helps you develop important relationships and produce an abundance of values. Abundance is the power that drives every successful life, so it is a critical ingredient of success.

Of course, this all comes from effective communication, which is the glue that binds life together and a necessary tool for success. Effective communication enhances useful knowledge and balances life because without it, there would be no business and no life. Useful knowledge is a prerequisite to success, which can be achieved by enhancing and maintaining a reasonable self-confidence.

This book is about helping you achieve more success and find long-lasting professional relationships with quality colleagues. Success begins with good performances and with a clear vision. This book is about building value and creating opportunities to advance, learn, grow, and develop in new ways; acquire new knowledge; achieve more success; and live more life with less stress. It's important to remember that learning is a key aspect of building a strong business plan and creating real, powerful, and lasting change. Building trust creates value that fuels passion and allows you to enjoy the ride, which creates exciting results in all arenas of life.

CHAPTER 1

CREATIVE INTELLIGENCE

The key to growth is the introduction of higher
dimensions of consciousness into our awareness.
—LAO TZU

We all have different dreams, careers, plans, and goals in life, but our main goal is to succeed and enjoy a better life and a great future. Creative intelligence will greatly help us achieve that because it's a potent force that harnesses, connects, and inspires. It's a creative power that lies in the very heart and soul of our blessings and in the center of our attractions, as well as in the root of all manifestations. Creative intelligence is necessary for all intelligent life and medium of expression, for all creative insights, for all powerful intuition, intellect, and emotions that are guiding positive actions. It supports the creative power of useful knowledge, profound understanding and creative wisdom and allows all realities of life to be properly established and developed.

The transcendent aspect of absolute truth underlies all objective planes of useful knowledge and higher levels of understanding. This means that creative intelligence lies at the very seat of conscious action, the storehouse of collective consciousness, and the powerhouse of collective wisdom and awareness. This justifies why it's the glue that holds together our sound thoughts, reason, and logical insights.

The absolute truth exists at the permanent seat of memory, creative understanding, and rational thinking and can lead us to greater happiness, satisfaction, and fulfillment, which can eventually help us foster a real, dependable, and lasting knowledge that supports our purposes and guides our lives. It is the conscious pilot of the mind, the body, and spirit, the conscious pilot of the spirit of enthusiasm, the spirit of passion, motivation, and inspiration that rules our lives and directs our goals. Our inspiring goals are at the very center of our positive habits, sound thoughts, and feelings and create a stream of positive experiences that will certainly help us add more value to our lives and modify our belief systems.

Creative intelligence comes from a sound mind that sparks positive actions and produces positive results. It's a conscious spirit that expresses itself through creativity and through the positive spirit of truth that consciously waits for the right condition to unfold itself and manifest its inherent powers to satisfy your purposes in life. Creative intelligence is a logical awareness of the mind and a rational embodiment of truth that supports all facts. It serves as the power that enables us to peacefully enter other mind-sets; successfully relate with them; and explore interests, useful knowledge, skills, and values.

Exploring values and beliefs that are important to you is the best strategy for living a positive life because knowing your interests, skills, and values plays a critical role in helping you discover and develop important relationships and appreciate life more. It helps you understand the qualities in life that guide all successful relationships and all successful businesses. All potential values should be based on creative intelligence, and a lack of them turns life into a breeding ground for fear of failure, poverty, pain, worry, suffering, misery, fear, and self-doubt, which all feed procrastination and leave you feeling overwhelmed, incompetent, or even stupid.

When this occurs, you become incompetent and unable to meet demands. You may even lose interest and self-motivation because of feelings of inadequacy, lack of self-confidence, and low self-esteem. But conscious meditation and contemplation can put you in a resourceful state, help you increase your emotional health, and improve your psychological well-being. It also helps you exist in the present moment and consciously relax your body and mind, which eventually enhances intuition and increases emotional intelligence.

This is exactly what you need to stay awake and present during timeless moments of truth. So if you want to live a full, authentic life, you need creative intelligence to make positive things happen. Creative intelligence is the only logical way of thinking and creates a positive tendency for success and personal growth. It is perhaps the only active filter that retains and supplies positive thoughts, constructive ideas, and realistic goals and plans and brings you effective results. Basically, it filters useful information, valuable feedback, and positive thoughts from those that are not useful. It is guided by conscious observation, which rules all of our minds and hearts.

When you develop a practical, dynamic, and effective discipline, you will have a conscious, intelligent mind. So if you're truly seeking to succeed in life, you should remember that a consciously repeated practice and discipline will transform into creative intelligence and useful skills, which support a diligent disposition of the mind, body, and spirit and enriches your sense of self-confidence. Furthermore, it will help you cultivate value that will certainly enhance your sense of purpose. When you repeatedly practice movements in a deliberate way, you become good at those movements because the mind and body are interconnected and interrelated. Creative intelligence gives you conscious control of a mindful action that engages the heart, drives the mind, and delivers quality results. Basically, you should be very aware that conscious exercise increases your overall health and eventually helps you develop your strength and flexibility in all aspects of life. Let your mind- and body-awareness practices involve bringing your consciousness into the present moment, focusing on now, and consciously moving your body and living in the present moment. This will increase your energy level, improve your emotional health, and even provide you an active spirit of enthusiasm that will guide your soul and inspire your mind for better action and greater purpose.

Obviously, we all have different goals, but we all want to succeed and enjoy better lives, and creative intelligence enables us to achieve that.

It helps us make better choices and prompt decisions and ultimately shapes our perceptions so we can have deeper thoughts, develop higher cognitive concepts, and improve our analytical judgments. Most important, it gives us the freedom of self-expression; the freedom of choice; and the independent initiative of judgment, self-discovery, and spontaneous action. Certainly, it provides us the opportunity to embrace and accept our innate natures, and ultimately it gives us the power to accept and develop our inherent abilities to fulfill our hearts' desires and serve our highest good.

Creative intelligence serves as source of inspiration, motivation, courage, passion, and guidance because it produces a conscious body and a deeper sense of awareness. This, in turn, deepens our sense of perception and enhances our sense of purpose, which helps us produce a higher intelligence. This creates a mental map that is endowed with higher powers, inner truths, intuitive awareness, creative imagination, and wisdom from which we receive the intuitive messages that spark positive actions in our businesses and relationships that bring us positive results.

Now you can see that creative intelligence is that aspect of body awareness that strengthens the center of your emotional health and psychological well-being, or perhaps that part of the mind that determines all the positive results that happen in your life. If you can feel the mind and sense the body, you will certainly realize that both are interrelated and therefore work together to shape intellect and enhance emotional intelligence. By increasing your body awareness and using that to increase your energy level, you can fuel your daily life with renewed enthusiasm. This is the way to enhance the power that guides all the basic truths about being unique. This helps the body and mind connection and increases concentration, helping you focus on the present moment, where you can balance your emotions and respond to life promptly and act effectively.

When you center the mind, you can consciously respond to life because focusing on the present moment gives you access to the intuition that deepens your knowledge and helps you make good choices. It serves as a deeper consciousness, as a unified field of useful knowledge and creative wisdom, and even as a unified field of purpose that provides you with a deeper sense of understanding and a reverential interest and attentiveness. In addition, it promotes a higher level of consciousness and a greater degree of intelligence that yields multiple returns. It actually helps you stimulate positive energies that produce better seeds of creative thinking and constructive actions that will continue to provide you desirable results. Furthermore, it gives you more insight, peace, and clarity of mind and heart, which greatly serves the best spirit of passion, courage, and motivation. Eventually it will enhance your clarity of purpose, which in turn provides you a much more desirable state of well-being.

If you can concentrate and focus in the present moment, you will certainly enhance your well-being and enrich your purpose. If you observe carefully, you will discover that extraordinary people concentrate and focus in the present moment to achieve their purposes. You will equally discover that they are centered and align their minds and prioritize their goals to accomplish all their purposes. Often you can see that an extraordinary person has a self-revelation of truth, a self-realization of reality, a self-acknowledgment of fact, or a self-recognition of oneness with the infinite mind. Creative intelligence unfolds the truth, manifests the realities of the future, and ultimately provides you guidance for future needs that may open a larger window of opportunity with great expectations to achieve the economic freedom, self-sufficiency, and peace of mind you desire.

This is the pinnacle of transformational change, the evolution of mind, and the transcendental power of knowledge. That's critical to an individual's economic freedom, self-enhancement, and well-being. It will and can even broaden the horizons of the best possible skills, which is one of the most essential building blocks of success, prosperity, and health and a vital element of the mind–body connection that enriches your life purpose. The most important thing to note is that education builds confidence and self-reliance and is the source of our infinite supply of intelligence and the means by which we influence others.

The future is better than you think and even wider than you can imagine. Creative intelligence will provide you the divine light, the spiritual eye, and the mental vision through which the inner eye sees clearly so you can act effectively. It also provides you the eternal light to embrace spiritual realities, to understand divine knowledge, and to embody intuitive wisdom that will enable you to see the wholeness of truth and achieve a profound understanding of life. It's the power that leads to every great success. The strength that comes from unity and orderliness also provides peace of mind, energy, passion, vitality, that rejuvenates the pure spirit of freedom. Another exciting thing to know is that creative intelligence provides you divine inspiration and motivation, the ultimate light by which humankind knows the divine truths and acknowledges divine purposes.

When you plug life into creative intelligence, life will become greater than what you see now because creative intelligence provides you all the art of ecstasy and dynamic meditation. Because it's the mirror of the mind for problem solving, the reflection of the heart for dealing with situations, and enjoying real life. In one sense, this shows that creative intelligence is a synthetic understanding, an intuitive perception, and the spiritual realization and revelation of all the truths that will govern your life. Here you begin to feel more centered and more creative in daily life and experience a higher state of consciousness. A science of fertile knowledge and a fruitful intelligence will provide you a higher level of sensitivity and a greater sense of purpose. Then you can better understand why it represents spiritual unity and the light of the world— a unity of peace and harmony, a reflection of wisdom, and a mirror of intelligence that supports your life, enhances your purposes, and enriches your state of being. In addition, it purifies your mind, refines your heart, and gives you eternal happiness. It also gives you an eternal peace that provides you with an indispensable creative innovation.

So living in creative intelligence is what you need and want because it provides you the eternal attribute of nobility, a receptacle for divine creation, and a cognitive capacity for artistic vision that generates the essence of new spirits, new souls, and new bodies that can provide you better opportunities in all your daily endeavors. Remember, your best days are ahead.

But you should also remember that effective action is what determines results; inspires the spirit of love, courage, and passion; and then becomes the mother of eternity and creativity and the father of orderliness, purpose, and productivity. That comes with a clear sense of gratitude and appreciation, a cognitive state of awareness, a higher realm of consciousness, and a new and greater purpose of existence that will truly captivate your heart and enhance your mind. Because as a good soil is measured by its fertility, creative intelligence is measured by value and awareness of sensations. All of this proves that nature has substantial evidence that shows why creative intelligence is a constructive mind-set that grows with the awareness of the body and then becomes the ultimate power that helps you discover the secrets of all creation.

When you focus on success, creative intelligence becomes a powerful force of attraction; the birthplace of all truths; the source of all knowledge; and the pinnacle of all positive, powerful, and lasting success. It's also a powerful force that draws value toward you, enhancing dynamic, authentic, and enduring relationships. Because it is an effective way of enhancing and attracting value and drawing profitable businesspeople.

I guarantee you that creative intelligence makes life rich and meaningful because it serves our hearts' deepest desires. When we are able to align with our values, it will result in a collective wisdom, a unified power of purpose, and creative energy—a vital life force that moves through us and around us, drawing positive results and serving as the fertile field of all inspiration, all motivation, all passion, and all active dreams and goals in life. Therefore, it's the science of positive thinking and sound feeling, which comes through effective communication that sparks productive actions to greatly enhance our lives, refine our senses, and enrich our well-being. Creative intelligence is the science of modernization, the act of creation, the science of newness and innovation, and the ultimate legend of productivity. It grows the creative powers of the mind and brings us positive, dynamic, and lasting change.

Come rain or come sunshine, creative intelligence is the refinery for the mind–body conversation. It is the filtering power that discovers and shapes the truth, guards the truth, and properly links the truth to emotion, intellect, and intuition. It is the agency of thoughts and is our inner thinker, creator, observer, builder, developer, and prolific producer. This means that it can benefit anyone who reasons in a certain way to produce certain results, devotes much time to positive thoughts, or has a well-developed faculty for thinking. It fosters the self-contemplation of intelligence, the self-discovery of truths that can serve as the power of self-acceptance and the power of empathy that comes from deep listening and profound understanding. All of this shows why it's the coordinator of all senses, all sound thoughts, and all positive feelings that support active emotions. All of the facts justify the reasons it serves as the main source of wisdom; the true manifesto of knowledge; the keen observer of consciousness; and the collective faculty of mind, body and spirit. This further explains why it's an intellectual property of the mind that enhances the spirit of success; the spirit of work and passion; and the overall spirit of life, passion, and motivation.

Obviously, all this will be the turning point of intelligence and wisdom, and ultimately it will be the turning point of prosperity consciousness, success consciousness, and health consciousness. Certainly, it will be the viewing point of creative awareness, conscious alertness, keen observation, and profound understanding. Creative intelligence is a powerful guide for the soul, the active camera that watches the mind and projects positive visual pictures as signs of active duty that allow us to see clearly, act effectively, and get quality results. Perhaps it is even the center of positive thinking that presents a different core set of psychological symptoms of quality of life that will greatly serve and support our utmost good and possibly help us use the best of our abilities, powers, and resources to the greatest possible degree to reach the highest attainable goals. This is the highest degree of power that will ultimately transform unlimited potential into material reality and translate all creative vision into practical value. That's why it gives us the ability to shape our own futures, provides us guidance from within, and ultimately increases our responsiveness and receptivity. It represents the greatest possible power to absorb anything, use it in some way, and hold the divine blessings that creative intelligence showers upon us.

When we are ready and willing to accept observable reality, then our creative wisdom and understanding will play out well at profounder levels of awareness, deepening our knowledge, actively refining our experiences, enhancing our memories, and expanding our consciousness. Properly improving our subjective sense of well-being will ultimately empower us to achieve greater success and then attain a higher degree of control that will help us enjoy unlimited potential future and the endless potential and unlimited possibilities of intelligent life.

That will deepen our consciousness, helping us consciously relax our bodies, minds, hearts, and emotions and increasing our energy levels to fuel our daily lives. All of this shows that enhancing our strong emotions and increasing body awareness can lead to a deeper understanding of doing what we truly love. This is the cornerstone of having abundance in our lives. Creating the basis for being awake and present in the moment will certainly help us live full, authentic, and dynamic lives. We all need to advance into a much better future. That's why we need creative intelligence to provide us with infinite, potential possibilities that will continue to enhance and enrich our lives and provide us much more sustainable futures. We all need to satisfy our deepest desires and thereby live quality lives. Creative intelligence will help us accomplish all that, because it's a mental quality that guards all positive experiences and feedback and basically becomes an exciting journey to positivity that can support a living consciousness and healing condition of all life. We all desire and deserve a synthetic system of understanding, a synthetic system of knowing, and a natural way of refining our skills and enriching our talents that will serve our life purposes.

That will help us get much more value out of life, find our passion in life, and discover our real life purposes and the core life intentions that can help us move with greater focus and clarity. That's why we need creative intelligence—it represents a universal truth and helps us take the reins on our life journeys. It's a profound system of cultivating consciousness, harvesting rich minds, and enriching others' lives. It helps us explore broader meaning and make smarter choices that keep us moving forward in life, trusting our purposes, and providing opportunities for us to grow into our best selves. All of this serves as one of the greatest reasons why it's a creative power that generates more creative ideas, sparks more creative thinking, boosts high energy production, and enhances the ability to remember things that can leverage our careers by sparking a positive spirit of passion and enthusiasm. This in turn will continue to enhance more creative powers that are flowing with quality ideas that generate positive feelings, which are receiving all that life has to offer. This positive feeling allows us to express ourselves, helps us get what we want, and eventually helps us advance our lives because it is an adventure for curious minds and receptive hearts. It's great if we can express sound thoughts with artistic, creative vision that expresses our real spirit and true character. This, of course, must come forth from an inner consciousness and ultimately from our inner sense of purpose.

As we gain a unique sense of purpose living and working in a positive environment, we will be better able to experience the changes in life with inner peace, great joy, and higher-quality health because creative intelligence works best in a well-balanced state of mind and properly relaxed state of well-being. It also works effectively among reliable emotions and a confident spirit. It ultimately works best in a positive environment with favorable conditions.

Creative intelligence is necessary for the development of useful skills, business creation and personal growth, bringing value, for consciously streaming movements of creative innovation. It also helps us discover effective strategies for creative thinking and profitable innovations that will serve both big and small businesses. Perhaps it will become the most exciting experience to be gained on our financial journeys because it will help us take the reins in life. This is an adventure for curious minds and receptive hearts, and we all know that we can achieve success by embodying useful knowledge, which will help us live wisely; adjust our attitudes, behaviors, and feelings; discipline our minds; and ultimately live better lives.

We also know that we can grow by eliminating our fears and resolving our inner conflicts, our mental disharmony, our self-doubt, and our self-sabotaging behavior. When this happens, creative intelligence will give us the power to overcome temptation, subdue frustration, and even help us conquer fear of rejection, poverty, anxiety, and worry. It also will help us defeat self-doubt and procrastination that kills our ambitions, goals, and plans in life.

Creative intelligence helps us develop an action plan to enhance our life skills, have greater purpose, and better understand why we are here and what we are working to achieve. Setting a clear goal gives our lives direction and boosts our motivation, revealing a clear conception of value and a strong conviction of truth that supports our unique talents and guides our unique purposes. Creative intelligence refines our beliefs and convictions in life and properly stimulates our minds to produce more powerful, more inspiring beliefs that can support our lives and enhance our well-being.

Positive thoughts and affirmations can help us attain a variety of health benefits, including mental, emotional, physical, and spiritual well-being. We can use these affirmations to build important relationships and attract more profitable outcomes. This shows how almost every significant breakthrough in the field of creative endeavor comes through creative intelligence because it cultivates mental powers and activates inner strengths through which all sound ideas are formed to control and direct our life forces. It's the checkpoint of the mind, the clearinghouse for awareness and knowledge, and the source of logical reasoning and understanding of the natural law that governs our conscious bodies and regulates our creative minds to properly serve and actively support our well-being.

This gives us the faith and stability to experience life's challenges, enhance our skills, and achieve the goals that are most important to us, making us truly happy, satisfied, and fulfilled in our lives. That's why I believe in creative intelligence—I have patiently observed and strongly perceived that this great power lifts people from poverty to success, from fear to courage, and from sickness to health. Think of Helen Keller, Nelson Mandela, Martin Luther King Jr, Steve Jobs, Barack Obama, Oprah Winfrey. They all have mental power and strength to shape their destinies and reach their goals. Obviously, I believe in creative intelligence because it's a rational way of thinking and a constructive action that helps us live up to our highest values. It's an inner quality that unfolds as we learn to trust our deepest experiences. It's also a constructive mental attitude that reveals itself through sound thoughts and positive feelings, which guard and support our well-being. As we learn to think constructively and act effectively, we will see why it's a positive mental disposition, representation, and reflection—a mental reflection of sound thought, positive feeling, and action that produces an unquestionable mental state of balance and inner harmony that fits a unique purpose.

Creative intelligence is how we can get the best from life and fulfill our unique purposes. I believe in it because we are born to fulfill our unique purposes to reach our unique destinies. We can understand and apply our hearts to wisdom, producing meaning and creating pathways to a better life. That enhances our core values, shapes our perceptions, and influences our belief systems. When it comes to learning, creative intelligence enables us to turn up the light of consciousness and acquire useful skills, positive experiences, and valuable feedback. In addition, it helps us have insight, sound thoughts, and practical ideas that can enhance our minds and enrich our hearts. As we learn and believe, it is important to remember that we have gained useful knowledge in the form of a sense of perspective understanding and have acquired insights in the nature of human knowledge. This marks the reasons for learning and perhaps reveals why, when it comes to learning, we don't have enough patience to deeply understand the core concepts of the true nature of things if we lack creative intelligence.

As we begin to think constructively and believe profoundly, we will certainly understand things at higher levels because creative intelligence will digest information to its highest good and to its deepest meaning, which will give us the best outcome. In addition, it will give us positive energy to do greater things in life. Finally, it will satisfy our deepest value and support our innermost convictions, which can open the doors for more and more success.

Is that not what we want for our futures? We need creative intelligence to make better things happen in life. We need creative intelligence to live a life that is full of meaning and purpose, the life we are striving for and longing to achieve. Creative intelligence is a potent force, a deep exploration of intuitive wisdom and a profound understanding of self. The key to understanding the self requires that we understand its basic emotional needs and then use these needs to satisfy and fulfill our lives. If we trust and believe in creative intelligence, it will become the power that charges our emotions, sparks smart choices, and grows by investing our energies in a single purpose. This is essential to the mental health necessary to sustain our emotional well-being. As we start to explore the core emotions of the heart, our strong emotions can put us in a state of awareness, in a deep sense of perception, and help us live in a realm of mindfulness that will provide us with a mental map and intuitive guidance. It will also put us in a state of inner harmony that will ultimately provide us a unified field of consciousness.

Therefore, the ultimate joyride to success comes from an inner atmosphere of truth, love, peace, and harmony in daily life. To achieve peace and harmony, we must strive to build strong and lasting relationships that are guarded by creative intelligence; without it, there can be no lasting love, no lasting peace, no harmony, and no happiness. So to build real and lasting relationships and enjoy successful lives, it's critical to enhance and link important relationships and use our imaginations, intuitions, and intellects in harmony to produce powerful results. Creative intelligence helps us unify our sensibilities, intuitions, and imaginations and properly aligns our senses of cognition and perception to support a singularity of purpose.

Creative intelligence is endowed with a well-refined sense of humor that is characterized by charm, uniqueness, and quality that deepens our consciousness and enhances our artistic vision, creative authenticity, and our senses of perception and intuition. That will certainly show a well-bred feeling, a properly purified sense of imagination that creates infinite value and brings people from every conceivable walk of life to share a common aspiration to do better and achieve greater goals. This is one of the very important elements of success and a critical tool for creating our lives in a rich and satisfying way. When we believe that we should be something other than who we are, we create an image of who we expect to be and eventually change. As we change, we are enhanced with rational minds and endowed with the higher power of intuitive cognition, as well as greater awareness, spiritual and intuitive perception, foresight, and wisdom. This is the most helpful approach to understanding the underlying experience of the heart, mind, and body. When we believe in conscious awareness, we will unfold our infinite potential resources and display our infinite values that come with perceptive power, clearness of truth, a clear vision, and creative insights. This is one of the reasons that creative intelligence produces rhythms and melodies of heart that enable dormant powers to awaken and open their doors to breathe and breed more life, produce better results, and enjoy more success.

It's important to know that whatever passes through the doors of the conscious mind rules over us and determines the quality of our lives. Therefore, it's important to enhance creative intelligence to guide our destinies. Because creative intelligence is blessed with the spirit of a sound mind, which is created to support our present existence, it helps us live in the present moment with the power of now. We need to enhance our analytical minds using the power of now because there is no better time than the present moment. This allows us to harness the full potential of the present moment and use it to guide our emotional well-being, as well as our spiritual enlightenment. That in turn encourages a healthy, happy lifestyle that provides a clear understanding of the true nature of things and opens up new gateways to success. Creative intelligence is the key that unlocks the doors of perception that lead us to a more fulfilling and more profitable life.

We can enhance creative intelligence to provide us active memories and good emotional health, allowing it to become the conscious driver and the intelligent pilot that run our lives and determine our destinies using a higher level of consciousness and wisdom. That gives us the ability to consciously control our lives and fully exercise our freedom by empowering us to create our own realities, experience our own small worlds, and live our lives in our own ways.

Creative intelligence supports our evolution toward peace, love, and unity because it's a synthetic symbol of success, progress, happiness, and triumphant joy, as well as a synthetic power that controls and directs our perception and expands our beliefs to enhance our lives and enrich our purposes. It also helps us increase our fields of awareness, creative insights, and conscious wisdom.

It's crucial to know that the sole purpose of creative intelligence is to protect and guide our spirits, bodies, and minds and then promote our senses of humor, creativity, and perseverance. We should believe all the truths about creative intelligence because the logical and analytical mind is what controls our dreams and regulates our goals. All of this shows why it's the captain of our ships of success and the conscious pilot of our healthy and happy lifestyles. It will certainly provide us a reasonable direction and a constructive arrival.

It is wise to adopt and establish a constructive dissemination of information and implementation of knowledge. This is a constructive approach to develop effective strategies to deal with life because our techniques play a vital role in building our economic health and future needs. As long as we sharpen conscious awareness and believe in creative intelligence, we will prosper in life because creative intelligence plays a critical role in shaping the future. A logical, analytical mind is the basic building block for action, a strong foundation for a good life, and a critical determinant factor of long-term well-being. It is also the powerhouse of consciousness, wisdom, and understanding—the concepts that help us grasp useful knowledge and experience all the underlying factors of life.

As long as we are using our minds constructively, they will serve us effectively because they're conscious minds that are clear in meaning and in action. Therefore, creative intelligence is an undeniable spirit and an unmistakable intelligence that enhances our lives and enriches our well-being.

When you think constructively and look closely at people who have attained success, you will see that they all believe in creative intelligence because it's the inner power and strength that guides their purposes. If you can form a similar belief system, your life will change because positive habits can change the direction of your life. This will change your life in more ways than you can imagine because creative intelligence is a whole new way to better your life. It comes from the perceptive abilities of the mind, heart, and body that represent significant values. Your sensory acuity and sound reasoning are what bring you the essence and the meaning of life. Ultimately, a greater sense of reality will result from the breakthrough created by your clear thinking and thorough analysis of your actions. In turn, that will arouse all the senses from your inner mind, heart, and body and provide you with excellent results.

You will communicate value to attract and retain important relationships and take advantage of all the value to build the future and get benefits. By knowing what others value and giving them more of what they value, you can increase and maintain the value of your important relationships and also attract new ones. This is a whole new paradigm-shifting breakthrough that will forever alter the way you think and act. Creative intelligence will enable you to take advantage of opportunities and help you build trust, live in trust, and benefit from trust. It will also help you build value, live in value, and take advantage of value to attract even more value.

When you learn to value yourself, take control of your feelings, and guide your emotions, your best self and best efforts will certainly come forth. Creative intelligence is the power that grows with flexible knowledge, with an adjustable and adaptable mind, and with patience, and it will support all your basic needs in life and business. By helping you attract a consistent stream of high-quality prospects, creative intelligence will get you what you want by helping others get what they want. This is the greatest power that arises from creative thinking and acting. It improves your standard of living, increases your level of understanding, and eventually expands your creative vision that serves your greatest desire and supports your best needs.

Creative intelligence increases your receptive power, enhances your responsive mind, and provides you the highest and broadest sense of expression of self-reliance, self-determination, and self-confidence so you can attract more prospects by providing them more value. You can get what you want and grow in power and influence because more power comes from a well-heightened sense of awareness and a creative imagination.

All this explains why creative intelligence creates an inner vitality, inner power, and practical wisdom that produce a cooperative association of positive senses and the elements of a comprehensive strategy, interest, and undivided attention. So if you're striving for a better life, you should know that it will provide you the best and clearest images of thought that will communicate the best possible meaning and bring you much clearer purpose and the best possible answers. You can advance into a better future because creative intelligence inspires efficiency, effectiveness, and productivity in any calling. It's the power that shines the light of awareness, brightens the light of consciousness, and ignites the fuel of desire that sparks positive actions and brings multiple returns.

Creative intelligence is a transparent spirit that flows from a positive mental action or a constructive channel of thought that illuminates knowledge. It a potential power that draws spiritual energies, enhances creative efforts, and converts potential energies into material blessings. A functional mind, a representational wisdom, and an excellent execution of intelligence are the most widely recognized marks of excellence in the field of knowledge. They are the ultimate sources of knowledge that is equipped with the right insights needed to execute actions with highly measurable positive results.

Practicing creative intelligence allows you to continuously improve your daily performance and helps you strive to be the best you can be in everything you do. When it comes to knowledge, creative intelligence is the ultimate source of inspiration, motivation, passion, and action that drives you to pursue excellence and achieve greatness. When you pursue greatness, you pursue your vision for excellence. As far as useful knowledge is concerned, there can be no permanent success, happiness, or healthy life without a permanent and steady consciousness. This means that creative intelligence provides you a steady stream of profitability and innovation and a constant flow of business that brings you a constant flood of good and an inpouring of blessings.

To have creative intelligence and experience life is to have operational excellence in all of your business endeavors, and to have operational excellence in business, you must have a potent competitive weapon. That's why creative intelligence is at the core of business operational excellence. When you realize that so many businesses are striving to improve their reach and connection with customer-based business innovation, you will see that creative intelligence requires having a rational mind and sound heart that believes in its intrinsic self, lives wisely in its inherent powers, and then ventures into the future for better life and for greater future.

So whether you're consciously thinking or not, something is happening within you and around you, and it needs to be recognized to unleash both the power to grow better and the resources to live wisely. Creative intelligence is a strong, positive, and lasting power that comes from a conscious spirit, a responsive body, and a receptive mind. Your mind is the mover and the doer, the river of destiny through which you can move your life to a greater length to achieve success. So you should expect to see some serious growth and some aggressive advancement in your business because it's a logically thinking and acting mind that effectively communicates and performs quality actions to help you generate positive returns. It's powerful to have a knowledge-based intelligence and a value-driven and profit-seeking mind that clearly represent the essence of uniqueness and serve the most significant and meaningful purposes.

When it comes to business, creative intelligence will enable you to build valuable rapport, help you exchange useful information, share positive feedback, and ultimately help you connect with valuable minds. It will give you a positive attitude of gratitude and appreciation of life. In addition, it will enable you to prevent negative situations rather than spending precious time resolving them. So as you think constructively and act effectively, creative intelligence will guard your mind and give you the power to prevent negative situations. It will help you preserve your values and enjoy life with less stress. Finally, it will provide you the ultimate ability to move with certainty, clarity, and intensity to achieve a specific goal.

This is the pinnacle of business success that will help you grow in wisdom and get extra value that will bring worthwhile changes in your personal life and in your important business relationships. It clears the road for a positive spirit and vibrant energy that will produce better results and yield greater returns in business.

You will gain a sense of how effectively and efficiently organizations are using available resources to generate profits or get business results using creative intelligence. The more you are able to direct your business intelligence toward business success, the more powerful and lasting value you can get. This is an integral element of life that shows that you have an intellectual sense of purpose, integrity, and value that can help you function better and ultimately help you perceive greater good. If you can think constructively and act wisely, you can advance into a better future and live a much better life. Creative intelligence enables you to harness your creative powers and helps you unleash your inner strengths to pursue greatness, excellence, or perfection.

Creative intelligence is a unique quality that highlights the inspiration behind success and brings about the changes that help you live a healthier, happier, and more productive life. For these reasons, we who seek greater success and better futures should know that creative intelligence grows in our minds when we set big goals and have realistic plans that guide us to achieve our dreams and purposes in life. When our minds grow logically, their processing abilities and data volumes grow as well, which boosts production levels, increases business intelligence, and inspires greater business performance and more effective management techniques. We can achieve our business goals and create an active focus that comes from undivided attention, which allows us to make a meaningful difference using our influence and investments when we define our goals and identify a clear way to attain them. Aspiring to our goals will greatly enhance our well-being and strengthen our sense of awareness, which then opens up a new way to observe and understand life. We will sincerely seek to live more wisely because we now have a richer sense of purpose and a heightened awareness that exists only within creative intelligence.

When it comes to meaningful purpose, creative intelligence provides us with a bright point of view and an effective means by which to apply our knowledge and wisdom. These are prerequisites for achieving goals and therefore require a centralized point of view, a synthetic point of understanding and distinguishing values, constructive thinking, and effective action. Only then can we produce logical, consistent results that improve our lives.

We all need to feel good and eventually get tangible results for our efforts. If we can expand our consciousness, together we can reach a place of undivided attention and interest, which creates a flawless action that produces quality results and ultimately helps us produce a roundtable of courage and wisdom that restores great hope, ignites passion, and sparks positive actions in the marketplace as well as in the workplace.

By growing our minds and expanding our consciousness, we can enrich our purposes so much that our purposes will serve and support our businesses, and our businesses will greatly enhance our well-being. There we will find our innermost peace, joy, and happiness in life, as well as our deepest comforts that will empower our spirits of passion, progress, and success. In addition, it will open more doors for profitable businesses and more windows of favorable opportunities to bring us even greater success and progress.

If we can live wisely in the potential possibility, practicality, and profitability of the mind, heart, and body, then creative intelligence is a perfect match for us because it goes hand in hand with life. Therefore, life flows with it and through it, giving us valuable results. That's why it's the main power that rules our lives, determines our futures, and governs our destinies. It's the center of wisdom, the center of intuitive awareness, and the soul of knowledge and profound understanding. It's the ultimate secret to success because it exists to enhance quality of life, guide important relationships, and get profitable results in business. We need to get rich and stay rich by using our minds diligently to enrich our purposes in life. This is one of the most important decisions we need to make to get rich and stay rich. We need to make it a priority and have a burning desire to become rich and use our conscious minds to make it happen in business and achieve success in life. The only way to become financially rich is to enhance our conscious minds. This is the most effective and proven way to become rich, successful, inspired, and energized in life. So it's the energy that fuels all positive lives and enhances all profitable businesses. It's the ultimate power that holds the key to the good life and unlocks the doors to freedom.

Creative intelligence is one of the most important aspect of the mind that clearly stands out amid rising and changing difficult situations because it's all active, authentic, and lasting life. That's why it's a vital force that fosters a wealth of knowledge and brings us vitality and freedom in life. This shows that success is in our own hands, and it comes through creative intelligence—a creative mentality; a perceptive power; and a congruity of mind, body, and spirit. It enables us to make finer distinctions and ultimately helps us make better choices that perfectly satisfy our inner longings in life and fulfill our deepest needs, desires, and expectations. And as we continue to journey through life, it will ultimately present to us a clear vision and a strong conviction about the future that our dreams can be achieved. If we strongly believe and abide in consciousness of it, it will help us accomplish all our purposes.

Because creative intelligence is a properly established mind and a well-fixed purpose with a realistic goal that comes from sound character, flexible personality, and useful knowledge, it gives us a clear picture of what we truly want to accomplish in life. We all long for and strive for creative intelligence because it's the power that allows a person to believe in his or her own mentality and in a classic sense of significant purposes and values. We can recognize great opportunities, take quality actions, and get effective results using our inner wisdom and intelligence.

We can all unleash our potential power, and strength because creative intelligence provides us a properly refined thought process, a simplified knowledge, and a clear understanding of life. It plays a critical role in creating meaning, shaping our values, enhancing a greater sense of purpose, and providing us with courageous spirits that take passionate action to get real and lasting quality results. With this in mind, we can all unravel the mysteries of life by living and operating in consciousness and wisdom, which are derived from thinking creatively and seeing clearly all of our good actions to bring us more quality life and sound feelings.

This is the grandest edge of innovation that's surrounded by plenty of goodness and bountiful values that should serve the best possible mind-set to support the most complete life. Creative intelligence actively lives in its intrinsic nature, effectively operates in its inherent powers, and greatly multiplies through the higher levels of understanding. As we face the need to grow in business, we will realize that every new innovation has shown that creative intelligence reveals itself through positive thinking, creative imagination, and intuitive wisdom. Furthermore, it reflects itself in a brilliant business mind, in clarity of purpose, and in congruity of spirit that clearly expresses itself through positive mental action and absolute purpose.

In the most profound sense, creative intelligence expresses itself in value, quality of character, mindful satisfaction, and fulfillment. It gets results according to its soundness of character and a concreteness of purpose that's in line with its desirable condition and state of being.

Creative intelligence is the positive energy that holds life, enhances our purposes, enriches our well-being, and ultimately expands our creative vision. It brings out all of our artistic vision and all of our inherent powers and strengths to produce better results. All of this explains why creative intelligence provides us a way to positively engage our hearts, minds, and bodies to serve a greater good. That certainly comes from a clear sense of perception; understanding; a steady flow of conscious awareness; and ultimately a positive spirit of enthusiasm, motivation, and passion.

With all this truth in mind, I guarantee you success and assure you progress if you can shine the light of knowledge. Then the death of fear of poverty becomes certain because creative intelligence gives birth to uniqueness of knowledge, wisdom, and understanding. It also gives birth to new and better opportunities that will bring you a better life. Most important, it gives you unlimited possibilities and infinite potential to achieve real and lasting results, which ultimately will provide you with endless opportunities and an abundance of blessings.

As long as you're in the right mind-set, you can increase the inflow of your power and strength and multiply the inpouring of blessings that reinforce your mind and strengthen your spirit. And as long as you believe in creative intelligence, it will enhance your mental vision and expand your creative awareness to bring you a perfect balance of mind, body, and spirit. In addition, it provides you an improved spirit to pursue excellence and unique skills that will greatly serve your best interests and support your highest good.

Because creative intelligence is a creative sense that gives birth to better possibilities, it also brings about new purposes and greater opportunities. It's important to remember that a good business venture can create something better in your life. If you can set better and higher goals, you can achieve better and greater results. It's a creative sense, which is a conscious spirit in action and in effect. This is why we are spirits that think and act on desirable conditions with meaningful purposes.

To all those who have desirable hearts and minds, I give to you creative intelligence because it's a guarding force and a sustaining power that you need to advance your meaningful purpose. It requires focus to grow and needs mental agility and inner strength to maintain its value and purposes. It gives you what you need, shows you how and where you need it because it's the vehicle that transports you from one point to another, and it leads you to an end and helps you accomplish all your desired aims.

Get ready to shine your consciousness because creative intelligence comes from a creative sense of logical mind, positive thinking, and right actions. It also comes from inner truths and transparency of heart, mind, and body. It's the sustaining power of knowledge and understanding. It enables you to grow spiritual power, develop mental faculties, and maintain emotional guidance based on wisdom and logical actions. As you become more aware through self-observation, you will better understand why creative intelligence is the oxygen of the mind and the source of the power of awareness. As you become more aware, you will see how it provides you the best ingredients for action and the best possible results. Energy flows through creative intelligence, and through it all good comes, all hope arrives, and all blessings appear; poverty, misery, pain, and difficulty will disappear.

Creative intelligence is the very essence of reality for living a conscious life. For all growth, it's the very essence of endless creativity value, and productivity, and it creates a sustainable future. For all enduring life, it acts as oxygen for positive life, a positive spirit of life force, and a conscious spirit of enthusiasm, bringing us the best intentions and serving the greatest good to bring us real and lasting change in our lives. It's the power source of all progressive innovation, profitable life, positive changes, and creative efforts. It's the power source of all prolific producers of high-quality ideas and of all abundance, economic freedom, and blessings.

We can all advance our lives and purposes because creative intelligence comes from mental reality, emotional value, and spiritual unity that serve our highest good and best interests. It also arises from mental quality that flows from within and around consciousness, inner harmony, and orderliness. To bring quality results, it ultimately becomes the positive energy and life force that guides our lives.

When we see the truths around us and feel the goodness within us, life will be better than we think. To bring about true evolutionary change in our lives, creative intelligence opens the doors of useful knowledge and then guards the doors of awareness and understanding, ultimately helping us sharpen our senses of perception to enrich our lives.

It's important to perceive and believe in the truth that is born within our abilities to think correctly and act effectively as much as possible. When it comes to truth, creative intelligence comes with creative drive and willpower that shapes realities. This explains why it's a self-inspiring spirit that uses self-controlling techniques and makes it a self-governing intelligence. It produces strength of character and ethical and moral values, as well as personal power and inner strength that ultimately provide us with sound ideas and a profound understanding of the concepts that can help us take more effective actions that serve and support people from all walks of life.

The principal goal of creative intelligence is love that flows from a transparent heart, the wholeness of mind and body, and perhaps from a good conscience and active faith. We can start to perceive and believe at all levels of understanding because faith serves as the unity of consciousness that illuminates our minds and hearts, or perhaps as the unity of all purposes that support our overall well-being. Therefore, it serves as our overall reservoir of peace, happiness, health, success, and progress. Faith is a conscious spirit that gives us a sense of purpose, security, confidence, and belonging. Even on the higher planes of thinking, it's a conscious power that exists in the wholeness of spirit and in the presence of the mind–heart–body connection.

This is true in all areas of development because when it comes to action, active faith evokes the same transparent action that comes from the indwelling spirit of passion, the sustaining spirit of goodness, and the self-knowing spirit of love and action. All this shows that it's a properly systematized and integrated knowledge and a well-organized intelligence that supports an excellent execution of mindful action and a perfect disposition of mind–body conversation.

It's also true with individuals as well as with organizations because with faith, creative intelligence provides all aspects of life with ceaseless energy production and a tireless spirit of enthusiasm that serves an endless reality of purpose that inspires our hearts and heals our minds. It's the power that shines the light of truths, and then truths become pathways to positive life that brightens the light of wisdom and awareness of all good. Therefore, when it comes to self-knowing, creative intelligence produces a self-conscious knowledge, a self-conscious spirit, and a positive energy that represents excellence and greatness. It's a positive spirit that shines the light on life and success. It's a potential energy that flows freely from a pure heart, a transparent mind, and the overall unity of spirits and sound thoughts.

Creative intelligence requires willingness of heart, certainty of mind, and directness of purpose because conscious thought is what makes all good things happen and enriches our well-being. It represents a unified field of active spirit, positive energy, sound feelings, and powerful emotions. It shines the light of business success and typically brightens the light of successful relationships to increase inner joy, peace, and health. We need to shine the light of life and the light of our overall well-being that draws us toward better lives, greater futures, and even offers us bigger opportunities to obtain higher-quality results with greater incentives.

That will inspire and move us to work and change our lives for the greater good because when it comes to enhancing values and enriching our life purposes, creative intelligence supports a unique business mind that frees us from self-doubt, procrastination, fear, and worry, which can lead to poverty, misery, and suffering. But if we realize this and develop a unique business mind-set that will provide us the vital fruits, vital energies, and necessary ingredients to foster progressive life, we will greatly enrich our lives. That's why we need creative intelligence—it's a rewarding channel of a possible source of attraction; of continuous blessing; and of inspiration, motivation, and passion. Most important, we need creative intelligence because it inspires optimistic spirits to take voluntary action, make diligent efforts, plan ahead, think constructively, act effectively, and eventually receive bountiful returns.

As we evolve through life, we can start to see why every solution in life begins with self-awareness and stays alive in creative intelligence. As long as we're thinking constructively and acting reasonably, it will enable us to mobilize our greatest potential, our powers of thought, and strength of character so we can use them in the most productive and effective ways to serve our purposes. As long as we're in the right mind-set, it will continue to provide us a positive spirit of persistence, determination, and perseverance. We all need to achieve our principal goals in life. That's why creative intelligence fuels our burning desires and expands our creative visions to transport us from one level of power to another. Ultimately it will help us make prompt and concrete decisions that will in turn help us embrace and accept positive changes in our businesses, as well as in our homes and environments.

As we become more aware of our different environments, we are capable of developing deeper insights. That's why creative intelligence is the legend of all success, the mother of all creativity and productivity, and the father of all inventiveness and drive. It actively prepares our minds for readiness, efficiency, effectiveness, and absolute determination that gives us a constructive expression of our spirits and draws a desirable atmosphere of peace and happiness, love and passion, ultimate joy, inner harmony, and lasting success. Therefore, creative intelligence gives us lifelong health and happiness, long-lasting relationships, and remarkable and enduring lives.

We all strive for a better future, a greater way of knowing, a richer understanding, and a more effective way of acting, and creative intelligence can provide us all of that. It is the transmutation of intelligence into conscious action, self-manifestation of passion, and realization of truth. It is also the conversion of wisdom into reality, into facts, and into material good. It's the light that illuminates conscious awareness of truth, reality, and purpose. This shows why creative intelligence is the basis of the ultimate creative spirit, wisdom, and life. It further explains why it's the thinking center and the acting point of all positive spirits, all productive minds, and effective hearts.

When marked by conscious alertness, energy, and vitality, creative intelligence gives us the foresight and insight by which to perceive reality through our own visual minds and to see the truth through our own mental eyes and imaginative faculties. That's why it provides us a pure knowledge and a synthetic wisdom that is marked by a symbolic expression of our spirits and a crystal-clear intelligence, which can be achieved through constructive thinking, understanding, and experiencing facts. That helps us stand out amid all the realities of life, producing a faithful truth and expressing a powerful, confident, and reliable disposition of the mind–body conversation. And that can bring us a unity of sensation and spirit of excitement that gives us conventional wisdom to act effectively and consistently.

Creative intelligence is the underlying factor that converts complexity into simplicity, transforms difficulty into blessings, and eventually converts our fears into multiple successes. As we continue to grow and mature, it absorbs our mental ignorance and resolves our internal conflicts, just as light absorbs darkness.

Here we're blessed with power, success, and progress because creative intelligence grows through creative efforts, logical consistency, and practical wisdom. It further grows in conscious awareness, profound understanding, creative wisdom, and mental harmony. On all levels of achievement, it's important to know that so much of our power begins with keen observation, conscious alertness, and a sound mind.

We need to use the best of our abilities, powers, and resources to do something as well as we can and advance our mindful purposes for the best possible outcomes. As we become more aware, we need effective means of acting as much as we need more efficient ways of producing multiple results. Creative intelligence will give us all that because it is a creative mentality, a rich sense, an observable reality, and a perceptible truth that enhances our well-being and enriches our lives. Creative intelligence guards the doors of awareness and understanding and therefore improves our mental integrity and spiritual alertness. It puts us in a state of readiness, awakening and internal vigilance, which enhances our emotional wisdom and sharpens our mental vision.

As we become more aware through self-observation and profound understanding, we are capable of creating more chances of success and development. This is what seems to make the biggest difference between success and failure—the ability to observe, recognize, and understand our emotions and the power to enhance our emotional intelligence. By improving our ability to observe, recognize, and understand, we can do better jobs and live better lives because creative life begins with the power of observation and conscious awareness and rests on logical analysis to equip our minds to face our challenges in life. As we face the need to become more flexible, adaptable, and transformational, we need to rethink and restructure our minds to cope with the complexities and mysteries of life.

Now is the time to influence the future and embrace emotional intelligence because it truly opens up new perspectives and provides powerful insights that eventually can be developed through open communication, practical ideas, and mindful actions. That's why creative intelligence is an integral part of real change that brings us a dedicated sense of commitment to achieve our goals.

All of this creates a lasting value that serves not only as a critical component of success but also as a crucial factor for personal growth and development that supports our physical and mental health. It becomes a necessary human resource that brings us psychological change, supports our well-being, and helps us build the best possible lives. It also brings us an immeasurable intelligence, which is indisputably valuable in both our personal lives and businesses.

We all need to foster our important relationships because they are a powerful force in our lives, and they are built on trust. Trust is the foundation of all relationships. Therefore, when it comes to building important relationships, we need effective communication, quality action, and to see things on a deeper level and in a much more fundamental way to achieve positive results. Creative intelligence provides us all of that. It produces positive pictures that enable us to communicate the best meaning and bring us the best logical expressions that serve the most rational insights. Creative intelligence is indispensable because it provides us a steadily ascending quality of life by converting positive intentions into sound ideas; transmuting sound thoughts into useful purposes; transforming useful purposes into practical actions; and changing practical actions into positive, dynamic, and lasting results.

As we face the need to become more adaptable and transformational, we need effective communication and sound, constructive minds to make things happen. Creative intelligence provides us all of that. It's a crucial component for building important relationships and standing out in the crowd. It enables us to effectively communicate from a place of conscious, transformational thought and to foster powerful, positive, and lasting relationships using a healthy language of success and the principles of progress and development.

When it comes to effective communication, creative intelligence comes with all the artistic realities of life that bring us an articulate style of knowing as well as pattern of understanding. This shows why creative intelligence is at the very center of knowledge as well as the very heart of understanding reality. It also explains why creative intelligence is an adjustable knowledge that must be supported by a flexible mind and an adaptable heart. Perhaps the greatest appreciation of life comes with both skill and talent, which can bring out all our innate values and sensitivities and in the process become refined knowledge, transferable thoughts, and practical ideas.

As we sincerely seek to understand deeply and embody useful knowledge, creative intelligence will greatly serve us because it comes with useful knowledge, and useful knowledge comes with real power that manifests the real images of our desires and the best possible means of attainment and satisfaction. It opens the doors to success and progress, and as a result, creates a better life. It also opens the doors for new purposes and for better opportunities. Therefore, it requires cognitive awareness, conscious observation, careful attention, and a sound mind, all of which provide us with a realistic plan, a proper strategy, and effective action. It also provides us a sound thought process, clear feeling, and concrete and flawless action. That comes from an individual's unique pattern of thoughts, feelings, and behaviors or from skills that make a person unique. It further comes from an individual's upbringing, a positive personality, and a lifelong habit of success. In addition, it comes from sustained, strenuous efforts of the mind and heart. All this shows why creative intelligence is a language of the body that brings us a richer, more refined language of the mind and heart. Therefore, it's a knowledge of your heart, mind, and body that produces a strong spirit of enthusiasm, love, passion, motivation, and inspiration in all creative endeavors.

Once again, when it comes to building important relationships and producing lasting value, creative intelligence produces sensory information through a harmonious association of sensibility, positive experiences, and feedback. Through conscious awareness, we need to enhance and grow our businesses and better our lives. We also need to enhance valuable relationships that support a creative, powerful, and lasting change. But, remember, it takes great effort and sound thoughts to spark a positive emotion and drive a smart decision to take a quality action that brings positive results. We need to bring out one another's potential and help one another use our energy and creativity to serve the common good and empower people in all walks of life. So when it comes to building powerful relationships and sharing value, creative intelligence produces a clear picture, an observable substance of thoughts in the most dynamic and productive ways possible. It's an active power that enhances the substance of unified consciousness that serves great ideas and supports sound feelings and productive actions. It enables us to actively perceive things from one holistic viewpoint that both creates a better life and supports a greater future.

We can see, trust, work, and eventually get benefits. So when it comes to seeing the future, enhancing our purposes, and growing our minds, creative intelligence comes with powerful forces because it works within its intrinsic values to produce powerful, positive, and lasting results. It's also the vehicle that lifts valuable minds and great hearts to the highest mountain of success and enables them to continuously climb into the unknown to explore the best possible values. It eventually helps us see the uncharted future and exploit great benefits, which certainly gives us the power and strength to convert a potential future into material reality. This is the ultimate power that lifts us from the level of thinking to the level of actualization. It's also a dynamic power that reveals itself through a prompt and smart decision and profound understanding and through a keen observation and conscious awareness.

This is the substance of knowledge, the sum of life, and the means by which we can triumphantly and consciously enjoy life more, live wisely, and produce better results. Creative intelligence supports intellectual knowledge, interests, and integrity and serves all the meaningful purposes, which can represent absolute life and support strength of purpose that guides excellent execution of intelligence and wisdom.

Therefore, conscious awareness helps you improve your knowledge and helps you grow your life by connecting sensory acuity, reclaiming vitality and present awareness, and expanding your consciousness. As you find and retain wisdom, you will continue to grow in wisdom and knowledge. So to explore the deep connection inside yourself to the world around you, you need creative intelligence. Sensory awareness involves collecting useful information from your senses to take quality actions that will produce effective results. This can be achieved by expanding and improving your mind and enhancing your emotional awareness. This dynamic approach can help you enrich your daily life and boost your personal growth. This can also help you expand your memory and ultimately live a better life, enjoy more success, and experience less stress. Creative intelligence expresses constructive efforts of the mind, heart, and body working in harmony and shows a symbolic knowledge and wisdom that indicates practical intelligence and creative insight so you might grow in your knowledge of self. It prepares your mind to observe hidden values that can drive your interests and faithfully deliver you to your destination. It's also the principal reason your creative awareness and perception increase and your creative vision expands.

All of this boils down to growing your business as well as improving your personal life. Once again, let me remind you that creative intelligence is the ultimate edge of success for generating multiple results in all phases of life. This is also the ultimate hedge strategy for guarding your life and leveraging your business. So if you're desperate to grow your business and improve your daily life, creative intelligence is the right tool and weapon to make positive things happen because it unites all profitable innovation, all creative insights, all functional minds, and all great hearts. It adds value and eventually turns all practical ideas into a unified field of energy and a singularity of purpose that will give you the opportunity to win, acquire, progress, and succeed in any creative endeavor.

So no matter what your goals are, creative intelligence is what you need. It produces a strong chain of positive energies, constructive thoughts, and profitable ideas that can support the best action and bring the best possible results. It will provide you the best possible power and strength to support the best possible efforts of heart that represent the uniqueness of mind–body connection. It will also provide you the blueprint of the future, the blueprint of all effective action, and the positive visual images of your thoughts, which will enhance your belief systems and support your overall well-being. If you're endeavoring to succeed, it will enable you to envision a brighter future and help you design your life in your own way for a greater future. It serves as a gateway to better options and greater opportunities to better-paying jobs with higher goals and greater ambitions.

Remember that creative intelligence is an irresistible power that will conquer and transform all things and make positive things happen. It will transform your intention into action and convert action into multiple results. Keep in mind that creative intelligence represents the highest and best aspects of consciousness, is a major component of success, and is the science behind an extraordinary life. It's an individual's gateway to financial and economic freedom and unique opportunity, as well as a pathway to organizational resources. In the most profound sense, it's the power that causes people to live better lives and increases an individual's access to opportunities for personal growth and development. It's a priceless resource for people in all walks of life and the main highway to a healthy, happy, and successful life.

CHAPTER 2

THE CAPABLE FOLKS

He can who thinks he can.
—ORISON SWETT MARDEN

I n the world today, there are unique individuals who are intelligent, very effective in life, and capable of generating positive results. These capable individuals are the reason we have civilization, progress, and development, as well as an abundance of health, happiness, joy, and success. They're the ones who foster creative innovations that greatly improve and enhance our lives and therefore encourage voluntary actions in all the important areas of life. They have the powerful, unique, and healthy brains that support other brains, the successes that enhance and guide other successes, and the lives that enrich other lives. These folks are skillfully trained and destined to become the best possible minds that enhance the most comprehensive values, feed real economic growth, and expand the economic opportunity that fosters all of our businesses. Consider and think of Steve Jobs, Henry Ford, Adam Smith, Thomas A. Edison, Martin Luther King Jr, Nelson Mandela, and Barack Obama.

They're powerful individuals because they all have had a sense of direction, a sense of who they are and what they stand for, live for and die for. They know what they want and concentrate all their energies on what matters.

With their intelligence and proper analysis, capable folks are always learning and experiencing things in positive ways, and then they feed others valuable information that promotes healing and enhances performance and creativity. Their useful experience enables them to make prompt and smart decisions that support their purposes and make a real and lasting impact. Most of their decisions are based on useful resources that yield greater value and produce more powerful results. All of this plays an important role in shaping their perceptions, enhancing their belief systems, proclaiming their perpetual existence, and maintaining their innate creativity. This increases their inherent wisdom and their spiritual awakening, and eventually they find within themselves an ever-present basis of existence, which ultimately helps them discover the condition of being genuine and achieve great success in life.

Their upbringing might have played a crucial role in shaping their belief systems, enhancing their strong convictions, and improving their sense of self-confidence. They're properly guarded, well equipped, and fully prepared to unleash their potential and achieve the best possible goals in life.

Their shared belief systems enable them to focus on singleness of purpose to satisfy their specific needs and eventually help them take a well-calculated action to further enhance their future potential expectations. They all have pursued a course and determined to find an end to the root cause of fear of poverty. So they're the ones who are fully enlightened, willingly embrace challenges, and voluntarily accept their responsibilities to render accountability.

Basically, their inner powers and strengths always come from a courageous spirit, love, passion, willingness, readiness, persistent determination, and logical consistency. Therefore, they live and breathe in wisdom and in conscious awareness. That's why they're the ones who can face new challenges, embrace and accept positive changes in any environment, and then convert changes into better opportunities for rapid growth and development. Their quality upbringings equip them with a constructive mental attitude that clearly positions them to navigate an ever-changing world and helps them stay in business and therefore continue to breed success.

These people focus on producing results and using all the best strategies to achieve the most beneficial outcomes in every profitable environment. They're driven by their goals and continue to be motivated to take quality and consistent actions to satisfy their desires. They continue to build on their existing values, thus compounding better qualities and greater values. Fortunately, They see changes as favorable windows of opportunities and fertile fields to plant more value, therefore producing multiple results. All of this shows that they embody the energies that empower and inspire positive actions in every creative endeavor, which of course means they are the bedrock of all meaningful purpose. They also represent the managerial excellence of all creative disciplines by following instructions, obeying the rules of stewardship, honoring the rules of fellowship, and then committing themselves to the principles of success.

To maximize their potential profits, they choose their words carefully and act diligently to produce great results. That's why their colorful actions clearly identify and define them—they're individuals with practice-based training and solid principles. They all have acquired unique talents and have organized skills. They have all the properly established facts and well-organized knowledge, and they are fully prepared for unexpected events. They are ready and willing to make prompt decisions and take congruent actions.

They're winners who live in their intuitive wisdom, which empowers their creative insights to help them develop winning ideas. They make daily conscious efforts to observe reality while maintaining their distinct lines of success and building better values. Basically, they're the ones who live in vision, see abundance in value, and survive in consciousness. They're also the ones who always promote a healing, faithful condition in every environment that enhances performance and creativity in every arena of life. Ultimately, they're the living legends of creation, ultimate constructive thinkers, infinitely creative inventors, and prolific producers.

You can see how fundamentally unique these individuals are because they don't just see through their physical eyes; they perceive things in their minds' eyes, hear sounds in their minds' ears, and feel things deeply in their minds' hands. They see things differently, do things differently based on past experiences, and then produce unique and better results. However, if they face difficulties in the process, they mobilize their greatest potential, gather the greatest possible powers to make the biggest impact, and continuously improve and expand their conscious awareness. That's why they always follow the right instructions, obey the basic rules, and eventually follow the precise guidelines that support creativity and enhance their specialized skills. The basic reason they always maintain and develop their sensory systems is because it serves their best interests and supports their overall well-being. All this may be the ultimate reason why their sound minds and creative thoughts draw rapid development and notable success.

As we look around us and within us, we can recognize that there are people who have in-depth knowledge, great resources, and the unique skills to do something better. They have clearly defined their purposes and therefore have criteria for selecting and satisfying their basic needs. Those people are unique individuals with unique values; they take notes and record everyday events, thus using their unique experiences to impact the future and enhance others' lives.

They're competent individuals whose make the effort required to make positive things happen. Their unique skills and powers are based on useful knowledge, and they know that valuable information provides them the key to a better life. That's why they're able to create a triumphant, compelling future that changes businesses and brings better and bigger profits. So with success in mind, they build value, work smarter, and enjoy greater success because they're talented, brilliant, and clever enough to meet demands in a completely satisfactory manner. They believe in their creative intelligence, which boosts their emotions and makes them more efficient at climbing the ladder of success. They successfully grow and develop profitable businesses through quality actions and produce quality results in all aspects of their lives. They have a logical approach to satisfy their basic needs and a systematic way to deal with everyday phenomena. Their superior intelligence distinguishes them and makes them unique, and their internal structures and mental make-ups define and identify them in all areas of life. All of these attributes represent their ultimate values and become the determinant factor in all their successes.

I have carefully observed these people work their way from tatters to riches, from extreme poverty to major success. I have also witnessed them transform negative to positive and then lift other people from a state of fear to a resourceful state. Consider the faith of Mandela, Martin Luther King Jr, Barack Obama, Steve Jobs, Henry Ford. They all have conquered and transformed their fears into courage and achieved great successes. Therefore, I believe in them because they focus on what matters most and eventually act on valuable prospective trends. They have different, economic vision, and see innovative trends as profitable opportunities for rapid growth and development and favorable chances to advance their goals. So they always prioritize their needs and eventually channel all of their energies toward a singleness of purpose. Thus, their dedicated sense of purpose opens the main doors of success that lead them to many valuable rooms full of opportunities for unity and diversity.

So the path to success comes when capacities are born and opportunities unfold themselves to ultimately help our lives grow. Therefore, success comes from knowing that we did our best to become the best we are capable of becoming. The most important thing to remember is that when capacities are born, we grow in spirit, courage, and wisdom, and eventually passion grows, and then inspiration sparks in our minds and hearts.

Therefore, the principal goal of learning and experiencing things in our lives must be conquered, transformed, and achieved and then represented by creative intelligence. This, in turn, creates men and women who are capable of producing new things. That's what capability is all about because competent individuals are creative people who have practiced, experienced, and lived in creation and eventually maintain their inherent values. That's why they're well-rounded in knowledge, practical ideas, and wisdom, and properly equipped with positive experiences that can help them solve future problems and even prevent negative situations.

Capable folks always use their mental vision to see the uncharted future and adequately prepare their minds to climb unknown mountains and achieve definite goals. But before this happens, they have to examine their own minds through the conscious practice of mindful meditation, which means that they live in the potential future within their own minds.

They have effective minds and substantial energy to initiate change and impact the future. This eventually brings courage, energy, and hope to the entire society. Most important, they're self-disciplined individuals who are properly equipped with wisdom and fully stabilized in thought. Their sound ideas and rich sense enables them to take clear actions that can bring them multiple beneficial results. Capable folks always use their logical minds and imaginative senses for creative purposes. Therefore, they choose their words carefully to maximize their potential profits. They carefully analyze their risks, define their purposes, and then take well-calculated and flawless action to produce a powerful and lasting result. That's why they're always practicing their diligent distinctions of personality through sound thoughts, clear judgment, and mental integrity.

Common sense can inspire and empower every wise man and woman to believe in the idea of abundance. It shows us that poverty is not a direct result of lack of physical supply; rather, it's the result of mental conflict, inability to perform, mental inadequacy, ignorance, and lack of self-confidence.

I believe in creative intelligence because it sounds good to me, and I eventually saw why capable folks are the powerful, influential, and vital forces of social influence who always have been in charge and in control of their emotions. That's the main reason their reliable emotions always serve and support their daily needs and wants. This explains why they see business rejection and failure as a challenge to excellent performance, as a challenge to perfect themselves even more for a better life and greater future. They use a considerable amount of energy to foster profitable innovation because they're inspired by the object of their desire and sparked by the burning desire to become even more successful.

I have carefully observed and confirmed that these folks are result-focused and goal-driven individuals who continue to grow in power and in capacity. That's why their profound beliefs and intangible and tangible changes have enabled them to focus on solutions rather than problems, ultimately enabling them to invest all their time, efforts, and powers to satisfy their desires. They lock their minds on their main goals and never allow rejection and frustration to rule their lives. They're effective in mind and strong in spirit, and they thoroughly understand how to make significant progress because their sense of confidence renders them more powerful and much stronger in life. That's why they always strive to increase in power and ability and develop their wisdom and intelligence. This means that capable folks focus on results and therefore use their whole energy and power of thought to create success. They think success, feel success, and ultimately produce success.

All capable minds believe in the potential of their minds and in a triumphant future. They believe they can transform their present circumstances into a greater future. They set standards, break the old, uninspiring rules and set new ones, and then they fill their thoughts with a positive, burning desire to do whatever it takes to accomplish desirable results. In fact, they are thoroughly governed by a progressive spirit of success. They plant similar thoughts of success and progress, so they harvest similar results. They take similar kinds of successful actions, so they produce similar kinds of successful results. They foster the spirit of passion, so they receive passionate outcomes. They gather adequate knowledge, so they reap unique blessings. They share valuable information, so they achieve and enjoy valuable outcomes together. They plant similar seeds of logic, so they receive reasonable incentives and better rewards. They have embodied a unique attitude of success, so they produce the same abundant, prolific results.

Capable folks are the ones who normally think deeply and act effectively, so they extract quality outcomes. Eventually they become the ones who think more and talk less, who stand up and express their feelings by taking action that will greatly satisfy their emotions. Ultimately, capable folks are the ones who always seeking the best methods for effective action and the rational means for producing consistent results. Therefore, they're the ones who always motivate, inspire, and empower and then fuel their minds to serve their unique purposes and support their emotional well-being. They have acquired flexible knowledge that guards and supports the active mind and helps promote humility of heart to stay active in business and continue to grow in life. That's why they have great patience and tolerance that enables them to adapt to change in all the areas of life and deal with any negative circumstance that may arise.

To handle situations, they control their minds; direct their thoughts; maintain their energy; direct their focus, action, and vision; and eventually take control to make positive, powerful, and lasting changes. To do this effectively, they use due diligence, logical consistency, keen observation, and a dedicated sense of commitment to create momentum, produce effective results, and pursue excellence and greatness. To ensure that they produce quality results, they organize their thoughts, sharpen their minds, and then use proven techniques to make positive things happen to serve and support their well-being. They effectively use their creative mentality and emotional intelligence for better purposes and for greater benefits. And they deliver all of this with a level of passion, power, courage, and determination to win. That's why they're winners who focus on results and skillfully use their best information at the right moment, in the right direction, for highest and best benefits.

These folks are the ones who provide us the greatest human resources and the highest standards of value that are changing the world for the better. They are unique individuals who have established higher standards, break old, uninspiring rules, and set new ones. Certainly, they have built value and earned self-respect through persistent determination; therefore they have sustained their self-images by demonstrating stability and inspiring entrepreneurial, artistic vision in all creative endeavors. As a result, they have effected a real and lasting change and encouraged entrepreneurial, artistic creativity. That's why they see business rejection as a wake-up call to effective action, a wake-up call that ignites actions to spark positive changes.

As all this continues to grow and develop in chronological order, they become more powerful and more effective in mind. This rejuvenates and energizes their minds and eventually grows their minds through practice-based learning and improvement that leads to an upward spiral of growth and development and brings them multiple successes. They're the ones who are always thinking and looking for new and better opportunities and higher levels of business performance. That's why they make conscious choices about how to direct their thoughts, energies, and focus to represent real, powerful, and authentic business lives. To accomplish that, they control their attention and direct all their energies, powers, and focus on what matters most. They are always consciously thinking about better future and looking for a better life, a favorable opportunity, and ultimately higher-quality results.

They take congruent action that transforms their lives, and they logically perceive and conceive realities that can yield substantial returns. They pay careful attention to specific detailed information and then focus on what matters most. They pay absolute attention to the most vital facts and essential values. That's how they maintain their internal memories and sustain inner harmony and peace of mind that comes with the finest and best qualities, which foster more positive lives.

By adding richness to the human condition, inspiring others through their creative wisdom, taking control of their focus, and eventually directing their attention, these capable folks are equally maintaining their optimal value, quality, and satisfaction. They know that opportunities are the potential sources of inspiration, motivation, and passion, which can spark positive action and yield extensive returns. This is why capable folks must shape and enhance a well-heightened sense of awareness and pay close attention to detailed information to convert negative situations into richer opportunities and transform their fears into successes.

We all know that our fear of failure and poverty accumulate in ignorance, and we can and will succeed if we think constructively and act wisely. Capable folks are the ones who embody these truths, believe in these realities, and then take consistent actions for positive changes. They're also the ones who have the quality character that attracts others, and they drive attention and interests in all areas of life. They're the great ones who never, ever allow themselves to be distracted or confused or allow conflicts to determine the course of their lives.

They always ask open-ended questions and wait patiently for positive feedback. They convert all positive feedback into profitable opportunities and meaningful purposes that produce outstanding results. As we learn from their formidable, outstanding, and everlasting actions and results, we will be able to measure and understand their unique character, desires, and actions and the scope of their participation in all levels of business success. Once we have realized this, we can see that they're driven by their goals and therefore committed to creating positive changes in their lives as well as in others' lives. They're driven by their inspiring goals, which are governed by rules and controlled by their moral and ethical principles. All of this explains why they're unique individuals ruled by sound judgments that help them promote healthy and wise living in all aspects of life. Their unique skills and positive experiences always lead them onward with steady advancement. They always think before they answer, and they examine and evaluate things from the most advanced points of view to achieve excellent results.

With their objective points of view, capable folks have proven to be indomitable forces and unique individuals with special powers and inner strengths. They're the ones who always think for themselves to enhance their well-being, explore and develop their own mental faculties, and eventually benefit from their own rational and positive thinking. That's why they're the ones with big dreams, realistic plans, and inspiring goals. Basically, capable folks are the ones who have the optimistic spirit of success that enables them to draw more good and attract more quality things into their lives.

Certainly, these folks are well equipped with the spirit of success, useful knowledge, power, love, passion, and vitality; therefore, they are flush with success. They are always improving and increasing their mental powers and emotional strengths through personal development, self-training, conscious awareness, and self-enhancement. Through all this, they're building reasonable self-confidence and then enhancing a realistic self-reliance. And through continued education and extensive training, they're also expanding their talents and growing their unique skills to help them face challenges and take advantage of opportunity when it knocks. These are the benefits of growth and development, and that's why capable folks are always growing in useful knowledge, profound understanding, and practical insights. All of this further enables them to become more than they ever thought possible. It helps them form better thoughts and sound feelings that are empowering and inspiring their minds and hearts, which in turn attracts better things into their lives. For these reasons, they always strive for something new and superior in quality to satisfy their minds. And that's why they have mastered control of their minds and direct them wisely to serve their unique purposes. And all of this explains why they focus on what matters most and are inspired to move with single-minded purpose to achieve definite results. This, of course, helps them use their mental faculties and mind powers for constructive purposes and to influence their environments.

Their dedicated efforts and consistent actions have created a favorable condition for success. Capable folks help other people turn their potentials into realities, convert intentions into positive actions, and therefore transform their dreams into destinies. Their mental vision and congruent action have helped others shape their futures, which is inspiring and adds more value to the human condition. All of this shows that moving from dreams to plans to action and setting realistic goals is an effective way of enhancing positive lives. That's why capable folks' moral actions depend on sound judgments and technical skills, useful knowledge, and considerable initiative in expanding available resources.

Their extraordinarily resilient powers of purpose and incredible efforts have proven to reinforce and enhance their social skills, which promotes their unique skills and helps them exploit more opportunities. They always use logical analysis to exploit new changes and make continuous efforts to enhance their minds and enrich others' lives. They use good tactics, sound ideas, and constructive efforts to foster progressive changes and establish new and better purposes for people who are interested in developing and enriching their lives.

Capable folks are the ones who shape our perceptions and change our mental vision by inspiring our minds and hearts. They're the ones who create value, live in value, serve value, and satisfy their emotional needs. They're also the ones who have embedded in themselves real, powerful, and useful knowledge and therefore have transformed their fears into courage and use their unique skills to build solid strategies to achieve multiple results. They apply their talents to develop important relationships; maintain rapport; and then sustain real, valuable, and lasting relationships by helping others improve their performance, which eventually adds value to the human condition. They're able to manage people's behavior and eventually develop their personal strengths while consistently controlling, directing, and disciplining their own minds. They are also renewing and strengthening their progressive spirits by maintaining their personal drives and continuing to develop their unique skills and talents. Truly, they're the ones who always sustain and maintain realistic plans, develop strategies, and focus on the most important areas of their lives, such as career, health, economy, family, and education.

As they concentrate on major areas of interest, they make significant progress and build more value because they know that every success is endowed with the greatness of the spirit of love and passion. That's why they have the inner strength and personal power to fulfill the promises of greatness and better futures. Therefore, they're created to fulfill unique purposes, satisfy their personal needs, and eventually fulfill specific economic needs. They're moral in character and ethical in conduct, so they become the critical success factors underpinning the right investment strategies because they are exact and clear in meaning and action, which inspires creativity in all areas of life.

All of this, is accomplished by accountability in all the major areas of life. The quality and reliability of their actions have determined where they are at this moment; therefore, what they are doing today will determine where they will be tomorrow. In the process, they become the light of life and radiance of energy in the universe. Typically, they're the strongholds of profitable innovation who guard all the productive actions in all creative endeavors. These folks are the unique individuals who spark the light of wisdom and the ingenuity of minds, which provides us the goodness that brings us the melody of joy into our hearts. Capable folks are the faithful masters who spin the wheels of success and sustain the wheels of development in all walks of life.

This ultimately brings us all great successes that support harmony and steadfast love in our homes and environments. That's why they're strengthened with the spirit of love, passion, and courage and are overflowing with both a sense of gratitude and appreciation. And as much as they're flooded with courage and passion, they spark creative wisdom and therefore become the illumination of awareness. That's why they're the products of innovation; the kings of creative wisdom; and the queens of all notable success, progress, and development. They're always feeding our minds with life-giving energies that inspire our thoughts and enrich our souls.

Capable folks are unique individuals with strong belief systems and solid convictions of success that dominate the nature of their clear thinking, sound ideas, and possible progress. That's why they're always creating and enhancing the spirit of passion for their purposeful living, so that their passion will enable them to become increasingly active in life. This explains why they're so determined to pursue their dreams, goals, and values in the workplace. Their passionate lives enable them to rise above poverty and help them overcome rejection and frustration in any environment. Their spirit of passion and self-motivation clearly determine their levels of success—they envision the future and create their own destiny and therefore design their own lives in their own ways that serve and support their best interests. Typically, they're identified by their active sense of purpose and their inspiring goals that foster self-motivation, love, and passion, which lead to consistent action and positive results.

If you look closely at their history, it reveals that they're individuals born with a clear sense of purpose, quality upbringing, and inspiring goals. Therefore, they have clear goals and sound reason that help them live wisely and happily. Successfully achieving their goals have provided them evidence of a sound sense of self-worth and a clear sense of meaning and purpose. A life of purpose fuels their motivation and provides them a strong, compelling reason for definite action. Their goals inspire them and give them a unique sense of creative discipline that provides them a positive attitude of success that will never surrender until they have achieved all their purposes.

To achieve quality results and be the very best they can be, they always use rational persistence because they know that responsibility is an obligation and a necessity to fulfill an exact and clear purpose. So they see responsibility as part and parcel of their lives. They also know that everything has its uniqueness and beauty, but not everyone sees clearly and understands profoundly. So they believe that their self-discipline leads to optimum results, higher performance, and greater accomplishment. Therefore, they have the spirit of self-motivation and enhancement; a powerful, positive attitude for personal growth and development; and a dynamic, positive spirit for personal accomplishment.

With their higher levels of attainment, they have provided us a roundtable of wisdom, and they know how to share value and profitable information, exchange useful knowledge, and build meaningful rapports. They're the glue that holds every business together and the key that opens the doors of business opportunities. They're also the glue that holds every meaningful relationship together. This means that capable folks are spiritually and mentally attractive individuals who know that building rapport opens the doors to understanding and eventually to opportunities that enable one to have access to enter other minds, explore useful knowledge, and leverage others' values. They also know that building valuable rapport provides a strong link that bonds businesses together. Every businessman or woman knows that building rapport is a way of building trust in business relationships, and building trust in business relationships is building a solid, dependable bridge to business successes. Certainly, trust provides us a quicker and clearer way of doing business and then becomes the high road to business success. That's why these people are bonded with solid rapport and a powerful and lasting trust that makes positive things happen. They know that rapport provides them the opportunity and the privilege and confidence to gain access to other people's minds. That's why they have all built a strong rapport in business relationships—they know that the quality of their rapport represents the quality of their lives. They also know that the quality of their rapport will clearly determine the quality of their outcomes. Therefore, the true meaning of their action depends on the results they're getting, and good actions rest on good results.

If you further look closely, you will observe that capable folks are independent, prolific producers and inspired thinkers who are finding innovative solutions, changing our businesses, and taking spontaneous action to enhance our unique skills and purposes. They are the ones who are forever sowing the thought seeds to reap and sow again. They're logical and rational decision makers who can change the world, which in turn energizes them and inspires them to achieve even greater success. Living in a positive, favorable, and profitable environment gives them the key to win, succeed, progress, develop, live wisely, and produce effective results. So they always live in any favorable environment that can open the gateway that accelerates success and propels advancement. Truly, they're living and breeding and eventually gaining power in a dependable, desirable, and profitable environment, which helps control their minds and direct their lives. That's why their inspiration, love, passion, and motivation enable them to see things in ways that support their well-being and help them perform so much better in life. Basically, they know that the goodness of a thing lies in the realization of truth and in the specific nature of goodness. That's why they're good listeners, careful analyzers, creative thinkers, prolific producer, profitable innovators, excellent managers, and effective leaders who are shaping and making things far better for us all.

These individuals are self-conscious optimizers and visualizers who have mental powers that can consciously navigate their emotional wisdom. This allows them to manage efficiently and use all their creative mentality to support and move toward their goals and apply their minds diligently. Their minds are well-ordered and relatively fixed because their goals are deeply rooted in their best judgments and rational choices. They know that just as exercise is a preliminary test of emotional competency, so are both creative wisdom and useful knowledge. Therefore, all knowledge must be put into practice to determine its effectiveness. That's another reason that capable folks have to learn from the feedback and adapt to environments—it provides them with the power to consciously navigate their minds. This means that capable folks are those who have acquired all the positive truths that can make positive things happen. Therefore, they have embodied sound thought in practical wisdom; lived in useful knowledge and intelligence; and had practical experiences, creative wisdom, and practical insights. They use wisdom and intelligence to create and direct their emotions and eventually guide their feelings, ideas, and experiences in life. They're also the ones who have empowered themselves to expand their minds and increase their capacities and abilities. They continue to grow in wisdom and expand in knowledge, and in the process become more effective and efficient in life.

As capable folks live and breed more success, success draws them more and more blessings. Therefore, they represent a stronger and more stable future and a powerful and steady stream of consciousness. They're properly ingrained, well rooted, and relatively fixed in mind and heart. They're the ones born under the guidance of law, self-control, self-discipline, and self-direction. Their remarkable inherent power and orderliness are naturally ingrained in their systems because they have inherent ability, energy, and vitality that emanate from within their consciousness. They have the inner powers and capacities to learn from feedback. This helps them see and feel the glow of positive, radiant energy, and eventually enables them to look for ways to expand and improve their knowledge, which ultimately enhances their creative vision, shapes their perception, and increases their awareness. They are filled with physical energy and vitality. As a result, they are consciously creating, directing, and developing a realistic spirit of self-confidence that enriches and governs their thoughts and goals in life. This explains why their ambitions and goals are the main source of their self-control, self-discipline, inspiration, and motivation. It also explains how their courageous spirits of newness, love, and passion are always creating a powerful, positive, and active sense of purpose that sparks sensibility, creativity, and productivity in all areas of life.

Capable folks can balance productivity in all the key areas of their lives and create a real and powerful business growth, so they tend to earn more money. They know that flexibility drives productivity and improves business performance. Therefore, they are adept at employing purposeful, productive business solutions, which create focus, more action, and multiple results. That's why they're results-driven individuals with a remarkable mental toughness who know that quality results will clearly determine their strengths, convictions, and active belief systems. That's why they're explicitly committed to action and properly disciplined by their inspiring goals—they know it will greatly empower and motivate them to succeed because they know where they are going and how to get there. Through their ultimate productive drive, they clearly state what they want and strongly commit to it. They're ruled and directed by their inspiring dreams and plans, which always represent their highest interests, self-concepts, and values.

Values represent real conception of the best quality and character traits and eventually serve as the best source of information for the creation and maintenance of self-efficacy of human belief systems. That's why it's the life students of innovation that will provide us with dramatic changes in business performance and therefore become the life learners of modernization that will ultimately bring us the best value, the best possible quality, and the best business creativity and productivity in the marketplace. As a result of all this, their well-disciplined minds and properly directed thoughts, goals, plans, and ideas produce multiple results and bring us prolific returns. They are always learning from their past experiences because they know that past experience is the best teacher. They all believe in the inner qualities that enable them to work diligently and eventually help them produce more desirable products that bring us much better outcomes. Capable folks separate important things from unimportant—so they can focus on what matters most.

Capable folks are remarkably successful winners in all creative fields; therefore, they're the ones who make the finer distinctions and smarter choices because they are absolute-minded, morally guided, and clearly self-directed individuals who know what they truly desire and deserve. They're unique individuals who have developed dependable emotions and a reliable and steady stream of consciousness, inner power, and strength. Their moral character and soundness of mind are marvelous blessings that provide them guidance and propel them toward happiness and prosperity. They're both inspired thinkers and prolific producers, and in the process, they have become the unified reason for the modern world and the ultimate course of positive change that engages the mind in making the world a better place.

And so they deliver systematic results by applying the principal goal of change that comes in the most intimate, expansive, and surprising ways possible. This turns them into excellent thinkers, abundant producers, and bountiful harvesters who have reliable spirits and dependable intelligence and therefore design dependable business solutions and use their unique skills and talents to serve a steady stream of intelligence. As a result of all this, they create a vision and live in that vision and in the process become sound in thought and effective in action. They become part of the endless unfolding system of creative innovation and the ceaseless channels of continuous blessing, progress, growth, and development that propel success. This ultimately leads them to become the inflow of endlessness, the influx of boundlessness, the infinity of mind-power, and the inpouring spirit of all goodness.

The fruit of light and spirit of life are found in all that is good, right, and true. Capable folks always accept responsibility for all their actions, and in the process they become responsible leaders who make business decisions that shape organizations to foster business innovation and change the world for the better. They're responsible leaders who are highly principled and extremely determined to achieve their dreams and purposes. This enables them to experience personal fulfill-ment through conscious enlightenment. They demonstrate their com-mitment to creating a fairer society and a much more sustainable future by fostering a culture that encourages innovation, rewards the right at-titude, and fosters trust and faith. By supporting creativity, they access deeper levels of awareness and transform humanity, therefore adding more vitality into other people's lives. They help build more responsible leaders who make a societal impact and pledge their commitment to the common good, ultimately helping to improve more and more lives. Their unlimited potential power and strength of character produce a steady emotional attitude and a powerful, congruent, and lasting flow of mentality. This is one of the basic reasons that their guiding spirits and potential powers inspire and empower them to do better and greater things in their lives. It helps them constantly navigate conscious, intelli-gent minds that are bearing positive fruits, flourishing in power, and ex-isting in abundance. This helps them expand in consciousness, increase in value, and strengthen their powers and belief systems. It is the single most important factor that guides their positive self-images, which hold their innermost joy and deepest comforts in life. That ultimately serves as a critical component of success that clearly spells out their destinies and determines the degree of their health, happiness, and success.

Because they're effective in their minds and hearts, they have im-pregnated the minds and hearts of their employees and even touched the hearts and minds of other people. They are inspired thinkers, pro-lific producers, and effective communicators who consciously create op-portunities for self-sufficiency, self-reliance, and self-development that transcend and enrich their souls. They're courageous in spirit, smart, brave, and clever in action, and they always separate their personal lives from their business lives. They're also the ones who have acquired a higher standard of knowledge and have achieved a heightened sense of commitment to take positive actions to win and get inspired to achieve a definite course.

Capable folks energize the workforce and therefore become the leaders of innovation and the universal, conscious minds and hearts that always think about success because they know that for every creative discipline, there is a bounty yield. So they believe in positive thinking because they know that for every sound and clear thought, there is a hidden benefit and prolific return. This leads to effective ways to capture attention, get benefits, and change the future. They know that life is success, and success is life, and for one to be successful, one must face the challenges and the tests of life. So they see business rejections and frustrations as ways and means to test their unique skills and abilities and grow their unique knowledge and self-confidence. They know that for every business rejection and frustration, there is a hidden value and a notable success; therefore, they always provide sound and clear information to their sensory systems for better understanding and greater achievement.

Higher faculties support the best practices, therefore helping gain a fresh sense of purpose toward success. Capable folks know this. They know that their words create positive pictures and direct their emotions, which control their destinies and lead to a triumphant future. They always let their words and actions align to strengthen their purposes and direct their feelings and behaviors to support their well-being. They let their perceptions and behaviors balance to sustain and strengthen them. That's why they always deliver accurate information and a clear message to their sensory systems, which then inspires and sparks their minds and hearts to achieve greater things in their lives. This is why they always believe in their knowledge and eventually share it with others to help them improve their present circumstances. This renews their sense of coherence and reinforces all the structural benefits of learning. In the process, it becomes the protective grounds for building and drawing more value and satisfying their future needs.

Because they're individuals who have developed higher levels of education and richer levels of operation, they are able to enhance their specific strategies and develop significantly higher levels of life satisfaction. Their happiness levels are largely based on knowledge because they know that knowledge is the road to personal development and a richer life. Furthermore, they believe in education because they know it is a necessary prerequisite for economic growth and development. Their sense of responsibility turns their attention to both the aims and means of education to produce specific and useful results. That's how they add resonance and richness to human lives and therefore increase everyone's levels of growth and development. These are purposeful individuals whose inspiring goals enable them to take consistent and congruent actions and help them use their powers and strengths in the most active, productive, and bountiful ways possible. They're the ones who effect real and lasting change, make better things happen, and eventually become the distribution channels for all meaningful purpose. They're the ones with dedicated action, clearness of sense, and clarity of purpose that eventually give meaning to life-enhancing purposes. They're also the ones with better knowledge, richer intelligence, and greater priorities that serve innovative purposes. Certainly, they're the ones who consistently ask for and believe in success. They're the ones who consciously meditate and pray and clap their hands for better and greater blessings. Therefore, they're the ones who receive multiple blessings in all areas of life. They're the precious stones and treasures of our creative universe and the collectible assets of a vital force in the universe, which makes them irreplaceable and inestimable assets in all creative endeavors. They're readily perceivable and instantly recognizable in any creative undertaking. All of this explains why capable folks are part and parcel with excellence, perfection, effective self-expression, success, and progress.

Capable folks know that the single most intuitive element of success is the ability to take quality action and sustain spirit of enthusiasm. Their emotional power and mental harmony enable them achieve full potential results and help them enjoy complete blessings. Their spirit of harmony comes from the power of undivided attention, concentrated efforts, dedicated interest, and mindful action. They're the ones who always build a chronological system of perfect harmony, rely on themselves, and establish an ethical standard and excellent skills for developing and promoting the young, capable individuals who can do better jobs. They know that there is no permanent result without a permanent action, and there is no permanent success without steady results.

So capable folks live on and gain value, and fortunately they have acquired unique skills, creative wisdom, and distinct knowledge that help them live wisely and enjoy a triumphant future. They invest their time, energy, and efforts to enhance and develop their innate abilities to produce better results. They enjoy greater success by using effective words to express their desires and their eyes to communicate intensity of information and definiteness of purpose. All of this shows that when they create opportunity, they see only potential possibility and then focus only on what they want to see and what matters most, eventually getting the best of the potential future. This in turn helps them to see only benefits and get quality results.

This certainly proves that they're unique and outstanding individuals with a higher volume of ideas, a boldness of spirit, and fearless hearts. Boldness in the face of difficulty is at the heart of being capable of facing challenges with one spirit and one mind striving to advance and achieve all potential business success. They persevere with steadfast hope, perfect love, passionate spirit, and ingenuity of mind and heart. With their brave spirits, they are mentally fit and visually splendid and therefore can deal with core issues. That's why they're undeniably brilliant and powerful individuals cheering themselves into productivity, capability, responsibility, and success. These are the people who created the modern world of today and continue to be the creators of the triumphant future. Certainly, they're the ones who will always use their vacation as vocation: a passionate and precise place to play and produce desirable results. All of this shows that they use their passionate profession as a breathing space for productive actions. They use their calling as a place of liberty to take quality actions and bring about positive results. Eventually, they see their occupation as a place of favorable opportunity, a place to explore new knowledge and get new experience. They see their jobs as joyful expressions of their desires, a place of triumphant future, and the disposition of a sense of gratitude and appreciation. This means that they see their careers as a place of opportunity to grow and develop; therefore, they use their areas of calling as a perfect field of excellent disposition of creative intelligence and a perfect place to exhibit and play excellent mind games to win more hearts and grow better businesses.

Their positive mental communication produces a positive reception and responsiveness. They're the ones who exploit positive energies and have a dedicated sense of purpose and progress, which shows that they are powerful individuals who have gained a sense of purpose and commitment and therefore have the mental agility and ability to sustain their winning streaks, maintain their emotional competency, and live in potential possibility. Perhaps they're the ones who have decided to believe in success and in potentiality and eventually live in active faith and function from an active sense of purpose, from a favorable condition, and from a dedicated sense of self-confidence.

Self-esteem is about how you define and value yourself. It's based on your positive experiences in life and your perceptions and assessments of things. It's important to foster a healthy sense of self-esteem because nothing is more important to intimacy than your sense of self-worth. Self-worth provides you with a dynamic, courageous fighting spirit to change the course of poverty. Therefore, capable folks function from a superior state of consciousness that attracts success and grows in wisdom.

Capable folks create positive environments that support their strength of character and produce positive feedback. Eventually, positive feedback becomes their distribution channel for success, development, and progress and even becomes the overall distribution channel for a steady flow of peace and happiness. Basically, these are powerful individuals who generate a positive, inspirational power and gain motivational strengths that allow them to acquire practical ideas and wisdom. All of this shows us that wisdom tends to grow in proportion to one's awareness of one's environment, or one's awareness of one's ignorance. Capable folks always create powerful, positive, visual pictures and sustain good, vibrant energies that can support their well-being and promote environmental awareness and interests.

By fostering self-confidence and understanding, a house is built, and through wisdom it's established. Capable folks are dedicated to perfection and excellence and therefore have quality standards that surpass ordinary standards. They have a great variety of strengths and eventually embody the best way to create, share, and discover values. That's why they're individuals with extreme devotion and dedication to the rules of success. Every notable success provides evidence of mental power and emotional strength. Substantial evidence has shown that capable folks believe in positive mental action, emotional wisdom, and creative intelligence. Nature dictates that they're individuals with great potential resources, exceptional character, and extraordinary lives. That's another reason they're fueled by a reasonable self-confidence—they're the ones who embody the greatest possible actions and the best responsible minds, which bring about the most desirable outcomes. All of this explains why their sound minds are the ingredients of success and the substance of thoughts that bring abundant results. It further shows why they're the foundational building blocks that clearly spell out all aspects of success that support different organizations.

Capable folks seek a real and enduring life and lasting happiness that will warm their days and shape not only their own personal worlds but the world around them. This is an ultimate truth worth seeking because happiness enables them to live their lives as they wish, generating value, enjoying their innate creations, and designing new and better things because they have the mental vigor, passion, vitality, strength of character, and soundness of mind to give us energy and hope. As a result, they change people's beliefs forever and therefore change the world by motivating young people to seek a higher purpose and bring streams of delight, hope, and courage into our lives. They also have changed tastes and styles and transformed old, uninspiring beliefs into new purposes. With their considerable energy, they make frantic efforts to make better things happen and have therefore changed the face of things and built attainable dreams for young, dynamic, and profitable individuals. With their powerful, mystical, and profound knowledge, they face the ultimate challenges. That's why they are designed to be productive and therefore create wealth and consistently lift their lives to greatness.

They're highly productive individuals who tend to think differently from anyone else, and they regularly put their strategies into action, unleash their vision, turn passion into profits, go after their dream lives, and get quality results. They focus on quality to outsmart competition in organizations with great strategies that are more successful and productive than those of the competition. This helps them harmoniously coordinate their energies, powers, and strengths to grow ever more sophisticated with attainable dreams. They have the capability to make smart, vital decisions and fine distinctions. Their principal goals are determined by effective actions and quality results to win. They always closely connect all the delightful and joyful experiences that can empower them to produce quality results and achieve all their desired goals.

Because their inspiring goals are the ultimate driving power that gives their lives meaning and direction and boosts their motivation and self-confidence, which shapes their actions and enhances their experiences in life. These experiences create sound ideas and delightful feelings through their sensory mechanisms of thought. That's why their chronological order of communication and action are integrated to produce outstanding quality results. Basically, capable folks know exactly what they want in life, so they know what to look for, when and where to look, and how to get it. That's why they all have found what they're looking for—they look with their hearts and minds and with strong conviction, seeing with the power of perception. Their passionate minds and courageous hearts are the oxygen of their souls and the breath of their lives. They're the ones who are transforming their dreams, goals, and ideas into real destiny, consciously attaining riches, continuously feeling good, and thinking more positively to achieve multiple results. Their sensory mechanism of ideas is the pathway to mental health, emotional competency, happiness, and success.

As we continue to grow and mature, we become more aware that these folks are consciously observing and making mental notes, bridging all the gaps of failure, and making real business successes happen. Through their managerial excellence and best possible leadership styles, they make prompt and smart decisions that greatly serve organizations and provide boundless rewards for the best efforts and behaviors. Their effective leadership skills and efficient management styles define them and enhance their sense of righteousness and belonging, which produces a strong and inevitable feeling that exists in human nature, and then meets the greatest fundamental, psychological, and emotional needs.

Enhancing their fundamental psychological needs have enabled capable folks to use all of their mental faculties and emotional capabilities to get worthwhile results, which they truly desire and ultimately deserve. They're using both their positive attitudes and personalities as checkpoints for progress, and above all, as a clearinghouse for all growth and personal development. That's why they have successful attitudes, ethical character traits, and most importantly, courageous spirits of progressive development. That's also what drives their actions and dedicated sense of purpose, which enhance their mental superiority and soundness of mind. It enriches their well-being and enhances their positive self-images to become a transparent sense and a reflective force of attraction.

Their self-confidence is constantly growing and developing their senses of self-worth and self-concepts that support their active belief systems and the strong convictions of success, which of course dominates the nature of their thinking and actions and ultimately drives their minds to accomplish something notable, desirable, and profitable.

Capable folks have the ability to make an invention into something possible and practicable by focusing on the areas in their control and ignoring circumstances beyond their control. They control situations by understanding all the pathways leading to wellness and therefore direct their goals and influence their environments in that direction. This enables them to overcome hindrances and roadblocks. All of this shapes and sharpens their awareness and perception so much that they become more effective when facing difficulty. They ultimately use difficulties as stepping stones to greatness. It even drives them to produce more useful, productive energies for higher-quality results. Through their specialized knowledge, they have acquired emotional intelligence and cognitive consciousness and have gained the most important skills for working for a better life. This means that they can deeply understand their environments and thoroughly use each and every strategic window of opportunity that comes their way because they know that they're responsible for their own well-being. They strive to make every effort to do whatever it takes to satisfy their desires.

Capable folks add richness to the human condition and synchronize the business world of commerce by inspiring others to change the way they think, feel, and act. With their strong, powerful words, they have the ability to communicate their passion, purpose, and meaning to others and therefore change the way people think, perceive, and act to get different results. They cultivate all the positive emotional habits of sound thought; embolden a sense of gratitude and appreciation; enhance a reasonable confidence and positive mind-set; and encourage acceptance, encouragement and perseverance that will help them communicate effectively and discover their paths to fulfillment and satisfaction. Through positive thinking and a sense of humor, they learn from the past, share positive experiences, deliver constructive feedback, keep their promises, and live in the present. This in turn leads them to feel good, communicate with the right words, ask useful questions, get the right answers, and receive valuable information to innovate the future. By acknowledging the contributions of others, they develop ambition, aim high, pursue their dreams with passion, and never surrender. They focus on areas of influence and pay proper attention to specific, useful information so they can make adequate sense of their keen observation and take congruent actions to make better things happen. They work hard to earn trust, stand firm, and have the inner strength to build people up and take responsibility for all their actions. With continuous improvement, they thoroughly understand reality and properly organize their thoughts, experiences, and plans to make a better future happen. They trust their gut feelings and intuition. Capable folks patiently and actively listen and strongly link positive experiences, therefore connecting powerful, positive, and active energies that enable them to act in certain ways to produce powerful and effective results that bring about positive, dynamic, and lasting change.

Capable folks have a well-sustained vision of the future, and they set clear and inspiring goals that greatly impact every aspect of their lives. Effective communication also supports their goals and helps them build and improve important relationships by deepening their connections and better understanding others. It also helps them develop younger capable folks who can help them improve the future. We all owe them a great debt because they are unique, priceless, and irreplaceable assets to any creative endeavor and help us build organizations, improve teamwork, and be better decision makers and problem solvers. They foster environments where creative ideas, sound feelings, trust, caring, and understanding can flourish. This is one of the most important factors that shapes their destinies. It serves as an excellent example of success that embodies the truth about capable folks who move from poverty to riches or from a poor beginning to high levels of achievement. They know the right time to change their personal worlds, flourish, and impact the future.

Capable folks make a huge impact by using positive words to communicate and change the future. They serve as an excellent example and use an unstoppable, undeniable revolutionary and evolutional language of nature in which life and light hold the truths that enlighten our minds and trigger certain feelings that put one in a resourceful state or particular condition that sparks positive actions and satisfies human needs. We all owe them a great debt because they are changing our personal worlds into better places and constantly producing, directing, and leading the way to a far better future. They perceive the uncharted future and climb the ladder of success to produce powerful and lasting results. This makes them selective individuals who balance situations, resolve differences, and eventually build trust and lead without resistance because they know that positive words provide them a flexibility of mind that brings solutions to life.

Capable folks choose their words wisely to promote their emotional health and establish strong bonds, and they wisely sustain them, eventually molding their destinies and rising to fame and fortune. That's why they can deepen their knowledge and perceive things through profound ways of understanding and rational ways of thinking, which greatly molds their perceptions and helps them achieve all their goals. These are the main reasons why they always follow the right instructions, obey the rules of success, and respect the principles of entrepreneurial, ethical behavior and moral adaptation that hold the foundations for quality enhancement. They appreciate all useful human resources that bring worthwhile values that feed real economic growth and expand opportunities that foster success. Capable folks gather specific information, organize particular facts, and therefore embody ideas that enable them make prompt, firm, and valuable decisions that help them push the right buttons at the right places at the right time to move in the right direction to produce powerful, positive, and lifelong results.

Of course, all of this, is crucial to success, which typically becomes an integral element of life that builds the best possible minds and ultimately supports the most comprehensive value. The more capable folks think constructively, the more they see things at the higher levels and the more they believe, conceive, and achieve the best possible results. This requires a willingness of heart, dedicated action, courage, passion, and the spirit of enthusiasm. For them, every solution to every problem is based on dedicated action that flows from a unified field of conscious awareness, keen observation, and profound understanding. This is likely why capable folks are value-based, knowledge-based, and goal-driven individuals who find innovative business solutions and therefore change the world into a better place. This explains why their lives are rooted in their best judgments, sound thoughts, rational thinking, and smart choices, which certainly makes them value-driven individuals who pioneer better jobs, harness their purposes, and achieve their goals.

Capable folks use their great energy and talent to anticipate the future, prepare for opportunity, and continuously live in the present. They also spend their time listening, probing, and observing facts and then deepening their levels of awareness and following their hearts' desires. They are unique and indisputable individuals who have made their lives worthwhile and are separated from ordinary people because they have well-defined purposes and missions and properly committed goals. They always have the end in mind and know the end from the beginning; they take significant, effective actions to protect all their goals. They always protect their goals from the beginning and eventually protect their results from intruders because they know that the quality of their goals and outcomes will determine the quality of their lives. Capable folks always face the need to become more adaptable and transformational. They constantly rethink and restructure their minds and adopt new, effective strategies to maintain specific, progressive rules of success to improve their lives and futures.

The greatest sense of gratitude and appreciation must come with both knowledge and action, in addition to some level of experience and understanding. Capable folks have economic foresight and financial freedom, and they gather useful knowledge and take favorable views of opportunities that will make a big difference. By enhancing their emotional intelligence and improving their ability to recognize and understand their emotions, they can achieve better goals and live greater lives. They have found inner strengths and then turned their energies to variety of purposes, experiencing and expecting the most desirable outcomes that will greatly enhance their goals and transform their dreams, purposes, and visions into reality. This is what seems to make the biggest difference between success and failure.

As capable folks sincerely seek, think, and have success in mind, they draw positive energy, and get more powerful, vibrant energy; and become more vital forces. As a result, their potential belief systems greatly increase and eventually become an excellent means by which to foster a steady growth for everyone. They help organizations solve problems, complete particular tasks, motivate workers, and build a steady stream of profitable innovation while guiding their own ideas to achieve their own goals. Everyone benefits.

This type of exemplary intelligence eventually opens all our minds to useful suggestions, better opinions, and bright ideas. Everyone embraces positive change as an established opportunity rather than established fear because that's the foundation of economic security in any organization. This explains why capable folks' optimistic spirits attract positive energies and fuel career ambitions that greatly inspire positive actions in all aspects of business success.

With so much more value, accuracy, and precision, and with all the considerable initiatives, they have found different patterns of thinking and different ways of looking inward that allow the heart, mind, and body speak with objective certainty and produce streams of consciousness. This great mental attitude of gratitude impacts the mind and influences it to think and act in a certain way and produce certain results. That's why capable folks are undeniably brilliant individuals with sound ideas and proper focus. They can observe, think, and act their ways to greater success and better futures. They all maintain the right attitude that fits their unique skills, talents, careers, and professions to achieve great goals. They also maintain all the ethical characteristics and moral principles that ultimately support their personal growth and development and therefore enhance all their creative efforts. This in turn enables them to stay stronger and remain more effective in life.

Their growing minds are very rich in sense, and eventually they will become an immeasurable intelligence that serves a worthwhile life and represents a priceless and lasting value. That's why they always perceive and represent all the positive visual images of creative imagination that guide their thoughts and personal values to serve the most comprehensive qualities of life.

One by one, they're prepared to welcome and face every new challenge and difficult situation in life as a new opportunity to wrestle with, win, and gain more experience, more skill, and new power because they all have well-defined goals and fully spelled-out plans to create their own lives. They strive to improve the golden moment of opportunity and catch the good that is within their reach. So instead of being paralyzed in the face of difficulty, they look for opportunity in every difficult situation and take advantage of it to improve the future. That's why they are always feeling good, cheerful, and vibrant and eventually strive to prevent problems instead of wasting significant time and energy solving them. Capable folks are always developing preventive maintenance plans and creating alternative plans to help them preserve valuable resources. This supports their goals and ultimately helps them have the clearest vision to discern the chance to succeed, flourish with prosperity, and enhance their creative powers to achieve all their goals. Their knowledge flows through creative intelligence, and eventually it feeds on useful resources and market values that support their personal strengths. They are able to develop capable young folks who are equally inspiring and empowering to others who can move with clarity, inner strength, and certainty.

These folks inspire and move us with their powerful words, deeds, and charm because they hold the ultimate truths, the undeniable facts about life, and the essence of everything that governs life. That's why they're cautious and have well-guarded powers of knowledge and highly preserved qualities of character. They use their values for what they truly represent because they're fully centered and properly connected with others. They seize all opportunities and take advantage of them to grow their businesses and enrich their lives. They identify and provide the environmental stimuli necessary for optimal psychological and emotional well-being and physical health.

As we continue to grow and improve, we will find out why capable folks are strongly aligned and firmly fixed individuals whose clarity of purpose, moral character, and well-disciplined knowledge make their pursuit of happiness possible and produce wonderful results. And as we continue to believe and expand in consciousness, we will discover the reasons why they are such figures of inspiration, passion, and motivation. They're unique individuals who have experienced the past, exploit the present circumstances, and use what they have learned to venture into the future. That's why they're the fountainhead for so much of the civilized world. They're individuals with useful information who convey and share value and exchange positive, powerful, and exciting experiences in life. They're always expanding the measures of excellence and therefore adding value to practice-based training, standards-based learning, uniqueness of knowledge, and creative wisdom that sparks inspiration and passion. Their flexible knowledge passes through conscious awareness, keen observation, and mindful actions. Their higher levels of understanding and broader points of view shine through their elegant actions and clearly speak more loudly than mere words.

One of the major reasons that capable folks are heard loud and clear is because their powerful words work in concert with effective actions that produce clear results. This is why they're the inspirational power that guides human souls—they all have found different ways of looking inward, perceiving value, inspiring others to be their best, finding reasons to believe in the people around them, influencing their environments, expressing their desires, and achieving great goals. They are inspired thinkers with unique intelligence who are the crucial elements of success and the vital forces of progress. They're truly remarkable individuals who provide us all the stimuli necessary to improve and maintain physical, emotional, and psychological health by increasing awareness and enhancing positive environments that can empower and inspire more lives to peak performance.

Capable folks represent the best characteristics of the best possible life. Their positive energy rejuvenates our minds and hearts and becomes an attributed part of the best possible universal forces that ultimately help us unleash our potential energies and enjoy unlimited potential possibilities. This is why they are considered the life forces that enhance and enrich our well-being and help us experience happiness and enjoy optimism.

Capable folks have struck gold by making a positive difference in the lives of others through specialized skills, useful knowledge, and a clear vision of the future. Therefore, it's important to remember that he or she who has a clear vision of the future has gold, he or she who has gold has power, and he or she who has power has the authority to lead the way to impact the future and flourish and prosper in life. So far, capable folks are truly making huge differences and getting what they want in life through a realistic, sustainable, and authentic vision of the future because they have highly prioritized goals and greater business performance. They're the ones who actively communicate their inner conviction and motivation for making smart and firm decisions and taking quality actions. It's also critical to understand why they are consistently developing and enhancing their unique quality that inspires and moves us and why they have constructive attitudes that drive us toward success and progress. All of this helps guard their eternal peace and happiness. Remember that they all have unique skills and specialized methods of expressing their emotional needs. They're well-recognized and properly identified by their unique mental dispositions and constructive attitudes. They have disciplined goals that regulate their minds, inspire their hearts, and set them apart from the rest.

Those who pulled us out of our ruts and moved us forward into action have inspired us for a greater good. They are the ones who have moved us to perform better and achieve greater results. They have changed our belief systems and should be remembered as extraordinary people who only see success, think success, and act successfully to achieve positive rewards. They know what they want, and they have a burning desire to achieve it. They see the world as a properly established place to accomplish all their desired goals, so they strive to live in practical wisdom and in conscious awareness, and they reap the benefits as a result.

CHAPTER 3

MOTIVATION

With a new day comes new strength and new thoughts.
—ELEANOR ROOSEVELT

We all know that we're different, and different people see differently, think differently, and get different results because we all have different reasons for doing things. We all have different reasons for learning. However, all our reasons for acting are to succeed in life, support our emotional well-being, enjoy greater futures, and ultimately enjoy healthier and happier lives. The key element driving us toward achieving all these goals is determined by a proper motivation. Motivation is the driving force that rules our desires and the inner power that pushes us to do things. It provides us a reason to act that rewards our creative efforts and enhances our well-being. Motivation provides us the answer to a successful life and helps us stay consciously awake and breed more value.

Every solution in life begins with motivation and stays actively alive through motivation. That's why motivation is the power that controls and directs our behaviors, feelings, and actions. Motivation produces a strong chain of positive energies, constructive thoughts, and profitable ideas that prompt us to take the best possible actions to achieve the best possible results. As we inspire our minds, we stimulate them to see things in a certain way and act in a particular way to achieve particular results, which provides us with the mental pictures of our desires so we can see clearly what we truly want and make quality and concrete decisions to attain it. In addition, it provides us the positive visual images of our thoughts and the blueprint of our internal communications that support our active beliefs and guide our emotional well-being. As a result, motivation enables us to actively perceive things in one holistic point of view that reveals the substance of our ideas and unites all creative insights and practical ideas into a crystallized whole that gives us the opportunity to win, the opportunity to acquire, and the opportunity to progress and succeed in any creative discipline.

This is the most important attribute needed to achieve any type of result, which is necessary for any degree of success at any time. So if you're endeavoring to achieve success, motivation will give you inner vitality and purpose, inner power and strength that will support your specific actions and help you prepare your mind for physical fitness and mental readiness. It will awaken your spiritual and emotional awareness and open the doors to success, prosperity, and health. It will guide your mind, body, and spirit to work in harmony to achieve specific results and arouse all your impulses of thought that influence you to think and act in a certain way and produce certain results. In addition, it pushes you toward your destiny and enables you to arrive successfully, giving you a positive outlook that supports your creative spirit. This produces positive vibes that radiate and attract similar positive energies that move you toward your desired ends. It stimulates your interest and attention and enables you to make prompt and strong decisions that help you act efficiently and effectively to produce the quality results you need.

As you think constructively and act effectively, you will realize the importance of motivation. You already know that motivation is the combination of desires, values, and beliefs that drive you to take action. This means that if you consider something important, you assign value to it and are inspired to act and get it. This shows you why motivation gives you a good element of heart and then provides you the driving force and the drawing power that balances your mental and emotional well-being. So knowing what you value and desire will help you achieve your goals and give you the power and the strength to guard them. To understand what motivates you, you will need to understand what is important to you. You need to set attainable goals that will help you get to the level you want to achieve. Motivation inspires your mind by reintegrating knowledge in new and unique ways, which provides you with an outstanding value and completeness, enhances your self-esteem, and improves your self-worth to elevate your thoughts and achieve your inspiring goals. In addition, it puts you in a state of sublimity that provides you great benefits, enabling you to focus on higher priorities, reach higher values, find greater mental fitness and agility, and allow you to take action that will greatly help you maintain a consistent stream of success.

Motivation improves your productive capability and capacity to produce value and then enables you to maintain a steady stream of innovation. In addition, it improves your mental productivity and enables you to maintain your mental harmony. This will enhance your mental power and physical strength, giving you the ability to act effectively to get plentiful results. As you increase your motivational levels, you will enter a state of alertness and readiness that prompts you to action, pushing you toward the object of your desire. This is the driving force that enables you to persist and persuade until you achieve your goals.

As motivation increases, profits in business increase as well. Motivation gives you sound ideas that enable you to understand the intangible impulse of your thoughts, the impulse of your actions, and the spiritual value surrounding your purpose. It provides you a reasonable belief and a strong conviction that enables you to clearly understand the true meaning of your purpose. It gives you the freedom of choice, the power that will enable you to wisely own your mind, consciously direct your spirit, and actively control your body to work for you, not against you. It enables you to develop a self-disciplined mind, a self-controlled spirit, and a properly directed body that can ignite a meaningful purpose that inspires positive actions.

So once motivation increases, businesses grow in profits. When you discover and develop your skills, you will massively grow in business because even as specialized knowledge increases, motivation helps you render useful service and develop a burning desire that spins the wheel of success and prosperity. It transforms your dreams into organized plans, organized knowledge, and effective action that inspires productivity. Because motivation fuels a burning desire and supports a congruent mind and active faith, it enables you to ride an exciting and inspiring journey toward your burning desire. It translates potentials into material riches, material blessings, and great abundance and the highest good. It enables you to convert desire into reality, and plan into action and then translates sound ideas into money. Ultimately, motivation helps you convert money into happiness, health, and prosperity, which grows from business profits.

As you grow in knowledge to advance your career, motivation helps you convert all your fears into courage and courage into success. Success then transforms into happiness, joy, and peace of mind. As a result, motivation enables you to burn all the negative bridges of fear that cause you to fail and helps you build a strong, dependable, and supportive bridge to success and progress. In addition, it strongly links all reliable emotions that enhance and enrich your well-being, preparing the way for multiple successes and clearing the road for multiple developments. It opens a point of approach to human consciousness that gives you greater power for a higher achievement. It also gives you a sustainable and reliable power that sparks a great passion that supports a positive spirit of enthusiasm.

As you take your career to the next level, motivation enables you to get what you want and helps you stay active and live in conscious awareness. As a result, it strengthens your mind–body connection and helps boost your mood while giving you plenty of energy to lift your spirits. Motivation clears the way for a better life and a brighter future. As you think constructively, it drives you to inspired action that ultimately gives you the power of enthusiasm. It provides you an exciting experience and a greater sense of purpose that fuels your life and empowers your mind and body, providing you with determination to produce desirable results.

Learning to think creatively therefore opens the doors to self-motivation because it inspires positive actions that bring you multiple results. If you get the passion that fuels your desire, motivation will give you the strength, the spirit of enthusiasm to pursue your dreams, and the great sense of humor to achieve your goals in life. So if you want to get positive results, you have to think positive thoughts, have strong faith in yourself, and create a burning desire and sound feeling that can bring you a powerful and authentic result.

This is one great source of triumphant joy that gives you a lifetime of comfort and happiness and can be transmuted into one formal system of communication that is promising and readily available. Motivation provides you a sense of transparency, an acute sense of responsiveness, a dedicated sense of accuracy, and a pure sense of commitment and practice. Furthermore, it improves your sense of competency, enhances your physical fitness and mental sharpness, grows your mind, and inspires your spirit to propel action.

As you continue to think constructively, motivation will continue to provide you the potential power and source of reason, the power of guidance, and the inner strength of action. This enables you to transform your intention into one great success and helps you transmute a real success into inner peace, health, and happiness. It can even help you change a real success into a great future of awesome purpose, which enhances a far better future and enriches a far greater life. This gives you a constructive habit of success and progress and provides you a properly established pattern of thought, influence, and action. It enhances a constructive pattern of accomplishments, which gives you a strict habit of work and a dedicated sense of purpose that will ultimately provide you the power of concentration. That's why motivation creates an atmosphere of love, peace, and unity and produces an atmosphere of success, prosperity, and health.

This is one great source of courage that will spark development in any creative environment to better your life. It will help you expand your reach so you can live more life and enjoy more success with less stress because motivation gives you the power to enhance your purpose. So if you are a reasonable person seeking to succeed in life, I encourage you to be fully prepared in advance and properly motivated before seeking success. Motivation will help you recognize and accept the basic truths about life, helping you to become the rider of life. That's why motivation produces positive habits of thought that enhance the mind and then become the emotional food and mental oxygen for the living soul. This shows you why motivation is the main source of inspiration, the main source of power of passion, and the positive spirit of enthusiasm that's capable of shaping the truth that produces a conscious spirit and the ultimate life energy that provides you the essential elements of success.

This means that success in all of its forms must begin with motivation because it gives you the ability to persevere and achieve your goals.

That's why it's important to note that every success in business starts with motivation and permanently stays alive through motivation. You need a quality state of mind to achieve definite goals, propel your actions, grow your businesses, and apply practical wisdom in your daily life. In addition, motivation gives you the energy you need for a greater future ahead, adding value and the sincerity of a mindful purpose, a humble heart, and the sense of humor necessary to handle every business endeavor. Motivation boosts your morale and enables you to handle rejection and properly deal with any situation that may likely present itself. It also boosts your mood, which empowers you to work with an open and diligent mind.

But before that will happen, it is critical to know that when you lack interest or motivation, you see little or no value in business. So enhancing a motivational technique will enable you to see reality through your own mental eyes, expand your vision, and help you seize any opportunity when it knocks. It provides you a sound sense of purpose and a clear understanding in any positive environment.

Motivation stimulates the power of thinking, the power of observation, and the creative awareness that provides you the necessary ingredients of success and the ability to seize opportunities when they knock.

Motivation is the vehicle that lifts valuable minds and quality spirits to a higher plane. It enables them to continuously climb into unknown and helps them clearly see the uncharted future to exploit great benefits.

Motivation can take you to higher levels because it's the power that can lift any positive mind from the level of positive thinking to the level of actualization. It prepares the mind to observe hidden values, helps you drive value, actively live in value, and eventually produce quality results. Motivation is a universal language of body and mind that brings you great benefits and supports a clear language of business purpose that brings you a profitable outcome. Motivation is a universal language of body and mind that brings you a richer, more refined language of spirit of enthusiasm in the marketplace, workplace, and every aspect of life. That's why it's a legend of creation as well as passion that enables you to properly design your life in your own way for a better future and a greater life that serves much higher purposes.

If you have already set up realistic goals and have creative vision in business, enhancing motivational techniques should be your first priority. Motivating your employees could be one of the most important business investments and crucial decisions that will determine your business success. It's absolutely essential to lead to more sales, bring in more profits, and inspire more positive actions that will further grow your business goals. As a result, it will enable you to acquire a useful and important knowledge that supports your business concepts as well as your overall well-being. That's why motivation improves your standard of living, increases your economic sense, and enhances your useful life. It provides you the key to unlock unlimited potential possibilities to enjoy the future of awesomeness, the promises of greatness, and the power of acquisition.

Therefore, it's important for organizations to understand and to structure the work environment to encourage efficient and productive behaviors necessary to make better things happen. Motivation is the prime mover of all action and the rider of all success and progress, which brings you a significant flow of business and an overflowing love of life. This is a happy hunting ground for all successful life, for all important relationships, and for all profitable businesses. It's the principal element of a positive mind and an ideal maker of peace and unity. It enhances your gut feelings and supports a pure mind that is flooded with abundance of love, inner peace, and harmony, which produce a distinct line of success and a properly marked line of action that supports your life and enriches your overall well-being. As you keep this in mind, you will certainly know why motivation fosters a profit-seeking spirit, a profit-driven mind that generates more deals, more leads, and more sales, bringing you an abundance of results and guiding your spirit of passion that fuels your life, supports your business, and ignites positive actions in any organization. In addition, it gives you an intensive desire for success and a strong motive for achievement, stimulating the mind and empowering the living soul to get you to the dreamland of success and stay there. It inspires you to think and muscle your way to prosperity and health, enabling you to turn every stumbling block into stepping stones of success and awesome moments of joy and greatness. Motivation gives you ethical value and moral character, a moral justice and fairness of mind that provide you the ability to perform and achieve.

Enhancing motivational technique is the key to understanding your employees and achieving success. Motivation can often be used as a tool to help predict behavior that inspires new and productive ideas and instill confidence in any organization. It also inspires optimistic spirits to render useful service, make conscious efforts, take quality actions, think better thoughts, and live better lives. You can think and expand in business because motivation enables you to cultivate the spirit of success that enhances the quality of human life.

As you continue to grow and develop, you will see that motivation involves three emotional needs when it comes to business success: arousal, direction, and intensity. Arousal is what initiates both mental and physical actions, and it's fueled by your desire for something you actually need at a given moment. *Direction* refers to the path you take in accomplishing the goals you set for yourself. Finally, *intensity* is your level of vigor and work performance. These emotional needs result in four outcomes:

1. Motivation serves to direct your attention and allows you to focus on particular issues to bring about solutions.
2. It stimulates you to put forth efforts to achieve a definite course.
3. Motivation results in persistence, preventing you from deviating from the goal-seeking behavior, from your goal-driven mind, and from your practice-based training.
4. Motivation results in task strategies, mental activities, emotional strength, and spiritual awareness.

If you don't have self-motivation, you have no cushion on which to rest your mind and properly comfort your soul. Motivation is the cushion that improves your mental health and enhances your emotional well-being. As you continue to believe and grow, motivation will continue to give you the mental uniqueness and great passion for success that provides you a strong chain of reasons for a consistent growth. In addition, it provides you the eternal light for constant productivity, a fixed course of action, and a steady flow of good. It offers you a positive, continuous course of action and a lasting chain of business success, fueling the fire of burning desire that stirs up action that gives you the spirit of conscious life and meaningful purpose. Sharing useful experiences give you the spirit of conscious dissemination of valuable information that enables you to build valuable business relationships based on trust that helps you grow in business and live a useful life. Motivation gives you a distinct sense of separation of value from conflict, as well as separation of business life from personal life. This helps you create a unique line of progress and a positive circumstance of success, giving you a dedicated attention and unity of interest, love, and passion that enables you to focus on solutions rather than problems, helps you focus on prevention rather than cure, and ultimately enables you to seize control and maintain conscious direction. As you think constructively and act effectively, motivation enables you to make diligent efforts to move toward your dreams, goals, and plans in life, providing you a mental map for accomplishment.

Use the most comprehensive achievement guide possible to stay motivated because it will enable you to prepare your mind for future events, help you focus on what matters most, and eventually help you get the most vital facts. Motivation gives you a sound moral character and flexible personality and leads you to take quality actions, turning your noble ideas and sound thoughts into a higher level of creative innovation, practical insight, and profitable knowledge.

That's why motivation puts you in a state of wonder and enables you to become the ultimate source of creativity and helping you serve the inventive sense of imagination that produces a new spirit of moral excellence to pursue greatness. This is the ultimate power that produces a high-energy brain wave that releases your inner splendor and allows potential goodness to flow through you. As you think constructively and act effectively, it creates an emotional fantasy that provides you a mystic cord of good memory of sound thoughts as well as a good memory of experiences, guiding you to consciously choose your words and actions to serve your greatest and best needs, especially if you are in business.

When you're in business to serve and satisfy the needs and desires of prospective customers, motivation allows you to better understand their emotional needs and gives you the power and strength to satisfy those needs. So if you're looking for a better life, it's crucial to know that motivation is the cushion of life, the cushion that enables you to consciously live and breed more life. So if you want to make life super awesome, you need constant motivation to achieve that. It serves as a pillow for all good health as well as a cushion for all active and comfortable life events that will help you consciously think and act effectively. As long as you continue to believe in motivation, it will continue to produce a powerful, energetic force that will provide you the ultimate wind of positive action, quality affirmation, and the green light of success, prosperity, and health. Motivation also provides you with a consistent strength and courage that gives you a new spirit of empathy and a systematic pattern of conduct that will adequately support all of your emotional needs. It helps you produce a specific course of action and a definite line of behavior that supports your business. In addition, it provides you a clear destination and a wonderful adventure that requires a unique method of approach. It enables you to guide your emotions, giving you a deep aspiration that enables you to take that extra step and go that extra mile to achieve quality results, live a better life, and enjoy a greater future. Motivation provides you a positive impulse of thought that gives you a ceaseless desire for success, helping you unlock your potential future and revealing the positive tendency of life that enhances your strength of character and moral justice. When you realize the importance of motivation, it spins the wheel of success, prosperity, and wealth to give you better opportunities and a greater future.

Almost everything you want in life is guided, controlled, and directed by motivation because it gives you the key to direct your mind and produce the results you need in life. That's why it represents the reasons for action, enhances life, and enriches your well-being. It's an intellectual paradise, a happy hunting ground for intellectual purpose, and heaven for the intellectual mind. It gives you the infinite wisdom of existence, a sharp sense of observation, a clear sense of purpose and decisiveness, a prescribed sense of action, and a committed sense of advancement to conceive reality and achieve success.

In the most effective, efficient, and productive way possible, motivation is the main mental ingredient of sound thought and the intellectual powerhouse of good reason that inspires your senses and development and can reveal all the mysteries of life. If you can think positive and feel good, motivation will become a potent force, a source of continuous action, and an ideal state of mind of success, which of course plays an important role in achieving great success. That's why motivation puts you in a constructive state of mind that gives you the superior power of influence that produces an obsessive desire for a notable accomplishment. It helps you boost your creative energy to bring about a mental harmony that supports your overall well-being.

We live in a business world that needs constant motivation. As we have the benefits in mind, motivation will help us play the band of magic that reveals our savvy consciousness and enables us to fully enjoy the superior quality of intelligence. We will be able to see the big picture in life and move toward achieving our desired aims. In addition, motivation provides us a compelling desire and intense emotion that moves us toward achieving our goals.

This is the driving force of action and the propelling power of reason for a consistent action and continuous productivity. That's why it represents a set of energetic forces that originate from within us and around us and then gives us sound sense and sweet reasons for our diligent efforts. We need motivation because it's in the very heart of education as well as in the root of civilization. And as modern civilization unfolds the mysteries of life, it also reveals why motivation is necessary for life education, which gives us nobility of purpose that grows our inner splendor of consciousness. This provides us an intellectual equilibrium of mind, a positive bearing, and a state of balance that gives us multiple results and enriches our purposes. As long as we conceive and believe, we will certainly achieve our goals because motivation is the determinant force of action and leads to an ingenuity of mind that produces a dedicated sense of sharpness and a heart of bravery.

To all good people who are in the business world, I encourage all of you to strive to have quality business minds because motivation is the source and substance of your faith, the source and substance of your action, and the center of all opportunities and blessings. It gives you a strong-willed mind and an explicit and congruent belief, which gives you the power and strength that fuels positive actions and brings you positive results. Furthermore, it gives you a dedicated sense of purpose and a willfulness to act that sparks the spirit of enthusiasm and creates the summer of opportunities. In addition, it gives you a vital energy and life force and becomes the main spring of your soul's evolution and serves as the fountainhead of all life purposes and business endeavors.

As you continue to enhance and develop motivational techniques for your business efforts, you will continue to grow your business because motivation will help you sustain your energy levels and manage your business growth. Ultimately, it becomes a resilient force that produces a positive spirit of perseverance that supports your mental drives and ignites emotional and spiritual liveliness in all your creative endeavors. It will bring you practical ideas and actions and transform all of your spiritual blankness and emotional darkness into a bright light of life. Motivation draws all the hunches of success and all the good, powerful, and desirable feelings of progress and excitement, which enhance the gut feelings and intuitive wisdom that support your well-being and provide you all the utilitarian values and useful purposes that support your emotional health. This is the foundational building block of success and the positive stream of innovation.

This will help you continue to grow and mature in business. As a result, you will become more aware of the essence of motivation. Most important, you will know that motivation is vital food for the soul and the oxygen of the mind. This is a deeply rooted spirit that satisfies your desires within and ultimately gives you optimism and vivid sensory experiences, providing you legitimate reasons for action and bringing you a bounty reward that influences you to become part and parcel of the universal body of truth that serves real business purposes. Motivation produces a keen interest that enables you to explicitly express your mind with a clearly determined action, good intentions, and desirable elements of the heart filled with realistic and detailed plans.

Creating a realistic business plan is the key to creating healthy habits, reaching your ideal, and enabling you to change the unlikely into possible. This helps you create healthy goals so you can continue to grow and eventually enhance and develop your mind to achieve your goals. As this happens, you will see that motivation is a positive seed of thought that creates a healthier attitude that sparks positive behavior and productive action. It produces a keen interest that enables you to plant healthier thoughts. It helps you achieve success and ultimately helps you push forward with all your innermost being until you achieve all your business goals and have an abundance of opportunities for self-advancement. That's why motivation enables you to maintain a cheerful disposition, which gives you a strong desire to achieve notable success and get multiple results.

Motivation puts you in a state of readiness, in a positive state of physical goodness and healthy feeling. Certainly, this enables you to listen with empathy and speak with caution. It also enables you to listen carefully and observe patiently. Motivation produces good feelings that allow you to do what you love and love what you do.

Most important, motivation holds the key to meditation, through which you can access your inner mind to open the doors to happiness, peace, harmony, and real success. It's a natural power that comes from the spirit of truth and passion, which have been patiently fueling the mind. It also comes with logical thoughts that can hold value and properly transform value into physical reality. Basically, it holds your active belief systems and your strong convictions that determine your actions and success, increasing the degree of your happiness and health and enabling you to properly filter information and adequately transfer it to other minds. Motivation is the secret power cord that holds life, the intangible web that connects valuable lives and strongly preserves and retains values. This is why motivation is the key to success in business and spurs multiple business successes in any area of calling. It's also properly blessed with spiritual dominion, mental harmony, emotional wisdom, and a complete reverential alertness. This is why it's the power that rules your destiny, controls your future, and directs your life.

This is what we need to advance and grow because motivation plays a critical role in business success. That's why we need to understand that motivation is at the heart of our attention and concentration, and it's vital food for the soul and the center of attraction and manifestation. Motivation is the power that satisfies effective communication and the key that opens the doors of the mind and enhances the body of knowledge. It allows us to develop an attitude of gratitude and appreciation and increase the energy that fuels useful knowledge. This is the power that supports the business mind, the main source of our abundance, and guides the power of self-confidence and constructive mental direction. Motivation empowers creative intelligence, which enables capable folks to continuously satisfy their desires and find more and more success. In one way or another, this shows us why motivation provides us a positive tendency for success, a positive outlook for progress, and a favorable circumstance for effective action. As we conceive of and believe in motivation, we will have a positive power that is endowed with the positive truth, a strong spirit of love, and the spirit of passion for work. This will enhance our motivational techniques because passion provides us a new hope that invigorates our spirits in our daily living. It brings us a renaissance spirit of newness, the birth of the golden mind, and the awakening of consciousness for spiritual transformation in our daily lives. In addition, it rejuvenates our energies and regenerates our thought habits. It's a rebirth of beliefs and a renewal of consciousness that provides us a uniqueness of character and soundness of mind.

In the most basic sense, motivation enables us to exchange valuable information and helps us gather useful knowledge that will enable us to build momentum with great hope and high expectations. It will also enable us to sow wisely and reap abundantly. As we think and reap, it will help us ask open-ended questions, and it will give us the patience that is necessary for us to receive valuable answers that can support our business minds and enrich our business lives. As a result, this helps us know why motivation gives us the clarity of mind needed to achieve definite goals, providing us the pull and push that we will need to acquire a real, potential value and enable us to build a wealth of knowledge to acquire a wealth of material realities. In addition, it will ultimately help us plant diligently and germinate wisely the seeds of success that produces abundance of healthy life and brings us an abundance of peace and harmony in our relationships and businesses.

So if you have inspiring dreams, motivation will enable you to overcome self-doubt, which leads to procrastination and ultimately to failure. You will conquer your fear of poverty, which originates from a lack of aspiration that comes from a lack of motivation. Motivation gives you positive thoughts and feelings that provide you an active spirit, a boundless faith, and quality health. You will be physically fit and mentally competent to move toward your inspiring goals and produce dynamic results. In addition, motivation enables you to become industrious and helps you develop a self-reliant attitude and passionate desire, which gives you emotional intelligence, mental integrity, and stability of the mind. This in turn provides you guidance, awakens the passionate spirit of enthusiasm, and stimulates the vibrational patterns of thought that intensify positive emotions, enabling you to meditate on thoughts of the utmost value. Additionally, motivation puts you in a state of readiness, in a state of sharing and receiving values, and allows you to enjoy the privilege of freedom of choice and spontaneous action.

If you desire to succeed, motivation will enable you to overcome self-imposed fear, self-limitation, and self-sabotaging behaviors that convey negative information that causes fear and failure. Fear is the root of failure because it stunts your decision-making skills and keeps you from ever taking action, but motivation provides you the power and ability to move with certainty, clarity, and intensity to achieve your goals. Motivation clears the road for active minds and positive energies to live and breed more good and achieve more value. As a result, it gives you the power and opportunity to penetrate into other minds, learning and gaining useful knowledge that will enable you to adapt to different environments to achieve more and more success.

Motivation is the cushion of knowledge and the seat of action that brings you congruent results. As you conceive and believe, you will certainly achieve because motivation enables you to visualize and believe in something much better and bigger than you, create positive habits, and transform positive thoughts into physical action and productive results. That's why motivation inspires action in any creative business and provides you unlimited potential reality. This boosts your morale; lifts your consciousness; and gives you a quality life, a unique purpose, a specialized power, and potential knowledge, all of this supports your overall well-being. Because motivation enables you to develop a thorough mind, to really know yourself, and to harmonize and use your knowledge to serve and enhance your well-being. It blinds any potential inferiority complex and helps you charge forward to accomplish your goals. It enables you to harness your power and develop a consistent and persistent way of continuous pursuit of excellence and greatness. It enhances your mind to keep you well-informed and fully familiarized in your area of calling. As a result, you gain practical insight and inspirational value that inspires action and enables you to compound value and build an atmosphere of prosperity. Motivation draws to you the substance necessary for growth and development and attracts all good things to you. As you believe and abide in the consciousness of it, it begins to manifest in all of your affairs, channeling the power of persuasion and determination to win, the persistence to succeed and advance into a greater future and live better life. As you continue to believe and abide in the consciousness of it, you will continue to grow and live a better life and enjoy a better future because motivation gives you a better understanding of life, bringing you greater opportunities that enable you to deeply penetrate into the heart of an unprepared mind to explore value and enjoy greater life. Motivation gives you inner guidance, mental alertness, and conscious awareness that will greatly guard your life.

As you become truly inspired and properly motivated, you will have a strong foundation to act on your convictions because motivation gives you a sense of priority that enables you to preserve your energy and use it at the right moments to generate results you want. Further, it provides you the object of truths and all the vital ingredients that will enable you to rise to fame and fortune or rise to higher power and achieve greater success. This in turn gives you ceaseless energy and provides you endless possibilities that enable you to make ceaseless efforts to attract more abundant influx of goodness and inpouring of blessings. It also gives you an irresistible spirit that enables you to live in a state of good mental health, an embodiment of a mental state of comfort and stability, a state of self-paradise that brings you inner peace, inner joy, inner happiness, and inner harmony. All this occurs because motivation provides you a conscious awareness, a keen observation, and a conscious mind, which afford you higher intelligence and greater power. That's why motivation is a creative power guiding and supporting an active spirit of enthusiasm that serves your best interests. As a result, it reveals to you the reality of nature, unfolding to you the reality of life, and giving you the power of recognition and realization of all truths. In addition, it unfolds the reality of evolution and reveals the secrets of infinite wisdom. This is why motivation gives you a positive, mental enlightenment, a mental soundness that enables you to live an extraordinary life and empowers you to connect with great men and women of incredible wisdom who can help you succeed in life. As you think positive thoughts and strive to grow, you will eventually succeed because motivation helps you conquer fear and absorb your negative feelings and transform them into positive energy, providing you a passionate spirit of enthusiasm and bringing you to a state of absolute tranquility.

All of this gives you a powerful life filled with absolute purpose and definite meaning and direction. So if you can triumph in the struggle, you will live in the consciousness of it because the key to effective communication comes through motivation. That's why motivation enables you to become an effective listener and helps you become an effective communicator and a good analyzer who brings a solid and sound sense of awesome values. You need and want motivation because it's a crucial substance of a good mind and a critical element of a good heart. It enables you to follow your heart in good faith. It also helps you follow your gut feelings and obey the living conscious spirit of an "I can and I will" attitude. It instills in you a passionate desire to achieve a definite purpose, a sense of self-significance, a sense of adequacy, and a unique attitude. In addition, it gives you a sense of destiny, a goal-driven attitude, a unique plan, a dedicated sense of purpose, and business commitment, and it supports the innovative spirit of success.

Motivation is the single most important element of business success. To make life awesome, you need a constant motivation because it helps you enhance and enrich your life. Therefore, be prepared and ready when it comes to learning because the best tool for learning comes through motivation. Basically, motivation gives you the key to knowledge, which begins with keen observation and stays active through right thinking and congruent action.

Motivation stays intact as long as you're enhancing it and living in consciousness of it. As a result, you will continue to be inspired because it holds the key to your soul. When it is enhanced by careful observation and conscious awareness, you can unfold its powerful and lasting effects through smart decisions and effective actions. If you can leverage this investment as far as possible and the extent reasonable, you will greatly enhance your life. Without motivation, life lacks luster and useful knowledge. Without useful knowledge, there will be no permanent action, and without permanent action, there will be no permanent results. This shows that motivation is a critical aspect of a positive life, a successful relationship, and a profitable business. It's the guiding power of action and the sustaining force of positive attitude. Motivation drives you to actions that can refresh positive emotions, and positive emotions propel positive actions and reenergize your drive to accomplish a desired purpose. A dedicated sense of purpose fuels motivation in the marketplace, or in your workplace, as well as in your home and environment, and ultimately enhances your important relationships that can grow your business endeavors. That's why motivation inspires dynamic energy, intensity, and passion and fosters behaviors for many of the actions and thoughts that bring you a happy, healthy, and passionate life.

So the ultimate goal in effective living comes through motivation because it gives you a higher perception and a clearer realization of truth. It also gives you a self-sustaining power and provides you a self-reliant mind. Motivation is a vital part of your road map to success; your pathway to progress; and as a good, sustainable, and reliable source of advancement. It gives you the burning desire to advance forward and take advantage of the opportunity to grow and develop. If you believe, you will certainly achieve because motivation enables you to make productive efforts and channel your resources into a singleness of purpose that generates multiple results, benefits, and worthwhile values.

Motivation puts you in a state of preparedness and sharpness of mind, empowering you to take effective actions that support your business purpose. Motivation inspires positive thoughts that stimulate your interests and directs your attention. That's why it produces a superior quality of mind, which helps stimulate your attention and increase your powers of attraction and reception. This is the compelling reason for taking effective action to better your life.

Motivation certainly comes from a positive mental disposition, or from a positive, powerful, and captivating attitude of gratitude that guides your obsession, which is essential to success. As long as motivation is captivating your mind with a burning desire to win, you will be enriched with the inspiration of passion that gives you a dedicated sense of purpose, and you will greatly be blessed with a committed spirit of goodness, orderliness, and value. This means that motivation gives you a sense of infinite value that enables you to get a deeper and clearer conception of the nature of the positive mind, helping you create a better future by growing smarter, stronger, healthier, and more powerful. As you believe, you will achieve because motivation is a self-contemplation of desire that inflames the mind and ignites the spirit of enthusiasm to act in a certain way and produce a certain result that pleases your mind and satisfies your soul.

Basically, motivation gives you a visual sense of memory of experiences that can help you shape your life and your world and direct your desired kingdom to a definite destination of your own choice. If you believe and abide in the consciousness of it, you will definitely achieve your goals because motivation enables you to have a sense of self-control and a dedicated sense of passion that helps you plan ahead, stay ahead, and then seize favorable opportunities when they knock. Motivation rejuvenates your mind and heart and refreshes your spirit. As long as you think better thoughts, you will continue to achieve greater heights of energy and hope, which provides you the fundamental building blocks of success, the sound principles of accomplishment, and the guiding ethical rules of progress. In addition, motivation gives you a sense of responsibility, a spirit of accountability, and the power of self-assertiveness. It also gives you a compelling reason for taking action and brings you a direct result. All of this can serve as a restoration of the positive spirit of enthusiasm, redemption of great hope, the preservation of energy, and the boundless power of faith.

Of course, all of this gives you inner power and strength, a pure sense of reason, a clear sense of the joy of knowing and of feeling good and vibrant. As a result, faith gives you a sense of certainty, providing you an optimal sense of decisiveness and enhancing an intuitive sense of awareness. Furthermore, it gives you a broader sense of readiness of mind and heart. As an added bonus, it gives you the joy of self-expression, self-inspiration, and the courageous spirit of passion and determination to win.

If you have a strong desire to win, you will certainly succeed because motivation is the only vehicle that can lift you to see the uncharted future and help you have intuitive insights and passionate emotions that will guide your internal feelings and discover all of the hidden facts surrounding your values. As you believe and abide in the consciousness of it, you will grow in power and strength if you have the desire and courage to employ a proper motivational technique. Motivation is your road map that leads you to the desired end and therefore enables you to see the end from afar. It helps you produce a classic sense of sensory qualities, bringing you intangible blessings and inspirational insights that can enhance and enrich your life. As you think and act, you will receive better rewards because your best self is growing, developing your mind, and enhancing your meaningful purposes. If you believe in it, motivation will continue to prove itself, and as a result, it will certainly show you why it serves as a perfect ground for action, a place of quality memory of positive experiences, which gives you the gift of a genuine heart of happiness and a sensory association of reality. That's why motivation provides you a peaceful atmosphere of love and a favorably balanced state of mind, orderliness, and discipline.

All of this gives you inner harmony, happiness, health, and prosperity, and therefore serves as a prerequisite to success. To become successful, it's crucial to know that motivation is born of intuitive insight and passionate emotion, and it depends on benefits, incentives, or rewards that influence the mind to act in a certain way and produce certain results. Motivation is a creative power and a courageous spirit that comes with a clear sense of purpose, integrity, and value, and it enables you to function more effectively and efficiently. As long as you can think correctly and feel good, you will eventually get better results because motivation inspires a brighter point of view and effective application of useful knowledge, resource, and creative wisdom.

This is a unique knowledge that is endowed with a richer sense and a greater intelligence that exists only within you and actively transforms itself into irresistible power and absolute purpose. It blossoms in so many grateful lives and flourishes in so many businesses. That's why you need motivation—it enables you create a new path and a new purpose with better opportunities that will enable you to live better life and enjoy a greater future. It gives you emotional strength, mental clarity, and a sound mind, as well as a sense of belonging, a sense of adequacy, and self-assurance that brings you inner peace, happiness, and tranquility of mind and heart.

Motivation is the transcendental essence of life, the inner fire of truth that ignites positive actions that bring you greater benefits. Motivation is a boundless substance of the mind and a transcendental reality of purpose. It provides you inner motive of action that represents a transcendental significance of truths. It charges and fuels the power of your mind, which supports a boundless power of intelligence and develops a transcendental energy and enthusiasm.

When you are able to align your values, you will feel vital energy moving through you, exciting and inspiring your mind and enriching your soul. This is the proper motivation of spirit that empowers you to act rather than be acted on. It gives you a sense of security, a sense of confidence, and action of reason. In addition, it brings you a reality of ultimate truth, which provides you a sense of wonder and emancipation of power and strength. Motivation provides you a bright idea, a positive conception, and a living, conscious inspiration of good that reveals the essential aspects of life and brings you the potentialities of the future. Because motivation is a good element of mind and heart, it guides a conscious application of intelligence. This is the ultimate sense of purpose that can provide you a quality life and good vibration of spirit. It's also a science of new knowledge, new life, and a creative purpose, serving as a baseline for all sound thoughts, all sound feelings, and all inspiring actions. It's the vital cord that holds the future of awesomeness, guides the spiritual sense of vitality, boosts emotions, and eventually lifts the imperative sense of desire that supports the baseline of all success. Obviously, it helps you boost your emotions and lifts your spirits because it is a substance of a pledged life, as well as the vital element of ethical justice that represents a self-governing spirit. It's also a mind opener as well as a mind comforter that satisfies your present condition of existence and then enriches your spirit of oneness.

If you are ready and willing to succeed, motivation will enable you to create a compelling future and bring you a compounding life that will strengthen the chain of your success, prosperity, and health. This is the power that purifies the mind, opens the heart, and comforts the spirit. It creates a melody of hope and then helps you enjoy the songs of noble character and grow your life.

As long as you believe and abide in consciousness of motivation, you will continue to grow in consciousness, but remember, lack of motivation causes an inactive life and depression. Motivation is the power that comes with inner drive, inner hunger, and an inner fire for action that enriches your purposes, actively helps you stay awake, and ultimately helps you achieve your desired life. You need motivation because it gives you the power to advance your purposes in life, which in turn gives you the feelings of excitement, interest, energy, and enthusiasm that come from a positive spirit. Motivation is the push and pull of reasons that will bring you a lifetime of encouragement and patience to produce real and lasting success. That's why motivation is a stimulant of the mind, the maker of consciousness, and the creator of positive attitude.

As you continue to think and act, you will know that motivation is the guiding force that rules your life and also can serve as the umbrella that helps any struggling mind produce multiple results and guides striving hearts to produce more success. You truly need motivation because it is a guiding spirit and a guiding light of consciousness that enables you to fill the gap of emptiness and deficiency and cover the gap of mental ignorance. It also helps you close the gap of fear and worry that leads you to self-doubt and procrastination. It is the baseline for innovation and creativity that uses logical strategies to obtain the most comprehensive results. It gives you the license, privilege, and freedom to own your life and directs your thoughts toward your own desired goals, meaningful purposes, and achievement of positive results. It opens the door of awareness and unfolds the secrets of creation and the mysteries of all wonders, recapturing the wonderful awe and unfolding the mystery of life. Motivation directs your life with intention because the more you focus on achieving a desired outcome, the greater your likelihood of success. Therefore, remember that motivation is the mother of all creation, the father of all meaningful purpose, and the fountainhead of all productivity.

We all know that motivation is important in life, but many of us don't know the degree of its importance and intrinsic value. It's crucial to know that our level of motivation is affected not only by our pattern of thought but also by the underlying physical chemistry of our brains. Finding the right motivational strategy captivates the mind and enhances the quality of our well-being. As we take a moment to consider this, we will realize that if we don't work toward our goals and get ourselves into gear, we will never achieve our goals, and we will be trapped within our current circumstances. Finding the right motivational techniques is very much about implementing new patterns of inspiring thought that kill old, uninspiring ones. As a result, it puts us on the path of the dynamic train of positive thoughts that bring us the best possible values.

It's important to know that as much as we believe and abide in the consciousness of it, motivation will serve us ultimate good. That's why motivation requires a willingness of spirit, an openness of heart, a certainty of mind, and a directness of purpose to brighten our spirits, shine the light of business success, and enhance healthy relationships. So it's crucial to remember that motivation captivates our spirit of enthusiasm and gives us a sense of gratitude and appreciation that emanates from our inherent power of awareness that shines the spiritual light of consciousness, reflects the mental light of wisdom, and gets us real benefits. Remember that motivation is a mirror of wisdom, producing a round-table of courage and wisdom that restores great hope, ignites passion, and sparks positive actions in our businesses and in our personal lives.

CHAPTER 4

A CONSTRUCTIVE MENTAL DIRECTION

> As a man thinketh in his heart, so is he.
> —PROVERBS 23:7

Everything that has happened in your life must have happened for a reason; that reason may be good or bad. But if you can consciously think and deeply understand why something has happened and are willing to learn something from it, it will definitely serve you well. Try to see some good in it and find a way to profit from it. Before anything can actually happen in your life, it must consciously or unconsciously pass through the mind. Sometimes you may be aware of this fact, and sometimes you may not. But whether you're aware of it or not, whether you believe in it or not, energy moves and life goes on.

Someone, somewhere, has been thinking and planning how to succeed and progress and how to make life more desirable and live better. He or she may be your friend, your business associate, or partner. When you encounter this, do not be surprised by it because it is part and parcel of life. But it's also highly important that you shield your life and guard your emotions through a constructive mental direction before someone uses the opening as an opportunity to use you or even harm you.

We were all born successfully, and we are all living and looking for ways to make our lives better. One sure way to make our lives better is through a constructive mental direction that sees only good reasons for success. A lack of constructive mental direction makes life worthless and opens a window of opportunity for others to penetrate into your life. Constructive mental direction provides them the key to knowing and understanding, the key to shaping innovation of the future, the key to enhancing life, the key to success and progress, and the opportunity to advance and influence others.

So it's absolutely important that you use a constructive mental direction to guard your life because it produces a deep mental effect that enriches your life and supports your well-being. The path to constructive life comes through a constructive mental direction or through a creative thought that shapes the truth that directs your life to produce the results you want, which then enhances the nobility of your life and well-being and sustains the nobility of your purpose.

The betterment of your life as well as your health, happiness, and joy depends on a constructive mental direction. It controls the volume of your thoughts, the intensity of your emotions, and the direction of your actions. It causes your interest and attention to focus on what matters most and ultimately enables you to pay closer attention to a specific purpose. It properly prepares the mind and guides the spirit to mental alertness. It produces positive feedback when that train of positive thought is blowing the melody of truth, which gives you reliable emotions and a dependable feeling that sharpens your actions and brightens your consciousness. It provides you a constructive application of action and emotion and a constructive approach to cognitive awareness. As a result, it provides you good mental health, emotional awareness, and spiritual guidance. It strengthens your faculties and enables your mental and spiritual forces to continually move in the right direction, helping you move your life in the direction you want it to go. Finally, it provides you a constructive mental approach to success, progress, prosperity, and health.

If you look around you, you can see that there are common people who believe that they're doomed to poverty, so they give up struggling, surrender to suffering, and live in a constant state of misery and pain.

This is due to a complete lack of constructive mental direction. Very often, they become frustrated and consumed with fear, anxiety, worry, self-doubt, and procrastination that lead them to a deeper level of poverty and misery.

On the other side, you can also see that there are reasonable, realistic, and successful people who don't share these common belief systems because they all have a constructive mental direction that rules their purposeful lives. They all know what they want, and they focus on what matters most. That's why they're successful. You can do the same by enhancing and developing a constructive mental direction—a train of thought that can help you consciously stay awake, actively live, think deeply, and patiently look around and feel the inherent value of life. This will provide you an emblematic power and wisdom of understanding and a symbolic reason for congruent action. The resulting ideas, if you truly invest in them, you will surely achieve success through the emblematic power gained by intelligence or through a comprehensive force obtained by wisdom of mind and heart that makes all things possible.

When this happens, success follows you, and life becomes better. This new and better mind-set plus positive attitude lies in a constructive mental direction and exclusively focus on results. As you truly invest in a constructive mental direction, it will reveal to you a synthetic, symbolic wisdom, and it will unfold to you a transcendental reality of purpose that sparks the light of intellectual knowledge. This creative intelligence powers your mental, emotional, and spiritual lamps of intellectual excellence and absolute purpose.

That's the best possible power and the most skillful direction you can take to produce a constructive congruity of the heart, mind, and body and make a clear decision with a sound mind. This explains why it's the starting point of all progress and development and why it's a property of the imaginative sense of the mind and the secret sense of the heart that reveals the hidden sense within you. Ultimately, a constructive mental direction will unravel all rational insights within you and around you. So you can now think and see why it's a secret power that arises from within and translates all of your potential into physical realities, converts all your failures into success, and transforms all your fears into courage and multiple blessings.

This is a better way to make success happen and even an easier way to stream all new ideas and all creative innovations that can be achieved only by a constructive mental direction. Constructive mental direction absorbs all your negative thoughts or at least prevents them from leading you to a deeper level of poverty that often results to blaming others, such as your father, mother, or even your Creator. The good news is that a constructive mental direction is the firstborn and the lastborn of all creative discipline, efforts, and innovations. It's your source of infinite supply, infinite blessings, and notable success. It provides you the means of effective action and the excellent performance, which brings you prolific returns and promotes a blissful atmosphere of love, success, happiness, and health by enhancing a boundless spirit and power of thought and enriching your energy of enthusiasm. It provides you a strong link to all factual facts, all substance of thoughts, and all elements of truth that serve your mind and heart. It promotes your mental vision, enhances your creative wisdom, and improves your conscious awareness so you can raise better children who have high expectations and greater understanding of life, which improves struggling family with a promising future. A constructive mental direction creates an atmosphere of peace and love, a guaranteed station of success, and a meeting place for the positive thoughts and impressive characteristics of good mind and heart. It further provides you a classic sense of purpose, a unique sense of value, and pure reasoning that comes from your heart and mind to guide your wisdom and profound understanding.

As you continue to look around to find the truth, you will eventually discover that common people have conflicting and unrealistic beliefs that often sabotage their behaviors and control their actions, which leads them to fail. But if they can allow intelligence to govern their lives, they can rise above poverty, fear, and worry.

If you don't have intelligence, you will likely struggle in life. Intelligence makes you a reasonable servant and the masterpiece of all meaningful obedience, the master of all meaningful purpose, and the servant of all realistic goals. It's your intelligence that gives you a proper sense of humor, tolerance, and humility in business. It's your intelligence and determination that shape and convert facts into physical realities and transform negatives into positives with definite purpose.

Your intelligence and determination make your life worth living, enable you to manage your time wisely, and help you carefully use your energies and efforts in the most productive ways to support your well-being.

As you truly invest in a constructive mental direction, you will surely see that your intelligence is a mental power that provides you ceaseless energy, ceaseless movement toward success, and limitless purpose. It also provides you a pleasant circumstance of success and with great hope, passion, courage, and abundant blessings. Basically, it's your creative intelligence that inspires your actions, empowers your mind, motivates all your creative efforts, and inspires logical and constructive thoughts. Finally, your intelligence gives you power and well-established thoughts that give you a responsive mind and a receptive heart.

A constructive mental direction is the root of creative intelligence and wisdom. It's a mechanism of sound thought, a well-coordinated idea, a properly controlled emotion, and a well-directed spirit of enthusiasm. It's a constructive power that arises from a well-stimulated energy in your mind and heart. It produces a unified substance of power and strength for a centralized purpose, which actively provides you the fuel for peak and inspiring performance. It produces a well-crystallized energy that connects with your body and links your mind and heart, which then enables you to create a new purpose and have better sense of purpose to live a better life.

As a result, a constructive mental direction provides you with self-education, self-training, and self-discipline and even gives you the strictness of self-direction, self-command, and orderliness, which bring you a flourishing source of greatness. It further enables you to produce an abundance of fruits for a better life and future. So it's the driven power of intelligence and the spiritual force of your life. And last but not least, it's important to know that just as the economy grows in self-discipline, constructive mental direction grows in wisdom, lives in intelligence, and depends on your determination and persistence.

Obviously, you need to live wisely and constructively to succeed in life, and you need a constructive mental direction to accomplish that. A constructive mental direction opens the main door of opportunity that leads you to productive actions that yield positive results. As a result, it produces a lasting medicine for fear of poverty, illuminates your mind, and converts your fears into multiple blessings that will fill your heart with the melody of hope, courage, and passion. It provides you a complete energy that gives you a full swing of success, a complete power of courage, and a consistent method of action that brings you full results. You also need creative thinking and useful information to unravel certain truths, and this may well become a means of producing a transparent result that gives you a clear sense of purpose that shapes the innovation of tomorrow. This is a powerful, positive, and lasting change that leads you to a great height of wisdom and effectively clears the path to progress and success.

So learning to think creatively therefore opens the windows of opportunity and the doors of understanding to every arena in life. If you fully develop your mind and wisely direct your life, you will realize that every sound thought lies behind the power that comes from a highly disciplined personality, a well-developed mind, and a properly maintained spirit of enthusiasm. You will equally know that every successful life is strictly preserved by self-control, self-discipline, and self-direction.

You can believe in constructive mental direction only when you use it constructively. You must see that it provides you a properly guided power and a supplemental energy for your imaginative sense of purpose. You must understand that it's the faculty that helps you pass the level of positive thinking to the level of realization. You'll know this when you see it provide you a clearly marked line of action that yields multiple results.

However, first you must have sufficiently developed your mind to control your actions for your self-sustenance. Then you will definitely believe in constructive mental direction because it will continue to supply you adequate energy for your self-sustenance and become the root of all miracles, which can be realized only by developing your mind and directing your purpose. A constructive mental direction produces a centralized idea of all effective action and provides you a distinctive value of all purpose that produces the highest outstanding quality of character and gives you the best desirable mind to serve a unique purpose.

Basically, it will unravel all the truths that illuminate your heart and enlighten your mind for a greater purpose. This is a power that's capable of shaping certain truths and therefore enhancing all creative innovations, which can then become protected ground for a steady flow of blessings, peace, and prosperity. This in turn multiplies the inflow of blessings, potential, and vitality into your life. This can be achieved by uniting with infinite wisdom and enhancing intellectual integrity and ingenuity of mind, which can be expressed inwardly because your mind is a spiritual substance of your soul that produces an endless circle of success and progress. It's also the substance of your creative vision and artistic ideas that can be gleaned through creative discipline and diligent efforts. It provides you the flexibility, the adaptability, and the adjustability of the mind and heart, therefore improving your mental growth, emotional awareness, and logical analysis. It gives you a sense of fairness and justice, brings you much more favorable conditions, and provides you justified reasons for effective action. In addition, it ignites the flame of your burning desire, draws definite lines of action, and ultimately provides you a complete army of absolute purpose that produces exact and clear results, which further ignite the flames of human passion, human spirit, and successful relationships through conscious direction and logical action.

Constructive mental direction is a standard logic that provides you a sound reason, a sound idea, and a clear plan that releases energy of enthusiasm for a real and enduring action and productive results, which can give you a soundness of character, a nobility of mind, and a moral justice.

Let those who are struggling and striving to succeed know that when a constructive mental direction is blended with self-confidence, it becomes a powerful force that can lead anyone to the height of excellence and perfect performance, and eventually will help anyone achieve great ideas and sustain a logical consistency that recognizes no failure.

It's absolutely crucial that you understand your purpose in life and construct a map that will lead you to achieve your definite aim. Constructive mental direction brings you new ways and means of accomplishing your desired aim. It's one way of knowing and the best way of understanding and thinking in the most productive ways possible. It's the main source of your mental powers and the major source of your emotional strengths.

As you continue to grow and develop, you will understand that a constructive mental direction is a mental power that comes from positive thinking, from a self-inspiration and self-motivation, which gives you a burning desire to achieve a definite aim. It's also a mental power that begins with self-awareness, stays with self-recognition, and actively lives in consciousness of the self-realization of truth. As a result, it requires a concentrated attention, a controlled focus, careful observation and consistent analysis to grow the mind and expand your consciousness. This is the faculty of knowledge that helps you pass from the level of conception to the level of realization. This is also a creative power that flows naturally from a positive mental revelation of a pure heart, from a progressive spirit, and from a positive self-expression of the mind. It arises from a spirit of passion and motivation and grows in a consciousness of a positive spirit of self-inspiration and a positive attitude of gratitude and appreciation that comes from your inherent powers, your intrinsic values, and your essential nature.

It's a creative way of thinking that attracts positive energies, sparks positive actions, and generates positive results that build, produce, and attract value. This further explains why it's a product of mentality—a product that comes from your mental activity, emotional wisdom, and cognitive intelligence. It's also a creative process that comes from creative awareness, spiritual blessing, and mental harmony. It demands passion, passion demands inspiration, and inspiration requires spiritual awareness and mental harmony. This shows you that what you need and want in life is a constructive mental direction because it leads to a self-conscious mind, a self-inspiring spirit, a self-sustaining purpose, and self-governing intelligence that will provide you a common point of view with reasonable people, a centralized thinking, and a unique purpose that comes with both cognitive and educational foundations.

A constructive mental direction forms the basis for the ultimate success, promising a better future and making surprising breakthroughs. Its resulting mental alignment is the very essence of effectiveness, efficiency, and mindful action through which you can properly achieve your goals in life.

It demands a constant motivation and a continuous inspiration that empowers the mind and heart for permanent success and progress. This is one of the most profound factors that will clearly determine the degree of your success, progress, and happiness.

Another profound truth comes from the power of the undivided spirit, from the power of undivided attention, from unified interest, and from singleness of purpose, which will certainly bring you a unified healing condition and serve the integrity of the mind, heart, and body.

When you get this basic truth well grounded in your heart, you will believe in it because it will provide you a unified field of purpose and a spontaneous action that need concentrated effort and sufficient power that will instantly help you get the job done.

This is the basic truth that explains why a constructive mental direction leads you to greatness and brings you perfect harmony and a steadfast love that calms your mind and pleases your soul. This is a profound subject that will enable you to shape your self-worth, design your self-concept, and ultimately produce a powerful, positive, and dependable self-image. It will further enable you to make finer distinctions and help you exploit vital information. This produces a roundtable of wisdom of purpose and productivity, valuable insights, a fertile ground for emboldening healthy ideas, useful knowledge, and positive experiences that may provide you a unified field of spontaneous reality and energy that is capable of producing multiple outcomes, enabling you to share valuable information and exchange intellectual knowledge.

This is the overriding factor that determines your results in advance by guiding your mind and helping you to be inspired in business. Constructive mental direction produces sound thoughts that enhance your creative energy, which may actually lead you to enhancing practical ideas and useful experiences that will determine how you live, how you act, and how you produce results. It gives you a consistent energy to move forward to win, to acquire, and to progress and then it provides you the power to think constructively, live wisely, and act effectively. It directs all your mental powers into a singleness of purpose to accomplish a notable success. It provides you emotional strength and supplies you the ingredients of effective action and abundant results that will lead you to steady growth and constant development. Therefore, it's the sum and substance of your creative thinking, sound judgments, favorable conditions, useful experiences, and favorable outcomes. Now you can see why it's a potential energy source for economic growth and development, for active progress and constant development, and for learning and succeeding in every aspect of life. You can also see why it's a potential source of inspiration and motivation that produces worthwhile value using worthwhile time and effort.

Your approach to a bright future comes just as inspiration and motivation inspire your goals in life, and constructive mental direction moves you to a definite aim to achieve that purpose. This is a mental strength that represents and enhances your overall well-being, shapes your perceptions, strengthens your emotions, and supports your actions. It is also a constructive thought that arises from self-disciplined mind, a definite reason to achieve goals and the propelling spirit of success in your life, which provides you endless stimuli, a ceaseless power, and strength of mind that ignites positive actions and reinforces and strengthens your belief systems. As a result, it enables you to design a powerful, positive, and effective way of communication and helps you shape a productive channel of expression. This provides you with sufficient power and strength of mind, giving you ceaseless energy of enthusiasm and putting you in a pleasant condition of mind that breeds within your wonderful world of imagination to produce multiple results that will greatly increase the value of your life. It may even determine your personal powers or individual initiatives that will ultimately create a personal world that determines the amount of space one occupies. Basically, it will properly spell out the quality of an individual's life and effective action and ultimately call out quality results. But before it works, it demands a properly self-disciplined mind and a well-directed sense of purpose, which arise from your sound thoughts and clear judgment.

This symbolizes your ultimate value that represents a higher quality of thought, which provides you the ultimate way to use values and enables you to carefully express yourself in the most productive ways possible. It also provides you a classic sense of inward and outward direction and a transcendent power of the mind and heart. Restructuring and reforming your mind produces a keen sense of cognitive awareness and development and provides you a unified spirit of an excellent mind. It also provides you a harmonious association of sound thoughts, positive mental discipline, and equilibrium of mind and body, enabling you to achieve a greater level of eternal blessings and emotional intelligence.

This is a constructive power that arises from your sound thoughts, emotional awareness, health consciousness, success, and happiness. People in every creative endeavor use a constructive mental direction to achieve their goals because it's an irresistible force and an indispensable value that recognizes no fear, no failure, and no feeling of inferiority or inadequacy. Think of Steve Jobs, Donald Trump, Henry Ford, Barack Obama, Nelson Mandela. All these people have different visions, but what they have in common is a constructive mental direction, a dedicated sense of purpose and direction. These creative people reveal the nature of a constructive direction; therefore, it has been tested by establishing results in new ways and has produced multiple outcomes by enhancing a keen observation of facts that shape businesses. That's why it's the indispensable power of a sound thought that produces a logical consistency, a dedicated sense of active purpose, and strong convictions that serve endless potentiality and possibility. It's the controlling power of the heart and the sustaining force of the mind that contains vitality, potential energy, and the spirit of enthusiasm, which enhance the vital force of conscious awareness and the oneness of all good that inspires vital knowledge and sparks positive actions. Ultimately, it gives you courage and strength that is overflowing with love, gratitude, and appreciation. Last but not least, constructive mental direction is an indwelling power and strength that enables you to recognize your oneness with the reality of life.

This is the ultimate way to express yourself and use your ability and value to motivate yourself and understand others. So it's absolutely important to know that a constructive mental direction comes through a logical expression, through integrity of body and mind, through congruity of word and action, through a mental harmony and spiritual balance, but then it depends on your ability to perceive reality. Its power lies in your ability to gather facts and ultimately rests on your mental capacity and strength to organize specific and useful information that can foster and enhance your mind, heart, and body. This shows why a constructive mental direction is highly effective in communication and action. Your body, mind, and heart communicate to you in a language you can properly understand and therefore increase the value that speaks in harmony, in spontaneous action, and in congruity with your purposes to provide you flexibility of mind and bring you solutions for life learning.

So learning to think constructively in one area opens many other doors to understanding in life. Therefore, creating and enhancing a constructive mental direction and enriching your life is a matter of understanding others and having the ability to cope with rejection. It's about knowing how to handle frustration and seeing rejection as an opportunity to advance your purpose and grow your business. A constructive mental direction is a self-contemplation of positive spirit of enthusiasm that produces an invisible good, which gives you a clear grasp of truth that actively prepares your mind, properly cleanses your heart, and effectively directs you toward a better future. This is the key to gaining financial freedom that will greatly increase the value of your life. This is also the controller of all creative thinking, creative efforts, positive emotions, and finally the director of all positive actions that will bring you great results.

As you progress to the higher levels of knowledge and deeper levels of understanding, it will significantly increase your self-confidence and help you adjust your attitude to rise above your limitations, fears, and worries. It will also enable you to stay ahead of the game and use the advantage of a favorable chance to open a major window of opportunity in your life. As a result, it will continuously put you in a state of positive anticipation and great expectation that will ultimately provide you multiple blessings and a steady stream of enthusiasm. In addition, it will serve as a productive power that supports all creative thought and serves as a constructive channel to all success.

For a better life and even greater future, I encourage every man or woman who is endeavoring to succeed in life to learn how to cope with rejection, handle frustration, turn no into yes, and transform fear into courage, and convert business rejection into opportunity to grow better. These things stand as the tests of faith; therefore, you must pass through them to open the doors of success. If you can pass the test of life, then you will eventually live more life with less stress, take more action with no fear, and gain more success with no worry, no pain, or stress. Success is hidden deep inside rejection and frustration and can be discovered only by patient cultivation. This is a profound truth that will give you a stronger and better view of life, and it will help you resolve and purify your heart, build up value, sharpen your mind, and expand your creative vision. In addition, constructive mental direction provides you a deep, profound knowledge and a strong conviction that can reform your attitude and enhance your mind, helping you produce wholesome ideas that will generate a higher power of intelligence and give you a richer view of what you truly want and need.

With a constructive mental direction, you will expand and grow in wisdom and understanding. You will create positive experiences that will trigger positive actions that you can use to produce the positive results you need to bring positive changes into your life. Basically, a constructive mental direction will enable you to arrest negative situations and develop a highly constructive approach to life. As a result, you will gain useful knowledge that strengthens your heart and influences your mind to act wisely and therefore draw an influx of blessings into your life that will calm your mind and heart and enable you to build more power, strength, and intelligence. You will also produce a cheerful, confident disposition and a positive affirmation that will draw even more good things into your life. A constructive mental direction is creative in nature; therefore, it controls and directs all your creative energies toward a singleness of purpose, an exactness of aim, and an absoluteness of desire to achieve a definite goal. This gives you a clear understanding and enables you to stimulate your mental faculties, eventually helping you draw good things into your life. As a result, it puts you in a state of anticipation and expectation and helps you produce a cycle of wisdom and productivity. It creates a fertile ground for embodying healthy ideas, useful knowledge, and positive experiences that will greatly enrich your mind, automatically serve your greatest needs, and open many windows of opportunity for success and development.

When properly directed and effectively applied, a constructive mental direction can help you gain a significantly better understanding of yourself and others. It will help you build strong and lasting relationships and ultimately help you position your business. As a result, it will give you the power and ability to transform your potential clients into life partners. It will also give you the opportunity to build decent and healthy relationships through a constructive channel of thought and action. In addition, it will provide you a sound rule, a perfect feeling, and a protective ground for successful relationships. It will give you an intellectual knowledge, a standard foresight and wisdom about the present moment for a better life and a greater future. As a result, it will actively reform your mind, refresh your heart, and properly restore your hope, igniting positive actions that will generate abundant results. As you continue to develop and grow in consciousness, it will link your mind, body, and soul and then strongly connect all your spiritual values and your emotional and mental powers to work harmoniously and produce better results. As you continue to increase in power and grow in knowledge, it will become your major source of all high intelligence and powers that will serve and support your utmost values and goals in life. It will help you convert all your hindrances into multiple blessings and all stumbling blocks into stepping stones of endless progress that will lead you to multiple successes.

You need to be prepared and ready to use your mind to serve your meaningful purposes and not allow your mind to control you like a paper airplane without a definite direction. Preparing your mind gives you the power to act promptly by putting forth the artistic idea that motivates you to action and inspires the mind to move with purpose to achieve great results. That's why it's important to refine your mind and change your old, uninspiring thoughts and unrealistic beliefs into new, inspiring ones through a constructive mental direction. A constructive mental direction fuels the creative process and enhances creative discipline in all your personal and cooperative efforts, therefore leading you to a more fulfilling and satisfying life.

Everything purposeful in life begins with logical thinking and sound feeling and depends on your inner direction, your flawless action, your excellent use of your talent, and proper application of your mind. Whatever you desire will motivate you to achieve success, progress, and development. In addition, it will enable you to overcome self-destructive patterns of behavior such as procrastination, self-doubt, fear, and worry.

I guarantee you success and assure you progress if you have good intentions. I promise you that you will achieve all your goals because a constructive mental direction will provide you a logical consistency, a congruent mind, and spontaneous action that will give you the ability to move with clarity and certainty of aim and purpose. In addition, it will provide you a better future and a greater spirit of progress. Ultimately, it will provide you a reliable and sustainable means of development and the best possible means of achieving real and lasting success.

If you can monitor the doors of awareness, you will certainly achieve great results because it will enable you to recognize and seize opportunities when they knock. You will find that it will provide you the power and ability to embrace profitable changes in your personal life as well as in your business efforts. This can clear the road for more creative opportunities and ultimately provide the means for you to probe deeply into other people's minds that are desirable and profitable to explore to enrich your businesses. When you believe and abide in the consciousness of it, it will further enable you to create the financial freedom and ultimately help you fix your mind and heart on what you truly desire and deserve in life.

Basically, it will play out well through a persistent desire and through a constructive application because a constructive mental direction helps you feel significant in constructive ways by helping you learn to think productively. This inspires your mind and gives you the desire to build a more prosperous life by creating powerful habits of success that come from willingness of heart and freedom of mind. It also requires sound thoughts, a flawless point of view, and clear action. It's an internal dwelling place for all reasonable minds, for all successful people, and for all good dreamers. It's your armor and armament that enhances your life, enriches your purposes, grows your intelligence, and ultimately expands your mind and heart for greater purposes.

Once again, it's important to know that a constructive thinking is a mental power that begins with self-awareness and stays alive through creative intelligence and strength of character. Through diligent use, it enhances your creative intelligence, improves your creative awareness, and supports your general good. In addition, it provides you a sense of creative imagination that enhances all your reasonable plans and inspires all your realistic goals. It's the birthplace of all meaningful purpose and the fountainhead of all intelligence, all sound plans, and all clear judgment that brings you emotional integrity and mental harmony. It's a sound idea that fosters progressive change, supports successful relationships, and serves better purposes.

I believe in constructive mental direction because I have seen it work in my life and the lives of others. I have seen it lift people from poverty to success. I have also seen it transform people from a state of fear to a state of courage. Most important, I have seen it heal all kinds of sicknesses from all walks of life. Think of Helen Keller, Nelson Mandela, Martin Luther King Jr, Steve Jobs, Oprah Winfrey, Barack Obama. All of these people achieved great successes because they have a unique, fundamental sense to reach their goals. Constructive mental direction played out well because it gives them a profound understanding, a pure sense of empathy of heart, a transparent sense of purpose, and an active spirit of enthusiasm.

It will serve you equally well if you believe in it. All power lies within a constructive expression and within a specialized field of knowledge. It can be created and developed only by reintegrating knowledge in new ways and training the mind to produce a positive self-image. This shows you why a positive self-expression of your mind and a constructive mental wisdom of your soul produce intangible wisdom and creative intelligence that empowers the engine of your desire and supports your mind for a perfect and precise purpose. It also shows you why it's the substance of your spirit and the fountainhead of your life that represents a guiding power and a steady stream of intelligence that brings you a steady flow of positive returns and ultimately gives you a transcendental reality of mind, a spiritual substance of heart, and a unified field of purpose. This explains why it's the sovereign reality and energy of the mind, the spiritual unity of consciousness, and the binding force of moral justice that provides you a clear tunnel of perception, mental competency, and practical wisdom. But to use it, you need keen observation, creative thinking, and functional wisdom that will provide you intuitive awareness, mental ability, emotional capability, and practical intelligence.

A constructive mental direction serves all those who are prepared and ready for it. It gives them the unique, exceptional value they need, and it increases their personal power and strength of character that provide them with healthy hearts, sound minds, and congruent bodies that serve their overall well-being. It serves their best interests that bring them the highest benefits. It enables them to remain focused and alert and to stay calm and listen to the inner voice that comes from within, helping them use that power for better lives and greater purposes. It reinforces their minds and strengthens their spirits and physical bodies, providing them a stronghold for their actions and effective results, and then it helps them climb the ladder of success and progress.

Just as unique individuals can exemplify effectiveness, constructive mental direction provides them with a pillar of support and adds more fuel to the fire of their desires, which increases the inflow of their powers and energies that ultimately give them more strengths and more positive ideas. In addition, it gives them a steady momentum for effective action and real and lasting success. It further gives them the inner peace of mind and mental harmony that free them from indecision and procrastination, self-doubt, and fear. It also frees them from self-sabotaging behavior and self-imposed limitations. As a result, it enables them to eliminate the causes of fear, poverty, worry, and anxiety, and it helps them destroy all the negative effects. As they continue to progress and acquire more useful ideas, constructive mental direction enables them to permanently destroy all the negative feelings of inferiority, loneliness, indecision, and procrastination and ultimately helps them achieve their goals. In addition, it helps them to overcome rejection and dejection and even helps them convert negative feelings into positive energies and then into joyful expressions of gratitude and appreciation.

Therefore, it presents to them a perfect system of mental harmony, which gives them an excellent, inspiring performance that needs to be recognized and used effectively. A constructive mental direction enables them to firmly fix their minds on the exactness of purpose with sound character, which helps them perform great services and receive great rewards and benefits. It further provides them with more power, more strength, and courage to pursue new goals, new dreams, and live better lives. In addition, it enables them to focus on what matters most and to recognize opportunity when it knocks. This gives them the power to overcome setbacks and provides them the ability to make positive changes in their personal lives and businesses. As they continue to think better and continue to grow, it unleashes their vision, transforms their passion into profits and helps them reach their goals.

It will serve you the same if you believe in it and deeply internalize the truth. It will become a constructive expression of an active spirit, a spirit of harmonious cooperation, and a spirit of shared value that brings you a highly effective spirit of enthusiasm, a pure heart, a sound mind, and a healthy body. This in turn will bring you the blessings of independence and an abundance of joy and happiness. And as you continue to think wisely and grow stronger, it will give you the patience, tolerance, and great sense of humor you need to acquire a unique skill, achieve great success, and live a better life. In addition, it will enable you to embrace profitable changes as great opportunities for growth. This explains why it's a constructive state of mind that gives you the energy and strength to shape your ideas, feelings, and actions. It further explains why it guides your spirit of enthusiasm and passion that inspires you to move with clear purpose and clarity of mind and heart. Therefore, I guarantee you success because every success begins with a constructive mental direction and stays there. It's the beginning of all progress and a powerful drawing force of all purpose.

A constructive mental direction is a unique power you can test in good faith and a unique skill you can practice with self-confidence. It enables you to make a prompt decision and helps you take congruent action that shapes the truth. It produces the highest and the best reservoir of wisdom and profound understanding by logical insights that fuel the creative process, which can then give rise to new and better thoughts in a variety of successful ways. As a matter of fact, every success comes from your inner drive and from a conscious direction, from a strong conviction and a mental attitude of gratitude, and from a mental disposition of perfect harmony and accurate thinking and acting. Finally, it comes from sovereign ideas that you can use to guide your prompt decisions and congruent actions.

A constructive mental direction represents a symbolic knowledge and therefore is the source of your eternal blessings and eternal happiness. It ultimately represents a unique power that connects all of your positive energies together like a strong chain of positive, dynamic forces. It's a dynamic power that inspires and motivates your mind and sparks your actions, and it carefully leads you toward the accomplishment of your desired goals.

If you do not act effectively, you will never receive productively. The net effect of an action is a result, and constructive mental direction is the unique blessing that comes from consciousness within the individual power of momentum, mental creation, and positive direction. This enables you to act effectively and helps you get a desirable and profitable result. It gives you the mental harmony that produces action and a productive outcome. It's the fertile mind and fruitful heart of all business purposes. It provides you the power and ability to acquire new and better knowledge and the power to understand others. It's the greatest power of self-reliance and the greatest expression of self-confidence, self-control, self-discipline, and self-direction. It's the power that prepares your mind and heart for the acceptance of all your basic needs and wants in life. As a result, it grows your mind, expands your knowledge, and increases your wisdom.

When your mind is prepared and ready to receive value, it strengthens in power and draws similar things that will enrich the mind and make your life more desirable and worth living. This means that a constructive mental direction properly prepares the mind and adequately sustains its values for a positive action. It also means that it prepares the mind and engages the spirit in a constructive and meaningful direction. As a result, it gives you a pleasing personality; a positive disposition; and an ingenuity of mind, heart, and body.

So it's a sound judgment that comes from a good state of mind and stays active with powerful, positive, and confident faith and a courageous spirit. As a creative process, it dwells on progress and therefore lives in a confident state. As a result, it reveals all hidden powers, all treasures, all assets, and values. In addition, it regulates high powers, stimulates your energies, and properly unites optimistic spirits that will draw more and more value, attract more positive qualities, and produce more profitable results.

A constructive mental direction has always been clearing the path to success and will always lead the way to a better life and stronger future. So be patient with life because a constructive mental direction is an inner power that sharpens your awareness and observation and enables you to use opportunity when it knocks. It clears the road for good spirits and active energies to come in and drive the mind for good, and then it helps you focus on a clear purpose that will make you truly successful. It enables you to concentrate and acquire new and better skills and ultimately helps you bring more and more qualities into your life. You will live in a delightful, healthy condition that helps you get the best of today and forever.

Because the business world is driven by data, it's also ruled by mental action and conscious direction. You need a constructive mental direction to prosper in business and advance in life. It's the thinking center and the acting point of all conscious and progressive spirit of innovation, which governs all active life. That's why it increases your receptive powers, enhances your responsive strengths, and then provides energy to your inner drives, impulses of thought, and the power of your will. As a result, it gives you the broadest sense that provides you the greatest value and highest quality of service, which gives you great courage and anticipation of a better future, as well as the hope of advancement and continuous progression. It also gives you a passionate spirit of progressive innovation and provides you the power, strength, and innate ability to act, succeed, and advance into a better future and live a greater life.

Now you can see why it enables you to eliminate the causes of procrastination and self-doubt, anxiety and worry, stress and sickness, and the unnecessary fear of failure and poverty, and ultimately helps you convert all these enemies of success and progress into courage and passion, which inspires action for a better future. This springs directly from conscious awareness and profound understanding.

A constructive mental direction in business produces constructive results. It provides you inner strength, spiritual substance, and receptive power to integrate the knowledge of the mind with knowledge of the body. This clearly represents a unique power that makes you realize all the vital truths that can positively shape the future of your business intelligence. That's why it's a faithful representation of reality and a constructive avenue to eternal peace and triumphant joy that creates an atmosphere of love and happiness in business and life.

Remember that all of your results are ruled by your actions and properly propelled by your belief systems. So it's important to know that your emotions control your actions, and your actions spell out your results. Therefore, it's crucial that you should direct and control your emotions, feelings, and actions constructively.

CHAPTER 5

A BRILLIANT BUSINESS MIND

Wisdom always makes men fortunate: for by wisdom no man could ever err, and therefore he must act rightly and succeed, or his wisdom would be wisdom no longer.

—PLATO

Thinking is what distinguishes human beings from the rest of the animal kingdom because we think differently, behave differently, act differently, and therefore get different results. We all have different beliefs and attitudes that come from different environments, upbringings, and parents. Sometimes our beliefs, behaviors, feelings, and actions sabotage us and deny us our effectiveness in life due to lack of a brilliant business mind.

A lack of a brilliant business mind prevents us from achieving our aims, purposes, goals, and plans in life. To bridge all these gaps of inadequacy, weakness, fear, procrastination, and self-doubt that will lead us to poverty, we must first have the best business vision, which centers around acquiring a brilliant business mind. As human beings, we must develop and use our minds in the most effective, efficient, and productive ways to enhance and enrich our lives and support all our purposes and aims in life.

Common people are used to believing that success will come easily and that they can succeed in life without any effort. That's an idle wish. As human beings, we form our beliefs from a variety of personal and emotional reasons based on our experiences. These values that shape our belief systems guide the way we think, act, and live and the decisions we make every day. In a deep sense, I believe that success is all about making smart choices, and we need brilliant business minds to accomplish that. I believe a brilliant business mind is a personally owned and operated mind, a personal matter, and a personal concern that comes from personal initiative and personal power. That's why we must actively integrate our best business minds in our daily living so we can think constructively and act effectively. We also must perceive life as a business because our lives desperately need brilliant business minds to achieve definite goals. That's the only thing that will bring us real and lasting change because it's endowed with absolute purpose and properly equipped with absolute spirit of success and progress.

Most people have insightful knowledge, but they're too weak to link their knowledge with action for sustainable development, so they fail to gain value. But if they can learn and live by developing effective strategies and a business vision and mind-set, they're practically guaranteeing their business success. And as they continue to live their values and ignore what others think of them, they will rise above poverty, and their lives will be full of power, which will be guided by a business mind and enhanced with unique skills, great faith and courage, and active belief systems. This will greatly increase their value and help them develop the spirit of love, joy, and happiness in their lives. In addition, their lives will be blessed with the power of acquisition, the power of actualization, and the spirit of harmony and spontaneous action. As a result, they will be enriched with an abundance of life, a surplus of power, the energy of enthusiasm, and a wealth of knowledge. And as they continue to grow and mature, they will discover that they are all well blessed with unique spirits that are full of heart and properly equipped with a meaningful purpose to achieve a definite aim.

Your mind is a personal treasure, an individual investment, and a personal resource that is born to grow in consciousness and expand in useful knowledge to increase wisdom and understanding, enabling you to see fresh ideas that play a critical role in business success.

Some of your business efforts will bring you good returns, while others will bring you pain due to lack of a natural fit for a powerful business mind. But if you can perceive the world differently and think reasonably, you can gain a better understanding about life. Life pays according to your own personal investments in everyday life. This is a business model that saves, changes, and benefits lives. Just as business success is considered the highest form of life, so the business mind denotes the highest form of thinking, acting, and getting effective results.

Creative people are those who believe and abide in the consciousness of a brilliant business mind and therefore always have enhanced a business mind-set. They know it goes hand in hand with a business vision and with the presence of mind, with creative intelligence and with a clear understanding. With a business concept in mind, they come up with ideas that are fresh, new, attention-grabbing, and appealing to their customers.

Entrepreneurs are also exemplary people who develop new products and take advantage of opportunities to venture into a better future because they often keep their minds only on business. They always have their business goals in mind; therefore, their business minds open the doors for them to clearly see the uncharted future. A good business mind supports the process by which it creates its business vision and the ultimate form of understanding the world of business commerce.

If you look closely at how successful people have used their best possible power to achieve success, then you will believe in the power of a business mind because it supports a definite purpose. It's an absolute power that proves itself by effecting productive results. It's a powerful skill that requires careful attention, proper analysis, keen observation, and conscious awareness. It requires consistent practice and useful knowledge that comes from practical ideas, wisdom, and intelligence.

Just as your personal world is full of business, so too are your relationships with others. If you're looking for better connections, you should know that some of your relationships will bring you happiness, while some will bring you pain due to an ineffective use of your mental power to serve your purposes. A business mind is the potential source of your inspiration, motivation, and passion, and it's a potential source of building valuable rapport, exchanging valuable information, and connecting valuable minds. A business mind provides you an excellent way to use your body of knowledge to guide your businesses and use your business successes to lift your life. It also provides you an excellent way to channel your moral values and unique character. It's the perfect way to express a positive attitude of gratitude of the heart, mind, and the body, which reveals itself through meaningful, purposeful expressions and effective actions. It's important that you use your body of knowledge to control and direct your life and enhance a brilliant business mind because it comes with a flexible knowledge that inspires productive thoughts and effective actions. It brings about sound ideas, realistic goals, and active plans that will provide you a clear mental image of what you want and positive thoughts that will properly communicate the best possible meaning and purpose that will ultimately bring you the best possible results.

We all have the desire to succeed, but we don't all have the uniqueness of mind that will make business successes happen. To make business successes happen in our lives, we all need a relentless and steadfast spirit, a resolute mind, and a persevering spirit. This is the key that will enable us to open the door of success because it's the power that grows from a positive influence, useful manipulation, effective action, and spiritual awareness. Basically, it's the power that comes through the passing of intelligence into reality.

I believe that a real businessperson is one who believes in the brilliant business mind and uses every possible power of mind, heart, and body to achieve positive results. A brilliant business mind comes with a spontaneous awareness and conscious development. It's the power that grows from following the right instruction, obeying the right orders, following essential rules of success, and ultimately maintaining a constructive mental application of sound principles through the embodiment of insightful knowledge. It's also a skill that arises from systematized development, diligent practice, clear understanding, and a sound mind. A business mind comes through the passing of intelligence and self-contemplation of spirit into self-realization of truth and a spontaneous reality.

Most of us are poor today because we lack the urge and hunger that breed success. We lack business drive, creative vision, and the spirit of enthusiasm. A business mind provides us the key to succeed and progress by properly fueling our burning desires and our passion to bring positive changes into our lives.

Therefore, the future will depend on our abilities to develop and use a business mind that will support our overall well-being. So if we are to succeed in life, we desperately need a business mind because it's a receptive power and a responsive spirit, a properly fixed and a well-determined mind with a persistent spirit of passion, enthusiasm, and never-ending desire.

This is one of the most reliable means of growing a business and sustaining a relationship, and ultimately it helps us influence others. A business mind is a conscious mind, a conscious mind is a business mind, and they both come from a conscious spirit and liveliness of heart. It's a deeply rooted conviction and a deep-seated belief that is running consciously or unconsciously in our homes as well as in our business environments. So it's built into our systems and ingrained in our blood, but it needs to be properly awakened before it can unleash its powerful forces. It's secretly waiting to be awakened and empowered.

This progressive tendency of success usually emanates from the fundamental principles of growth and from the fundamental rules of development. Life is business and business is life, and to live a truly successful life, you must have business intelligence, think and reach your goals and see life in terms of business. A business mind is part and parcel of your real being; therefore, it's a native residence of your real self that demands a conscious direction, a self-disciplined mind, and logical thinking and acting. It's also the ultimate creative spirit, the ultimate creative intelligence, and the ultimate creative life that come through the passing of wisdom into manifestation.

You need a business mind to succeed and prosper in life because it will make you truly independent and effective in life. I believe in it because it allows only positive thoughts to flow in and take control of business and properly direct its consciousness. It is the path to benefits, profits, and success. In addition, it's a function of creative wisdom that draws positive attention and profitable outcomes that open the main door of the mind, enabling you to draw even more blessings. As a result, it will further enhance your mental vision; expand your creative awareness; and bring you a perfect balance of mind, body, and heart. It increases the inflow of your power and strength for the better good, for the greater effort, for your best interests, and for your highest benefits. It also increases your personal power and strength, which reinforces your mind, strengthens your heart, and ultimately provides you a better spirit to pursue excellence and set better, bigger, and higher goals that will greatly empower you to seize opportunities when they knock.

A business mind is an analytical mind that provides you all you need because it's a cooperative channel of success, progress, and development that fosters creative innovation. It requires creative thinking and a lifelong value that gives you a lifetime of success and progress, which brings you a coordinated energy and multiple results. It fuels your burning desire for a better life, a greater purpose, more useful cultivation, and a better future.

Emboldening a business mind takes creative efforts and requires consistent action. The business mind holds a key to a lifetime of success because it is a major component of useful knowledge and deep understanding that lie at the edge of consciousness and rest in the heart of creativity. It's the power that trains the mind to integrate with the body and work with the spirit. It strives to get more useful information and more valuable feedback, which in turn helps you make finer distinctions and smarter decisions in life.

When you become excited and have your basic goals in mind, you will realize that a business mind leads to a self-knowing mind, a well-informed heart, and a delightful and captivating spirit. A business mind grows in conscious awareness, lives in practical experiences and useful knowledge, remains active in the field of understanding, and survives in the creative wisdom and emotional intelligence, which of course depends on your ability to recognize all facts that can help you make conscious, effective, and prompt decisions. As you continue to grow in business, the most significant fact to realize is that an entrepreneurial mind measures risk and ventures into the future for good, for benefits, and for great profits. This means that it creates a striving spirit that makes diligent efforts to achieve something for something. It's the most sophisticated component of success and the most critical element of effective action that captures all good results.

As you may already know, a business mind comes with an openness of heart, a dedicated sense of purpose, plainness and clarity of mind, and simplicity and lucidity of thoughts, which fuels the burning desire. This is the train of thought that produces a real and lasting result. This is also where artistic ideas meet inspiring performances and growing businesses. As you believe and abide in consciousness of it, you will certainly grow because a business mind is fueled by passion, inspiration, and motivation and therefore requires concreteness and directness of purpose. It's also fueled by desire that breeds on a focused purpose. This means that you can achieve anything if you hold to the desire with focused purpose, which breeds simplicity and enhances quality of thought, energy and spirit of enthusiasm. This also means that the business mind is a well-disposed spirit, nurturing your business goal with a positive, affirmative spirit of success and with a satisfying character and sound personality.

You can achieve anything if you believe in it and are willing to pay the price. You will certainly achieve great goals because creating a business vision and understanding and believing in the business mind are the keys to creating change and using opportunity to achieve goals. Remember that your goals serve your life and help you discipline your mind. Therefore, a business mind is a personalized mind, a personally owned and controlled body, and a well-directed spirit. It's a personal matter and a personal concern that comes with personal initiative, with ability, and willpower. It's also a personal treasure, a personal investment, and a resource. In addition, it supports a definite purpose that protects your goals and ultimately brings you logical results. It dwells on mental communication, a mental action, and an atmosphere of mental harmony, quality, and profitable results. It comes with mutual understanding and agreement, with personal conception and business ingenuity, and with the sole reason for action. So remember a rational thinking and self-knowing mind is alert and grows in wisdom and self-confidence, enhancing a courageous and passionate spirit that finds profitable solutions. It helps you do anything you set out to accomplish and even achieve more than you think because it fully expresses itself in wisdom and completely uses its personal powers to demonstrate the sole reasons for action. A business mind is a conscious mind, and a conscious mind is a business mind that comes from personal interest, mutual agreement, and a promising future.

When I look around, I see individuals who actively live and enjoy everything in life. They empower other people and widely use their business minds to optimize all their business decisions, which helps them enhance all their purposes. These are the successful ones who have achieved success because they have acquired brilliant business minds that are serving and supporting all their business purposes and further helping them make better and smarter business decisions. Consider the entrepreneurial, artistic vision of Steve Jobs, Donald Trump, Bill Gate, Ray Kroc, Oprah Winfrey. They all have had different vision, but what they have in common is business intelligence. They believe in business intelligence, and business intelligence is helping them acquire a tremendous wealth. That's why they are enjoying life and living happily and successfully. The business mind is the essence of life and a definite element of success. You should remember that business is life and life is business, and to survive in life, you must think and see life as a business entity and use human resources as a direct customer pipeline that fosters your business purposes.

At the other end, I can also see that there are other people who live in pain and suffering and end up in poverty due to a lack of purpose. These are the poor ones who live in ignorance and mental blindness due to lack of a business mind. These people live in blind faith and get blind results that are full of pain, suffering, fear, and self-doubt, and acquire a poverty mind-set that puts them in an undesirable state of worry and misery.

The good news is that as this basic truth becomes grounded in your mind and heart, and you are willing to embrace and accept the truth, you will find that the business mind will absorb all the pain and dissolve all poverty, difficulties, miseries, and suffering, just as light absorbs darkness. When light comes, darkness disappears, which means that when the business mind takes over, poverty, difficulty, misery, and suffering will vanish. The business mind breeds success and draws progress and development, and it harnesses all your creative powers, creative intelligence, and imagination. This is a creative power that increases in wisdom through a consistent practice that enriches your heart, which may bring you a well-heightened sense of awareness, a profitable value, a dedicated sense of purpose, and a meaningful direction in your life. As a result, it puts you in a superior state that produces the ultimate good and provides you a well-heightened sense of anticipation of greater good.

A business mind is business intelligence, and it needs substance to exist in business because your spirit in business is the essence of consciousness. This is a creative power that comes with a positive spirit and a passionate mind that reflects flexibility and shows a sense of humility and tolerance in business success. This is for good business purposes and for the spirit of passion, love, and courage that draws an abundance of good returns for greater success. This shows why successful people actively live in business intelligence and properly breed wisdom—apparently they know that the positive spirit of passionate business will always follow them around like a guard, will always guide them and actively live in them. Very often, they will perceive the positive visual images of good that will continue to reflect in their minds for a better future and a greater life.

This is a profound truth that reveals that a real businessman or woman must have a clearly defined purpose and a clearly defined mission, as well as a well-established plan and a properly defined goal. A businessman or woman must be well-organized and well-rounded with useful knowledge, positive feedback, and valuable information. He or she must be willing and able to take advantage of opportunities when they knock. To grow in business, you must build trust, live in trust, and take advantage of trust to innovate your business. It also means that you must build value, live in value, and take advantage of valuable experiences to draw more prospects, profits, and blessings. A businessman or woman is anyone who has acquired a flexible knowledge and an adaptable mind, patience, tolerance, and a keen sense of humor that foster and enhance all business purposes. He or she must be an open-minded individual who is willing to learn and experience something new and better. This requires a cheerful expression and a confident attitude, a bright and trusting personality, as well as a positive optimism, an explicit value, a perfect mind, and a congruity of heart and mental harmony. A business-man or woman needs specific and complete information to operate on.

In fact, your business purposes must come with a business mind and with the spirit of abundance to provide you a steady flow of progressive innovation. If it's well-constructed in an orderly fashion, it will help you live in an active state and function with actionable intelligence. Even if you continue to progress and advance in business, it will enable you to function from a superior state of consciousness that helps you perceive good energies and actively live in conscious awareness.

With constructive use and careful attention, business intelligence gives you an attitude of gratitude and appreciation. The purpose of such use may eventually reveal to you positive energies that will greatly enable you to attract more blessings into your life. It will clear the road for passionate spirits and for good and active energies to breed noble values. As a result, it will provide you better rewards and higher incentives that will greatly increase the degree of your creative efforts, positive interests, and attention in the marketplace and workplace. Ultimately, it will give you the power and ability to move with certainty, clarity, and intensity to accomplish your goals.

A brilliant business mind synchronizes the world of commerce; enhances personal relationships; and then brings multiple profits, great rewards, and higher incentives by providing you the best ideas that will make the greatest impact and bring real change into your life. Therefore, developing appropriate techniques for business purposes will serve as the power source for all profitable changes, creative efforts, and innovative purposes. So remember, it's the power source of all abundance; the power source of all economic freedom; and the main source of power of all spiritual, mental, and emotional strengths that serve as the real source of all your material blessings.

You can have a remarkable life and an enduring legacy if you can grow and develop your mind and enrich your heart with knowledge. That's why a business mind is a skillful power that comes with a positive line of action, a positive frame of mind, and a positive spirit of enthusiasm and life force that will satisfy your meaningful purposes. It serves the unity of your overall well-being and then becomes insightful knowledge that prepares the mind to discover something new and better. In addition, it will ultimately serve the unity of your overall reservoir of peace, happiness, and health. So it stands for endless creativity, endless value, unlimited productivity, and a perpetual purpose of all business existence that serves as the foundational stones of all success, progress, and development.

Every successful businessman or woman knows that the business mind is the thinking center and the acting point of creative intelligence, the conscious spirit that guides all active life. This is a skillful power that comes from objective awareness, from a passionate spirit and conscious action. Therefore, to achieve success is to think creatively and act reasonably because the business mind supports a highly effective mind and active life that comes from creative intelligence and spontaneous action, a sound sense, spontaneous awareness, and conscious development.

Nature has proven that you can succeed if you acquire the rightful skills to do business and achieve goals. Think of the fertile soil, a navigational river, the rain, the sunshine, a colorful sky, and moonlight. They all have natural power and ability to create and produce unique results. You can see Nature has significant evidence of truth, a gradual principle of growth, development, and accomplishment. If you believe in the business mind, not only you will succeed, but you will also grow, develop, and multiply because nature has proven the evidence of effective action and even reveals the evidence of intelligent use, careful application, diligent effort, and abundant supply. This is broader than you can think and greater than you can imagine because a business intelligence is the sum and substance of your unique business knowledge and of your synthetic understanding of a unique business, and your overall thinking, which provides you the best possible power, strength, and life in business and the best efforts of the mind and heart. That's why it's a critical skill that is endowed with the spirit of passion and an inner vitality, a practical intelligence, and a pure sense of imagination that is further blessed with power of attraction, motivation, and inspiration.

You can change your personal world through a business mind because it will significantly serve your best needs and actively support your greatest desires that inspire positive energies and will serve your best interests. This will eventually transform negative thoughts into greater purposes, thereby increasing the spirit of passion, enthusiasm, and progress in the marketplace, workplace, and in any profitable organization.

You can transform your life and live better because the desire to do so is the motivation that satisfies your heart; empowers you to clearly understand and accept your responsibilities; courageously face your challenges in life; and avoid irrational fear, unnecessary anger, self-doubt, and procrastination that kill your dreams and goals in life. You can even grow your business bigger because this improves your standards of living, increases your levels of understanding, expands your creative vision, and ultimately increases your receptive power and enhances your responsive mind, which provides you the broadest sense of the expression of your burning desire, self-reliance, self-determination, and self-confidence. All of this gives you the freedom of expression and improves your powers of thought. The truly remarkable thing is that the business mind improves your efficiency and ultimately helps you establish effectiveness in your life.

By creating useful skills and working with useful knowledge, you can break through to the new levels of inspiration and productivity that emanate from a business mind. You can change your personal world by enhancing a possibility of mind that fosters creative changes and opens the doors of profitable opportunities that will bring you multiple results.

A business mind is what you need to advance into a better future. It requires conscious awareness, diligent use of your mind, and intelligent direction. In the most basic sense, a business mind provides you a constant stream of profitable business and produces a continuous flood of goodness that brings you an inpouring of blessings. This is the potential source of your inspiration, motivation, and action that equally brings you an inspiring life, inspiring dreams, realistic goals, and sound plans. As a result, it strengthens your faith and moral values, empowers your unique character, and very often increases your mental capacity and emotional intelligence. That accelerates success and propels progression and development in your businesses and personal relationships. This enables you to create healthier customer services and draw in more prospects that will help you expand your economic resources.

Even if you are expanding your economic resources, it's equally certain that you can succeed and advance into a better future because you are born with an innate ability and power that represents a unique life. This shows why the business mind continues to yield surprises in the hands of managers and leaders and why they are highly effective and efficient in business. We all believe in them because they have acquired business minds that enhance their business purposes. They also have acquired business minds that provide them a roundtable of wisdom and purpose and profitable value, which enables them to exchange valuable insights and share valuable experiences to foster their businesses. This in turn will greatly enhance their lives and enrich their purposes. The business mind is a powerful resource that helps them exploit new goals and enjoy better opportunities, which bring them new business and therefore help them enjoy greater success and progress. As a result, business intelligence provides them novel ideas, sound thoughts, clear feelings, and sound minds that enable them to convert potential business into material goods, helps them transform material good into happiness, and convert happiness into spiritual blessings. In addition, it gives them a protective ground for efficiency and effectiveness in business, prepares their minds for unexpected opportunities, and ultimately helps them take advantage of future opportunities when they knock. It strengthens their imaginative faculties to enhance their emotional strengths and mental powers.

In the most basic sense, the business mind is the creative power that shines the light of consciousness and knowledge and brightens the light of awareness that illuminates creative intelligence. In addition, it's a conscious power that flows freely from a positive mental action and floods naturally from a positive mental revelation of a pure business heart and a pure business mind. It comes from a transparent spirit of passion, enthusiasm, and motivation. Basically, it's a creative power that demands a spirit of passion. Passion demands inspiration, and inspiration requires spiritual awareness—a transparent sense that draws spiritual energies, creative efforts, emotional strengths, and mental alertness that spark the light of wisdom and profound understanding and enhance a synthetic field of knowledge.

Every successful man or woman knows that the business mind plays a critical role in all business success and properly provides a legitimate reason for effective action. It gives them a richer sense of purpose and a brighter point of view that enhances all their creative intelligence and ultimately brings them success, progress, and multiple developments.

Once again, the brilliant business mind is a creative power that comes from an unambiguous mind, clear action, and possibly from your aspiration and ambition to become more powerful and more desirable in life. It's also a skillful power that grows from undivided attention, an undivided mind, unity of interest, and a burning desire to achieve a definite purpose. It represents a business purpose that comes with a strong spirit of enthusiasm and active spirit of passion, inspiration, and motivation, which brings you a richer sense of purpose and a greater intelligence that enhances your business purposes. The business mind is the sole property of the mind and heart that actively materializes itself into active force, productive action, and multiple results. This leads to a highly developed quality of character and a profound desire to grow, achieve goals, and admire the beauty that represents your life purposes. As a result, this becomes the code of ethical justice and moral progress. Yet it's a powerful source of attraction of all the good that will continue to provide you the eagerness to bring positive changes that will certainly make a huge impact in your life.

It's critical that you know the power that comes from a business mind and how important it is to take advantage of its values. The business mind is the vehicle that instantly transports you to the end of your desire and enables you to achieve your purposes. It's also a power that comes from within and makes the impossible possible. It gives you the sustaining power that makes all things possible, which means that it's the light that shines all wisdom and the light that brightens all useful knowledge. It lights your way to success and development.

Basically, it unfolds its powerful creative spirits through the inner chamber of your creative wisdom and through creative intelligence and profound understanding. Therefore, it's critically important for you to be properly aware that your mind is a creative spirit. A creative spirit is a creative wisdom and intelligence in action. This means that a business mind is complete in spirit and complete in meaning and in action. It also means that it's a creative power that feeds on a healing condition and senses a desirable atmosphere of healing and valuable outcome. It grows in knowledge and wisdom and actively lives through positive experiences that will open your mind, satisfy your heart, and spark positive actions that generate multiple results. For greater satisfaction, it will ultimately give birth to new, bigger, and better possibilities and conceive something new that will bring much better opportunities that serve even greater purposes.

In the most basic sense, I believe in the power and strength of the business mind because I have observed this creative power of mindful business lift people from poverty to success, from an atmosphere of fear to a state of courage; and from depression and sickness to happiness, health, and prosperity. As a result, I have carefully observed people using this creative power to lift themselves out from extreme poverty to great wealth, and I have also seen people use this ability to express satisfaction and fulfillment. I believe in it because I have carefully observed this creative power increasing in value and inspiring successful people and multiplying profitable values. In addition, I have seen it build multiple businesses and spread multiple values, and I have also seen it unite and diversify businesses in every aspect of life.

Consider the entrepreneurial, artistic vision of Donald Trump, Bill Gates, Steve Jobs, Henry Ford, Ray Kroc, and so many others. These people have a unique business vision and a brilliant business mind that guide them to achieve their goals.

You can see why a brilliant business mind is a value-driven mind and the partner of a profit-seeking heart that represents a significant value. So you can believe that it's an inspiring adventure of uplifting experiences, a career-driven and benefit-inspiring intelligence, a profit-inspiring goal, and a purpose-motivating action that brings you multiple results.

Truly, it's a creative power that comes from mental agility, inner strength, and ingenuity of mind that create artistic inventiveness, thoughtfulness, and creative imagination. This explains why it's a potential energy that builds valuable rapport, exchanges valuable information, and connects valuable people with highly efficient and effective minds who can make better things happen. This is a business model that saves, changes, and benefits lives. That's why it builds valuable contacts that skillfully communicate values and enrich more and more lives. So it's well-fortified with inner powers and strengths, which are built through mental toughness and inner vitality. It's a well-trusted power that transforms negative into positive, converts fear into courage, transforms courage into multiple blessings, and ultimately converts all potentials into realities. Truly, it's an incredible power that expresses possibility, potentiality, and competency and generates multiple results that will greatly increase in value and grow through due diligence and creative intelligence. That's because it's a creative power that comes from a cheerful attitude, relentless effort, and flawless action. It's also an artistic plan that grows from your active faith; your creative vision; your rational, persistent efforts; your purposeful mind; and your well-meaning heart.

You need to invest in something that helps you improve your life and enhances your purpose. The business mind is an effective tool that can provide you at least that. It's a tool that has been tested and properly used by successful businessmen and women in all walks of life. It's the power that arises from harmonious senses and from legitimate reasons, from sound thoughts and effective actions. It's the power that needs creative intelligence, a synthetic point of view, a point of understanding, a logical consistency, and an inner sense of awareness. Business intelligence comes through practice, practical ideas, and the effective application of useful knowledge and creative wisdom that sparks the light of intelligence and brightens the spirit of passion and progress. It ultimately helps you shine the spirit of success. It's also the artistic power that sparks the light of awareness that ignites the light of financial freedom, fuels a courageous spirit, and supports a conscious determination that opens more doors to profitable business and more windows of favorable opportunity to increase the value of your life and enhance more courageous and passionate spirit of creative innovations.

So the more often you apply the best business mind in your everyday endeavors, the more successful you will become. Now, you should know that enhancing a good business mind will enable you to sustain your business purpose, help you maintain a profitable innovation, and ultimately help you live wisely and maintain a desirable life. As this happens, it will restore your lost hope and ignite your passion that sparks positive actions and brings positive changes into your life. As a result, it will enable you to feel better and think healthier thoughts so you can live peacefully and happily in the present moment. If you allow a higher level of emotional maturity to take control, it will become a powerful glue that holds together your innermost joy and your deepest comfort in life. In addition, it will be a dynamic, artistic power that stimulates your interest that supports a higher intelligence and ignites passion that propels positive actions and provides you both visible and invisible goodness. You need to design and shape your own personal world. That always comes first, so remember that a brilliant business mind lives in potentiality and practical intelligence that reveals all potential possibilities, all profitable opportunities, and draws all potentials that will bring you multiple successes and prolific returns. The second thing you should bear in mind is that a good business mind is a transparent power that reveals bigger pictures and reflects its positive visual images in your mentality and in your meaningful businesses.

If you don't have a business mind, you don't record things or take notes of events, so you're not a businessman. A real businessman or woman will always be noting and recording events that can serve as valuable experiences and useful knowledge, which can eventually increase the value that can serve profitable businesses and bring multiple returns. A business mind is business intelligence in action, in manifestation, and in effective result. In the most basic sense, it's a fruitful mind that thinks within and acts around values and brings quality results. That's why it's the Mother Nature of the present, the maker, the doer, and the commander of the past; the leading founder of today's modern innovation; and the fountainhead of the stream of the future. When you realize the truth and believe in its concepts, you will certainly succeed and grow in power. A business mind is the power that brings you success, and all lasting success takes place within business intelligence. You will certainly be blessed with power and strength because all successful businesses grow in useful knowledge through a brilliant business mind and stay alive through absoluteness of purpose and clear judgment. This is why it's important that a real businessman or woman live in creative wisdom and intelligence. It further shows you why a good business mind must come from creative mentality, from creative wisdom, from perceptive power, from ingenuity, inner harmony, and inner sense of a dedicated purpose.

A business mind gives you creative wisdom and the possibility to succeed and progress. Are you ready and willing to take advantage of the opportunity and advance into the future? If so, you should understand that as the business mind expands in consciousness, it also expands in its greater purpose, in its greater good, in its higher power, and in its perfect gift of livingness of that goodness. When you lift your thoughts to their best, they will become the light that shines through your consciousness. This will position you for greater growth solidly grounded in goodness and eventually expand and stretch your wings for a greater blessing, abundant life, and eternal goodness that will certainly bring you greater assurance.

Whether you are looking to build lasting relationships with others, succeed in business, or provide excellent customer service, it's important that you learn to use your mind effectively. That is the way in which its goodness can be ascertained with greater precision, and your innate ability can unfold in the best ways and increase diversity.

As you mind your business and have business goals in mind, your business mind will reflect itself in clarity of purpose and congruity of mind. You can see why every business goal aims at the potential results and why every potential result comes with reasons of the mind and heart that express themselves in value, quality, and satisfaction. Deep inside me, I believe a brilliant business mind will provide you a better business and give you a greater sense of purpose, a passionate and courageous spirit of action, a stronger power, and a greater strength to succeed and progress. This is your personal prayer and a personal realization of spirit of success and progress. This is also a unique skill that lives in its inherent nature, in its inherent powers and strengths, and multiplies through its higher intelligence, which flows within and around inspiration and motivation.

The basic question is whether you are willing to change and progress. Obviously, the answer to the question is yes because no wise man or woman wants to continue suffering and slowly dying in pain. A business mind gives you the main key to unlock your potential future and helps you unleash your creative powers and strengths to increase the value of your life and serve all your meaningful purposes.

That's the whole point of positive thinking and acting that shows why a business mind is the pipeline for all creative innovation and sound ideas, which can be fashioned out of a profitable business. Therefore,

I think what can be fashioned from a business mind is to take note of events, see things the way they are, and take advantage of opportunities when they knock. That's why a business mind is at the center of all successful businesses, relationships, and lives. This will ultimately be at the center of all creative wisdom and logical insight, intuitive awareness, useful knowledge, and creative understanding that build all successful businesses. Remember, big is better, but small deals with the complexities of life. A business mind serves both big and small businesses. I encourage you to see and feel the reasons you are doing businesses and why a business mind sustains the life of business purposes and becomes a life vision and life purpose. You must understand the incredible power of useful knowledge, which is associated with a business mind because it fuels the energy of a business, which flows through a mental activity, through useful and profitable information, valuable experiences, and a profound understanding of new and better decisions to guide your goals.

Once you have acquired a business mind, your life will instantly start to change. I fundamentally believe in it because the more you use your mind diligently, the more you succeed. And the more you succeed, the stronger and more effective you become in life. I deeply believe in it because if you can think constructively, you can act differently and ultimately know how to convert a suspect into prospect, transform no into yes, and learn how to use rejections as stepping stones to acquire more value and get better information to help you profit from frustration and change your life forever. Once you have achieved this goal, your life will become a business life, and your mind will properly become a business mind that serves all business purposes. This is the ethical rule of a business life, the moral principle of an effective action, and a transformational pattern of thinking and acting that enhances all creative innovation, all unified energy, and all spirit of enthusiasm.

As long as you are in your right mind, you will always feel good about yourself. Good business ventures can create something better in your life, so if your business is not growing, it is because of a lack of a good business mind. By acquiring the best business mind, your business will start to grow, and your life will start to improve because a good business mind defines your business concepts and values and properly determines your results from the beginning of your action. It's an influential power that comes from your perspective sense, your significant values, your sensibilities, your sensory acuity, and your sound reason, which will provide you a positive cycle of development, success, and progress.

Now you can see that a business mind is what you truly need to succeed in life and build lasting relationships. It's the power that comes with a flexible personality, flexible knowledge, creative intelligence, quick mind, and adaptable heart. As water is an inescapable need, the business mind is an undeniable desire and an unquestionable spirit that is agreeable in all values and in all harmonious relationships. Therefore, it's exclusively owned, solely controlled, and properly directed by creative intelligence and ruled by the absolute power of creative wisdom. Once again, are you ready to change? So focus on the solution because the way you see the problem is the problem, and by focusing on the problem without having solution in mind, you become the problem.

You can make a great impact by lifting your thoughts, having greater assurance, and expanding your faith. This leads to a properly fixed purpose of mind, a firmness of belief, and a soundness of character that come with effective action, emotional awareness, and critical enquiry skills that can express the presence of passion, inspiration, and motivation that enhances all success. This also keeps you well-informed with useful knowledge to advance your career. This is a power that encourages voluntary efforts, independent actions that will enable you to plan ahead and stay ahead and properly take advantage of opportunities when they knock.

Just as useful information shines the light of consciousness and properly shields more lives, a business mind will brighten more lives and ultimately protect more businesses if used wisely. The business mind is a value-driven and knowledge-based intelligence. It's also a game of intelligence and a well-crafted plan that supports positive experiences, useful feedback, and sound ideas that equally bring you positive returns, multiple profits, and rewards that are inspired by a higher purpose. Your mind is pure gold, which means that your mind is a hidden treasure and a great resource that fosters creative changes in businesses.

The basic question is this: Why can't you embody a business mind that is enriched with personal power, artistic vision, and functional wisdom that provides you a means of livelihood and a positive line of action that sees only profits and quality results? The resulting efforts of the mind and sound ideas can give you the best possible reservoir of peace, happiness, and a triumphant joy that come from your creative thinking, quality actions, and great rewards. The more a unique business mind develops, the more fear decreases and problems are resolved.

This means that the more you appreciate what you have, the more your business mind provides for your future needs. As a result, it provides you all the vital fruits and energies that foster progressive changes in your life. This also means that the more you appreciate it, the more it opens the door to understanding your basic needs and creating positive changes in all phases of your life. Positive thinking is the business mind in action, which creates power that represents a cooperative channel of continuous blessing, inspiration, motivation, and accomplishment.

By working to grow and succeed, you can reintegrate knowledge in new ways, therefore breaking through into a business solution that begins with business intelligence, a reasonable self-confidence, and a self-awareness of truth. This motivates and inspires optimistic spirits to render quality services that can draw more valuable energies, spark positive actions, and germinate more bountiful results.

This is the appreciation of certain fine qualities for all good, powerful, and lasting life, and it's important for you to be aware of the benefits associated with a business mind. Through a brilliant business mind, all profitable opportunity knocks, incentives and benefits multiply, and unity and diversity grow because a brilliant business mind is clearly leading the way for reasonable people who are producing a long-lasting success and making better things happen. It's important to shape a new, better and profitable knowledge that comes with a conscious realization of facts, a valuable experience, an identification of spiritual unity and reality that manifest through creative intelligence.

Without a unique business mind, you might have general knowledge but fail to understand many of the real and productive truths and therefore fail to get the results you need. You fail because you lack a definitive mind. You can succeed and grow only if you have a unique business mind. That is because all profitable opportunity comes from conscious awareness, which arises from a sound sense of creative vision, personal power and initiative, and your mechanism of ideas and logical actions.

This represents a unique power that comes from your personal strength of character, moral discipline, and self-control, and it properly grows in wisdom and constructive sense that ignites positive actions and produces sound results. This is a new fabric of knowledge that unravels certain truths. It is the very essence of truth and of all eternal blessings that will properly demonstrate the powers and strengths of your mental realization of truth. Remember that truth can be experienced only when you understand how to think constructively. Realities can be gleaned from your mental recognition of facts, from your spiritual guidance, and from your mental affirmation of truth in your personal life, but when you are dreaming of becoming a good businessperson, you are eventually dreaming of having a conscious mind. This serves all your memories of thought and therefore should be recognized and expressed with the positive pictures of right action to gain positive results. Most important, let all your thoughts represent a symbol of a good business mind that will properly dissolve every mental problem, ignite positive actions, and then support your spiritual foresightedness to enrich your life and enhance all your useful purposes.

It's crucial to know that a business mind also helps you raise better kids through self-discipline, self-control, and conscious direction. It provides you properly refined thoughts and a simplified knowledge that further provides you mental power, emotional strength, and spiritual guidance and ultimately gives you the sustaining power of intelligence that rules your life as well as others' lives.

A business mind comes with a business foresight that is enriched with business insights. In addition, it provides you eternal energy and the power of spiritual realization in everyday phenomena. It opens up a means of effective communication and avenue of expression that expands your consciousness and allows positive energy to flow into your mind and heart. This then leads to a creative mentality that is born of intelligence to live and breed success. You must live in practical wisdom and effective action to produce positive results through a unique business mind to reap hope, blessings, and good results and ultimately enjoy true happiness, peace, and joy. Do you now know why the business mind is born of power and strength? You are born of power, and I believe it will unleash all of your potential power and unravel all of your potential strength because it's properly endowed with a higher power that is born of logical consistency, conscious awareness, rational thinking, and logical action that rests solely on its values and strong convictions. It depends on the certainty of your mind and possibility in your heart.

The people who have achieved their goals in life are prolific producers, builders, and creators, as well as talented performers who have made excellent choices and prominent use of their powers of mind. They all have achieved their goals by creating and building in consciousness, making the best use of their minds, and properly directing and controlling their minds to serve their unique purposes. You can do the same—you can control your mind and shape your life. Most important, you can direct your mind and advance into a better future and live a better life. But all these things will come only through believing in and developing a skillful business mind.

CHAPTER 6

APPRECIABLE VALUE

Do what you can, with what you have, where you are.
— THEODORE ROOSEVELT

Appreciable value is something that everyone longs for and works for, and typically we view moving up in the future as a sign that we are growing. Increased profit and business opportunity are also things we long for and strive for, and an appreciable value can enable us achieve all that and advance into a better future. It will enable us to see both the possibility and potentiality in business and ultimately help us get profitable results. Appreciable value is the value that adds even more value. It's the overriding factor that influences people act, helps them make valuable decisions and smart choices, and ultimately helps them focus on what matters most.

Appreciable value enhances a healthy economy, focuses on getting the most out of existing resources and aims at establishing a profitable business, sufficient enough to be readily perceived, recognized, and enjoyed.

If you want to be successful, you have to truly value people, understand and satisfy their emotional needs. Because an understanding of values is one of the most powerful and fastest ways to achieving success.

That's why creative people see good in everything, convert bad into good, convert fear into courage and into multiple blessings, and eventually transform negative attitudes into positive results. These people are grateful for life, and other people are grateful for them. They believe in gratitude and appreciation of life, and people believe in them. They believe in success and prosperity; therefore, appreciable value provides them all the tools and resources they need to accomplish their purposes.

They also believe that the world is a heavenly place and a paradise that will provide them everything they truly need, so they properly claim all portions of their blessings through appreciation because they know that appreciation holds their ultimate value. That believe it will ultimately reveal all their values and draw to them even greater value. They know that appreciable value comes from acknowledgment of good and that by focusing on results and appreciating good, they are drawing more and more good into their lives. In addition, their lives will continuously grow better.

Positive people always enhance appreciable value because appreciable value gives them financial freedom, emotional security, mental balance, and spiritual guidance. It enriches their lives, enhances their well-being, and ultimately gives them multiple rewards that help them focus on the absoluteness of purpose. Appreciable value is a gratitude that unlocks the fullness of life and provides us valuable outcomes that enhance more active beliefs that help us accomplish more positive results. It is the main source of our power supply that brings consistent energy to our minds and our hearts, helping us use our energy in a positive way. And then it becomes the light that shines on our consciousness and brightens our awareness.

Everyone should know that the more we are grateful for life, the more abundance we draw into our lives. And everyone should equally know that appreciation is the source of all abundance and the key to attracting more blessings, joy, satisfaction, and happiness. It opens the door of business opportunity, the door of courage and spontaneous action, and helps us make finer distinctions and better decisions in our lives. Everyone should explore something profitable or appreciable because it increases the power of appreciation that circles and embodies all growth. That's why it's the key ingredient of success in any organization that yields greater values and better returns. It's a product of mental activity flowing with love, passion, and vitality.

Everyone should learn to appreciate good because it increases value, enriches our lives, and improves our imaginative skills that come from rational thinking, a sound mind, and productive thoughts, which stimulates our minds, mobilizes our greatest potential, and unleashes our best possible powers. This is a wonderful power that lifts us to new levels of development and enhances our lives. It's a creative power that is born of usefulness and potentiality that demand passion. Passion demands inspiration, and inspiration requires spiritual awareness that lifts us to new levels of understanding.

As we continue to learn and understand, we should know that what we value in life is what we appreciate, and what we appreciate in life is what we value, and what we value determines our destinies. We become what we appreciate in life. We become our own personal love, our own creative energies, and our own creative thoughts. Ultimately, our own creative efforts define us in life. Most important, we become what we praise and appreciate in life. Therefore, I suggest that we embody positive attitudes of gratitude that strongly connect all the delightful, joyful emotions and positive experiences that can empower us and make us effective in our minds and hearts as well as in business. Appreciable value is a natural intelligence that flows and floods naturally from a positive mental revelation of a pure and transparent heart. It's a natural value that helps us grow and prosper in life. It's an inherent part of a successful life and plays a critical role in business success. It's our fundamental psychological and emotional needs and the ultimate key to success that provides us the flexibility of mind and the freedom of choice that give us the power and the opportunity to be in charge and effectively unlock the potential within us and around us.

Almost everything we need in life requires us to show a positive attitude because to deal effectively with others and succeed in life, a sense of gratitude is the gateway to a higher consciousness, growth, and fulfillment. This is where positive action spells quality results because when we show gratitude for something, we are expressing appreciation, and our attitude of gratitude helps us get through difficult situations, build value, and keep important relationships. This enables us to establish strong bonds, sustain valuable relationships, and eventually maintain effective communication that consistently fuels our desire to accomplish quality results.

Appreciable value plays an important role in our personal lives as well as our business endeavors. It gives us the ability to embrace change as a means of advancement that will bring us more favorable opportunities. All of this shows why appreciation provides us new opportunities and eventually spurs the best possible action that will ultimately bring us the most favorable results. It will further bring us the inflow of good, a flood of peace and happiness, so we can clearly see that all peace, happiness, and health come from an attitude of gratitude that is born in consciousness and grows with wisdom.

When we show gratitude and appreciation, we can begin to work with heart and prosper in business because it helps us serve in every arena of life, increases our value, and balances our lives in every calling. Remember that our effectiveness lies in balance, and balance is the very essence of effectiveness and efficiency in business. Therefore, as we grow and mature in business, our economy grows in self-discipline, and eventually profitable appreciation grows in our pleasant minds and hearts, as well as in all positive environments. As a result, it calms our minds, enhances our hearts, enriches our purposes, and provides us a cheerful attitude and a pleasant gratitude that brings us success, draws potential, and produces prolific results. In addition, it provides us a spiritual unity of mind and a reality of heart that enhances a positive state of consciousness, enriches all creative environments, and finally expands our mental vision to bring us a perfect balance in all our business endeavors. When we have a business plan in mind as we express our gratitude, it opens the door to simplicity and helps us use our energy in a positive way. That's why it's the source of our spiritual substance; the key to a powerful, positive vibration of abundance; and the infinite supply of our blessings, which continue to draw an abundance of value and prolific returns.

But before we begin to work and draw appreciable value, let us remember that when appreciable value stops flowing, economy stops growing, life diminishes, fear increases, and happiness and joy decrease. If we can get this basic truth well-grounded in our minds and hearts and know that when appreciable value comes, fear and poverty escape through the back door, our lives will increase in value, and happiness and joy will multiply. Then appreciable value will become a grateful attitude of gratitude that will enable us to enhance our business lives and ultimately help us grow our important relationships. As a result, it brings all of our ideas to life; helps us develop positive visual images in our minds; and enables us to sustain good, vibrant energy in our hearts. It provides us a uniqueness of purpose and a uniqueness of heart, mind, and body that determines the quality of our lives, the quality of our actions, and our overall well-being. This is a sure way to innovate the future, a confident way to express the freedom of the mind and the heart, and a sure means of a positive affirmation of our spirits. It's a proper avenue of expression and attraction, a clear and direct incentive channel any wise man or woman can properly use to draw good returns and attract great value. This shows us that appreciation is a self-expression of positive spirit; a clear, positive attitude; and a genuine and thorough expression of our spirits of passion and enthusiasm that enrich our souls and allow us to produce concrete realities in our lives.

So if we appreciate more, we get more and live more life, and eventually we achieve more success with less stress. Appreciation is the mother of invention, the father of innovation, and the unified field of all profitable purpose that produces a ceaseless energy of enthusiasm, a ceaseless quality of thought that shines the light of knowledge and brightens the light of awareness. It's the potential energy that comes from the spirit of enthusiasm and good that balances the mind, heart, and body to work harmoniously and produce effective results. It's an assimilation of value, a continued flood of peace, energy, and progress that fills our hearts, minds, and bodies with life-giving energy and life-inspiring thoughts that will bear positive fruits and yield multiple results. It supports all creative endeavors, enhances all profitable environments, and lifts all delightful minds to bring us the best value and opportunities to advance and succeed in life. As a result, it gives us the power to win, the willingness to advance, and the strength to pursue a more favorable outcome. It creates a cooperative channel of communication, learning, and better possibilities that brings us success, happiness, love, and passion.

This is the vital force that creates a path to life and lifts all positive minds in every aspect of life. It shows us the best possible action to reach the widest range of minds and hearts in every arena of success. Therefore, I encourage you to appreciate good because I have seen how good generates more good, increases value, and brings multiple positive results. I guarantee you success if you can learn how to appreciate something of value. This is worth talking about because successful people have used this to achieve their purposes. If we increase our appreciation of life and experience, embrace, and enjoy life more, success will follow.

We should know that the end goal is to increase our value and grow wisely in creative intelligence and creative wisdom through the diligent use of our power of appreciation and gratitude. This will all emerge from common sense and a proper application of useful knowledge that provides us foresight and insight and the wisdom of mind and heart that comes from profound understanding. Remember, appreciation is inherent in nature and integral in self. It unleashes the power of our desires and gives us the ultimate expression of our beliefs and self-confidence, which brightens our hope and ultimately helps us maintain a positive self-image, a positive outlook, and a constructive state of mind. Appreciation is a positive belief that builds a strong sense of conviction in our lives.

Obviously, appreciation is a positive belief in action, and action is a result of appreciation. This is a self-actualization, an unmistakable and indisputable reality that enables us to shape our perceptions, beliefs, emotions, and actions. So if life is appreciable, then it's worth living. Therefore, we must believe in life to appreciate it, and we must appreciate life to believe in it, which means that we are what we appreciate—we are our own beliefs. This ultimately proves that appreciation forms our root beliefs that crystallize into power that communicates action and determines results.

There can be no real success without appreciation and gratitude because appreciation supports our optimistic spirits of success, progress, and prosperity. It harmonizes our creative environments and brings us peace in our homes as well as in our business relationships. As a result, it produces a roundtable of intellectual values that share useful knowledge and positive experiences. This clears the road for all profitable opportunities and therefore provides us the means to penetrate deeply and have access to probe into individual minds to achieve logical ideas, better lives, and a greater spirit of success.

All real success involves appreciation. To enjoy success without showing a reasonable appreciation or gratitude is like building a mansion without a foundation. It's important that we know the value of a reasonable appreciation because it's a unified source of our power supply and the sole energy of our lives, our happiness, our joy, and our health. This is a positive tendency of success that causes us to strive for a better future, a better life, and ultimately for the best possible mind and heart. All positive thinking breeds within the power of gratitude and appreciation and feeds on valuable information, practical ideas, and profound understanding. It needs a blissful emotional attachment, a cheerful disposition, and a blissful attitude of gratitude.

As human beings, we are responsible for our lives, and the key to enhancing our lives and enriching our purposes must come through a real, powerful, and appreciable value. Appreciation provides us earnestness of mind, eagerness of spirit, firmness of heart, and absoluteness of purpose. It also provides us more power and more strength and gives us a new life and a greater spirit to pursue excellence, greatness, new dreams, and inspiring goals that will lead us to many profitable rooms of the soul. It can open the door to essential solutions that can serve many business and personal purposes and successfully fill all our needs.

If you can think constructively, then you can change your perspective and learn and grow to achieve more success with less stress because appreciation gives you a new body, a new mind, and a new soul that support a new and better lifestyle. This is why it's the firstborn of all creative efforts, all creative innovations, and all profitable businesses. It's also why it's the pillar that supports all creative discipline and the stronghold of all notable business successes, as well as successful relationships. To make your dreams a reality, you must appreciate life because that's what life strives for and longs for so that it can better serve all your basic needs.

Obviously, there is no permanent result without a permanent appreciation because appreciation enhances our personal power, our strong convictions, and our self-confidence. It enables us to refine our old thoughts into new, productive ways of thinking and acting. As a result, it enhances our beliefs; actively refines old, uninspiring thoughts; and properly forms new ones that shape our strong convictions and enrich our well-being. This means that as we appreciate and build value, it actively purifies our minds and enables us to build powers that will strengthen our mental vision and sense of imagination to give us a richer and brighter view of what we truly want and rightfully need in life. In addition, it enables us to live in the mental world of intelligence, creative wisdom, and deep understanding, which can help us adjust our attitudes and behaviors for the greater good and ultimately enable us to accept profitable changes as opportunities for growth. As this happens, we can think and understand in a more meaningful way, which shows us why appreciation is the vital force that enables us to pay greater attention to the essentials and help us live in usefulness. That's why it's the guiding spirit and the propelling power that determines our actions, rules our destinies, regulates our lives, and produces multiple results.

Remember, appreciation of what you have will enable you to build and develop fulfillment of your future needs. This shows that appreciation is the father of all enduring success, all modernization, and all development. It also means that appreciation produces great people with keen determination and indispensable qualities, people who can make finer distinctions and better choices. They are capable of communicating a clear language of the body and a clear purpose of the mind and heart. This shows that appreciation gives you inner strength of self-expression of your heart and instills the joy of justice, which transforms the mind into a confluence of an attractive and dominant force and influential power that builds a healthy body and enhances a pure spirit that serves all your meaningful purposes and supports your future needs.

The more one appreciates good and desirable things in life, the more one attracts them. The basic nature of appreciation is to act because appreciation is a function of creative wisdom and a responsive mind, which shows us that the oneness of love is the oneness of all good, which provides us a cooperative method of thinking, a coordinated effort, and a creative drive. This creates a desirable atmosphere of love, vitality, passion, joy, happiness, and eternal peace, and it enables us to live in peace and in harmony with ourselves, our families, and others. Appreciation provides us the enthusiasm that illuminates our hearts and spirits, enriches our self-images, enhances our self-worth, improves our self-esteem, and properly grows our spirits of passion and love. Appreciation is a function of a bright idea, positive thinking, logical excellence and perfection, and ultimately a practical intelligence that produces positive outcomes. Obviously, this is the basic truth that makes appreciation a constructive way of asking and requesting good and the means by which our positive spirits reveal themselves. It's also an avenue of praising, receiving, and recognizing value and a way of showing respect that builds trust, mutual interest, and understanding. This in turn brings us a mental harmony that increases the degree of our hope in the workplace and expands the degree of our excitement in the marketplace. This is one of the most potent substances of our inspiration, motivation, and action. This is also why it produces a dedicated sense of loyalty and commitment, a pure sense of regard, and a show of respect that builds trust and supports valuable relationships that encourages voluntary action.

Here and now we can properly use the experiences of successful people to begin to appreciate life and improve our own lives. Where appreciation exists, supply and demand exist too, and there will be true evidence of an abundance of happiness, joy, and love. Appreciation brings us great hope and an abundance of goodness in our lives. It demands self-organized thoughts, self-controlled attitudes, and well-coordinated plans. It's the indwelling strength and vital force that serves our lives and supports our goals in life. It's the invisible and visible truth that arouses our minds and sparks our hearts to better understand another person, and then it helps us build a strong relationship with him or her to improve our lives. It encourages empathy that comes from the heart and sparks positive feelings of enthusiasm in the marketplace as well as in the workplace. It's the power that comes from a well-established fact and a properly defined purpose. It gives us the courage to identify and recognize our oneness with the realities of life. It's also the power that comes from guidance of wisdom and intelligence. It's a self-creation and a self-contemplation of positive spirit that provides us inner vitality and enthusiasm. It's a sound mind that enhances our self-images, boosts our self-confidence, promotes our emotional well-being, and supports our creative efforts. Appreciation influences our habits of thought, our patterns of feeling, and our systems of acting. It empowers us, improves our wisdom, and ultimately sharpens our observational skills, which will enable us to attract better and greater things in life. It's a powerful force that attracts its own kind, builds value, and produces optimal results. It serves as one of the foundational stones of all facts, all ingenuity of mind and heart, and all congruity of purpose.

Creating a new life and producing multiple results begins with appreciation. Appreciation increases our receptive powers, enhances our responsive minds, supports our creative visions, and properly supplies energy to our inner drive. It enables us to acquire unique skills and sharpen our awareness and observational techniques to reveal our hidden assets and blessings in life. It works to stimulate our higher powers of intelligence and potential energies to shape our ideas and strengthen our faith. This in turn provides us a unique intelligence and wisdom and a unique value that increases our personal powers and strengths. It reinforces our minds and strengthens our spirits of enthusiasm, which adds more fuel to the fire of our desires. In one sense, the power of appreciation inspires our minds, sparks positive actions, and increases the inflow of our power and strength to expand our energy production for better efforts and for our best interests. As we abide in consciousness of it, we will certainly know that a reasonable appreciation is a conscious choice, a self-discovery of inner truth, a creative spirit, and a profitable purpose that enables us to see the future in advance and seize opportunity when it knocks. Ultimately, appreciation helps us be of great service and receive higher rewards and better incentives that will foster all our business purposes. As we live and learn, it prepares our minds for creative use and enhances our hearts for effective action, providing us the necessary tolerance, sense of humor, and patience we need in all our business endeavors.

So it's absolutely important that we appreciate life because appreciation provides us a healthy spirit of enthusiasm and a pure spirit of passion that expresses our unique qualities and inspires positive actions. As a result, it provides us a clear perception, a sound sense, and a steady flow of conscious intelligence that expands our creative vision and profound understanding so we can fully with synchronize the world of business and make better things happen. This is the best way to increase profits in business and the most comprehensive way to create a unified power of purpose. It's also the fastest way to increase positive energy that will actively supply us the fuel for a peak performance and greater chances of success. Now we can clearly see that appreciation purifies our minds for better performance and ultimately frees us from the limitations of worry, anxiety, fear, and failure.

As we live and learn, a reasonable appreciation makes us constant students of life, seeking useful purposes for useful lives and for a proper cultivation and enhancement of our habits. It enables us to recognize opportunity and helps us make prompt decisions that will give us the ability to embrace positive changes that will support our lives. As a result, it reveals all the mysteries of life that will bring us a miraculous outcome and serves as an element of heart that draws an abundance of blessings. Remember, appreciable value makes the ends meet, but it takes great initiative to create and develop because it's a deeply rooted conviction of the mind and a classic sense of value that drives clear actions that come from the heart. As long as we live and learn, it provides us a transcendental power that sparks the intellectual action that greatly increases the fields of knowledge and understanding. This brings us a synthetic, symbolic wisdom that lights the spiritual lamp of absolute purpose.

This is an excellent way to shine the light of life and one way to show an impressive character and attribute of the mind that produces a blissful family of great hope, high expectation, and anticipation of a better life and future. For the mind, heart, and body to connect and interact in much more fruitful ways, we must deeply understand the value of appreciation. Appreciation is a value that can be actualized only by appreciating value, which is why it's a continuous source of inspiration and motivation. That's also why it's the main source of our triumphant joy, victory, and eternal peace, which brings us a positive expression of our hearts and a constructive mental wisdom of our souls.

The use of appreciation as a source of reward is a worthy idea because it gives us inner strength, confidence, and the ability to sustain our value and bring us a harmonious blend of facts and the unified spirit of an excellent mind. It also provides us a steady and reliable emotion that enables us to take a consistent action and ultimately gives us the key to learn, understand other people, and act effectively.

To increase our levels of understanding and develop a higher degree of skill, we need a reasonable appreciation to accomplish this. We need to expand our levels of appreciation in many areas of our lives to achieve great results. A reasonable appreciation is a mental rule, a spiritual foresightedness, a perfect platform for all successful life, and the main source of all power and intelligence that will provide us the key to constant energy, consistent action, and the thus success in life. This has long been practiced by successful people in all arenas of life, in all phases of business, and in successful relationships. So it's a well-trusted power that enables us to use our freedom of choice and the privilege of our independent minds to clear our environments for better opportunities. This is an all-purpose tool that can be used to grow our businesses. The most significant fact to remember is that everything that occurs in our lives begins with appreciation and ends in action. This means that the positive energy we have generated by appreciating value comes from a constructive use of our sound thoughts, sound feelings, and sound minds and therefore demands a moral discipline and sound personality that transcends our mental poise and emotional balance and properly aligns the equilibrium of our minds, bodies, and spirits.

The obvious question is, where does appreciation come from? In fact, appreciation arises from accurate thinking, perfect mental harmony, excellent use of our intelligence, and due diligence. It also arises from a positive mental disposition and a constructive mental direction and from an excellent spirit of passion and creative wisdom.

Remember, appreciation is a reasonable cause that yields prolific outcomes and multiple blessings. Appreciation gives us a good element of heart and a quality frame of mind that accelerates progress and propels success. It's the power of gratitude that compounds value to bring us multiple interests. As a result, it gives us freedom of choice and peace of mind that release us from self-limitation and self-sabotaging behaviors. We should also remember that we are what we are today because of what we have appreciated in life, and what we appreciate influences our actions to produces similar results.

The wider your range of appreciation, the greater your range of success, and the more healthy a life you will have because appreciation is a potential source of useful knowledge, inspiration, and motivation that completes you. It helps you separate important things from the unimportant and to focus on what matters most, therefore providing you the best possible solutions in life for the best results. As a result, it brings life into business, and life in business brings equal returns in compensation, which increases the strength of your mental magnetism and power of attraction. Therefore, let those who are in business to profit be aware that a reasonable appreciation is a potential reason for effective action that brings consistent results. It enables them to build more strength and become more effective in life.

One cannot carry what one cannot hold, so one cannot appreciate what one cannot benefit from or use. Many people have suffered in life for appreciating nonsense without knowing that bad grows in negative beliefs, just as good grows in wisdom and understanding. So by now we should know that appreciation comes with a business mind, sound reason, practical ideas, creative wisdom, and profound understanding. When we dream of becoming good businesspeople, we are really dreaming of appreciating quality lives because the integrity of our words and actions brings us positive results. This all boils down to achieving success because appreciation is something that serves a meaningful purpose, increases in value, and strives for something better and superior in quality to satisfy our needs. Let it also be a mirror of positive thought, the passion of the heart that unites with the passion of the mind. Most important, let all of this come through a mental articulation of facts that guide our inherent abilities to perform much better and eventually enhance our intellectual knowledge to produce endless stimuli and ceaseless power. Obviously, this is a magic power and light that comes from our hearts, actively cleanses our spirits of enthusiasm, and prepares our minds for better performance. This makes a worthwhile business and inspires positive actions that will produce multiple results.

Sensing the purpose of appreciation and having a positive attitude toward it can help you improve your life. It will enable you to live wisely and act effectively, and ultimately it will help you control and direct all your energies into a singleness of purpose. In addition, it will enable you to improve and expand your point of view, increase the value of your life, and develop your creative vision and positive experiences. It will also enhance your creative energies and help you develop sound ideas and productive thoughts that can inspire your goals and support your spirit of devotion, passion, and commitment to bring about business opportunities.

Appreciation stands for positive change and therefore demands understanding and respect, which express our regard and devotion and actively arouse the impulses within us and around us. It also arouses our spiritual, mental, and emotional responsiveness. As a result, it provides us the fuel that ignites the fire of our desires, sparks our sensibilities, strengthens our senses of imagination, and eventually expands our mental and physical strengths. As an additional result, it serves as a positive emotional connection and a highly respected value in all walks of life. With this in mind, we can fuse our sensory impressions, positive emotions, and intellects in a unified way because a profitable appreciation gives us the ability to link all facts, all vital truths, and all substantial elements of success. The more we feel what we know and appreciate what we have, the greater our knowledge becomes. Appreciation provides us positive feedback and useful information that enables us to make valuable decisions, take quality actions, and ultimately produce quality results. It also enables us to maintain what we already have and to sustain our energies.

Your personal wholeness and fulfillment come from appreciation, so it's absolutely important to be grateful for life. Appreciation follows a particular tendency of good, a particular line of action, and a constructive channel of producing results that will give you a positive emotional connection that builds value and enriches your purpose. It gives you a deeper understanding and opens the door for new and better opportunities for more desirable results that can draw more positive energies and may eventually produce a powerful magnetic force. Therefore, expanding the circle of appreciation is what everyone needs because appreciation comes with a mental magnet that attracts whatever agrees with its ruling and healing condition to function simultaneously in accordance with the rules of nature. Here the principles of nature will show you why the power of appreciation enhances all the living and healing conditions of nature, and by believing and using it constructively, it infuses all the senses that stimulate your keen interests and guides your ideas with clear purpose. It's empowering to realize the power of appreciation, and by expanding the circle of appreciation, you gain crystal-clear, positive mental pictures that can inspire your mind and motivate your heart.

Of course, you need to appreciate life for life to release your portion of blessing. Therefore, it is crucial to understand the value of appreciation and how to tap into the inherent values in your life. You should know that a reasonable appreciation mobilizes all your powers and strengths, converts invisible goods into material goods, and eventually transmutes your potential into visible reality.

Successful people are the ones who cultivate a conscious awareness of good because they know that appreciation is the most powerful motivating factor that serves their lives. They also know that appreciation enables them to adequately use their powers and strengths in the most active and productive ways that will ultimately bring them better opportunities to expand their creative visions and enrich their lives.

Obviously, everyone has heard something about appreciation, but what everyone has not heard is an in-depth explanation of the value of appreciation. It's important to deeply understand the intrinsic meaning and inherent powers of appreciation. It comes with enormous power that makes a huge impact on our lives. It opens the main door of business opportunity that leads to many valuable rooms of profit. It's the power that lifts great minds to even greater heights of success so they may receive great rewards and welcome more blessings into their lives. It's the life juice that feeds and sustains our spirits of passion and enthusiasm and greatly expands our consciousness to opens the doors of abundance.

Some people don't appreciate life because they don't understand what life is all about. Basically, life is business, and business is life, and a real life comes with a logical sense that arises from a reasonable appreciation and gratitude. In fact, there can be no real life without a proper appreciation of life because appreciation enables us to feel better, think healthier thoughts, and live peacefully. As a result, it stimulates our interests in business, ignites our passion that propels action, and provides us a visible and invisible good that influences us to appreciate more and expect more for ourselves. It also enables us to deliver good services and distribute quality products that can open multiple windows of opportunity to get more benefits in life and improve our businesses. This is where quality action spells quality results because a reasonable appreciation brings us certainty and congruity in all our business efforts and spurs us to spontaneous action that supports a higher power of intelligence and profound understanding. In addition, it enables us to focus on a definite goal and get a definite result. Obviously, appreciation builds a better business and supports sound business relationships through good judgment, so we can develop a proper channel to enter other valuable minds to build better businesses and receive greater profits.

If we can think properly, we will believe congruently and achieve full results by appreciating positive lives. This is the very essence of our intelligence and nobility of our purpose in life. It's the key to enhancing our lives and enriching our purposes. Now is the time to get the power to unravel the mind and unfold the potential future because everything in life involves appreciation, which holds our innermost peace and our deepest comfort in life. It's the single most important factor that determines our happiness, health, and prosperity. It creates harmony that calms our minds and pleases our hearts. In addition, it's the power that enhances all living things and supports the courageous spirit that sparks the light of awareness, wisdom, and ingenuity. It empowers us to become more active and efficient in life. Profitable appreciation inflames and arouses our minds and hearts and eventually becomes a central reservoir of ideas that will continuously fuel our desire for growth, success, and accomplishment. It's the driving force behind our inspiration that empowers our spirits of passion, progress, and success and properly sustains our spirits of enthusiasm so we can stay more active and more alive in business. Positive appreciation creates real and lasting change and a logical consistency that comes from a reasonable appreciation and rational persistence. When we use our innate powers and strengths to unfold the future, we will believe in a profitable appreciation that produces constructive thoughts and positive actions. These things draw good into our lives and provide us a massive collection of wisdom, intelligence, and profound understanding that serve our lives and support our overall well-being.

When it seems like there is no way, profitable appreciation creates multiple ways to innovate your life. All it takes is a positive attitude and enthusiasm to look around, perceive positive energies, believe in positivity, and appreciate life, for which Mother Nature will reward you. This is the great promise of the future, and it will never fail as long as you believe and abide in it.

So to grow is to appreciate, and to appreciate is to increase in value because reasonable appreciation actively refines and enhances our minds, restores our hope, ignites positive actions, and ultimately brings us positive changes in our lives. It also refreshes our hearts, redeems our spirits, and opens many doors of favorable opportunities that give us the chance for success, progress, and accomplishment.

I fundamentally believe that the more we appreciate good, the more we achieve success. The birth of courage comes with appreciation. That's why it makes successful relationships that promote businesses. That's why it's the power that opens up receptivity, responsibility, and accountability and fulfills our dreams and goals in life. A reasonable appreciation plays an important role in life by properly harmonizing our thoughts and enriching all our purposes. There are loads of values we can appreciate that can produce a harmonious attitude that brings us a clear sense of imagination and enable us to fix our minds and hearts on what we truly desire in life.

Obviously, appreciation of good clears the road for good spirits and active energies to breed more good, motivates and inspires positive actions in any creative endeavors, and ultimately lifts any profitable mind to greater heights. As a result, it provides us reliable emotions and dependable minds through which we can produce the greatest possible reservoir of wisdom, which will eventually bring us the best possible reservoir of power, intelligence, and understanding of life. This in turn gives us a clear road map for growth and prosperity. In addition, it will help us sustain the driving force of enthusiasm that increases our energy levels. This is the infusion of power that provides us a unified field of action, a real purpose, and a lasting result that brings us success, attracts future potential, and produces multiple outcomes.

Every careful thinker and doer must know that a profitable appreciation serves as an indispensable value in all walks of life. It unlocks our potential, enables us to acquire full power, and helps us enjoy our blessings. Almost everything we need in life requires us to show appreciation. Appreciation provides us all the resources we need to advance into a better future and serves as a strong pillar that supports our businesses and anchors our emotional well-being.

CHAPTER 7

THE SPIRIT OF ABUNDANCE

> As you sow, so shall you reap.
> —GALATIANS 6:7

Ever observe a farmer at work? It seems like a dedicated sense of purpose, and the farmer seems to have a sense of humility, perseverance, and a clear commitment to life. To achieve his aim, the farmer performs series of steps before harvesting and reaping the rewards. To begin with, he selects the right seeds, prepares the land, and sows the seeds. Then he diligently weeds the land, and properly irrigates the crops for growth. Soon he fertilizes the soil, and after the crops have matured, he begins to harvest. Then he is free to enjoy the abundance of good returns, health, happiness, and bountiful success because as one sows, so shall one reap.

Mother Nature produces abundance because she thinks and feels abundance. She brings us bounty and prolific returns because that is the only thing she sees and feels. The feeling of abundance is blessed with the spirit of love and passion. It is an integral part of success and progress as well as thinking, feeling, and producing long-lasting success, progress, and stability. It's a way of enhancing our thoughts and a means of bringing more love, happiness, and joy into our relationships, homes, and environments. It's the main source of our inflow of power and energy that shapes and strengthens the condition of our minds. Eventually it creates certainty, self-reliance, inner harmony, and absoluteness of purpose. It inspires our actions, motivates our minds, and frees our spirits to express what's in our souls. This shows that it provides us an active spirit of enthusiasm, an active spirit of passion and a quality frame of mind. It also shows that it's a potential source of our inspiration, motivation, and action.

Of course, thinking and seeing abundance gives you the chance to win; the chance to attract more blessings; and the chance to draw plenty of joy, happiness, and health into your life. It enhances your well-being and gives you harmonious joy, inner peace, and quality health. It gives you the courage and strength that accelerates success and propels growth and prosperity. Ultimately, it provides you a strong, positive chain of power that attracts good, expresses quality, and communicates value. As a result, it gives you the power to make success happen and helps you keep the commitment to strive for success. It also gives you the power to produce a constant stream of innovation, a continuous flood of good, and an inpouring flood of peace, happiness, and health.

When properly approached and used well, your sound thoughts and positive thinking will give you an abundance of knowledge that protects your soul, lights your mind, and illuminates your heart. It will greatly increase your value and move you to absoluteness of purpose. As a result, it will provide you a positive spirit of persistence, determination, and perseverance. It will stimulate your interest and attention and enrich your senses, free your mind, motivate your spirit, and inspire your actions. It will greatly increase your desire to satisfy your heart and empower you to clearly accept your responsibilities and face your challenges in life. Certainly, it will improve your standard of living, which will increase your level of understanding and expand your creative vision.

As you make and keep commitments, it will enable you to live in the present moment, and eventually it will help you advance into the future by providing you the power and strength to influence your environment. It will also help you build important relationships that will enable you to access any valuable mind and achieve a definite purpose.

Even as you establish and build trust, it will give you a dedicated sense of purpose, a clear commitment, and the superiority of mind and heart that will enable you to see a broader point of view. Obviously, the spirit of abundance enhances your belief systems and solidifies your convictions to help you drive value and produce multiple results. If you believe and abide in it, it will give you the possibility of mind that fosters creative changes, opens doors of opportunities, and enables you to take advantage of opportunities when they knock.

Almost everything you seek and receive in life is driven by the spirit of abundance. It is an important component of success and one way you can better understand your business and optimize your operations. It's a worthwhile investment of time, effort, and attention. You truly have been blessed with an abundance of good that comes with a gifted power of acquisition, a power of actualization that contains the spirit of harmony and spontaneous action. There is an abundance of information that gives you the power to build a profitable business and constantly replenish your pool of potential customers. It also enables you to follow up with your existing customer base and maintain and develop relationships that will help you grow your business, expand your knowledge, and increase your wisdom to enrich your life.

It's important to note that thinking in terms of abundance is the key to a successful life. It will bring you inspiring dreams, realistic goals, and sound plans that allow you to use a constructive mental application of sound principles of success. This provides you protective grounds for an efficient and effective action that governs your emotions and prepares you to face unexpected circumstances and take advantage of the future. As a result, it enables you to make prompt and concrete decisions and helps you embrace change as an opportunity to expand and advance into the future. The spirit of abundance will always lead you to better knowledge, to better understanding, to a better future, and to greater success. It enables you to mobilize your greatest potential to provide you with a massive collection of ideas that will spark the light of creative intelligence and empower your spirit of passion and progress, and success. It will provide you a blueprint of your future endeavors, positive visual images of your actions, and a conception of your own personal world that will enrich your life. You can create healthier customer services, attract more prospects, and expand your economic resources. This is a positive approach to success that attracts an inflow of blessings, draws inpouring riches of good, and produces inspiring results. It provides you a round-table of wisdom and opportunity that enables you to exchange valuable insights and share useful experiences that will support and foster your business.

Remember, nature produces the evidence of abundance. Consider the fertile soil, the rain, the sunshine, the stars, and moonlight. They all supply us abundance of values. In the most basic sense, all of this shows that the spirit of abundance opens the doors of business opportunity, courage, and spontaneous reality and even enables us to sustain our energies. It encourages active discipline that brings us progressive development that supports the positive spirit of enthusiasm and further enables us to exploit new, favorable chances of progress that will greatly increase the value of our lives and give us a profitable chance of accomplishment. As a result, it heals our minds, inspires our hearts, and sparks positive actions that strengthen our faith and moral values. As we have a long tradition of harvesting nature's bounty, then nature will bless us, empower us, and even enhance our unique character to increase our mental capacities and emotional strength. Remember that all positive approaches provide us the richness of mind and the passion of heart and satisfy an excellent desire in our souls.

That's why it's important to remember that abundance of good comes from a sound mind and effective action. It comes from the mental mechanism of sound ideas, sound thoughts, positive thinking, clear feelings, and even from successful actions. It also comes from a creative sense of imagination that enhances all logical plans and promotes all realistic goals. It provides us better rewards and higher incentives that will greatly increase the value and the degree of our creative efforts and positive interests in the marketplace. It gives us the best possible reservoir of peace, happiness, and a triumphant joy that comes from the soul. It also gives us the power and ability to move with clarity, intensity, and certainty. This means that the spirit of thinking in terms of abundance will provide us a power that will consistently fuel our desire to accomplish more quality results and strive to reach more profitable and realistic goals.

Remember also that your sound mind is the creator and the doer that brings you abundance of value and clears the road for positive and active spirits to breed greater energy. This is a creative power that permits flexibility and adaptability in any creative calling, in any profitable business, as well as in any successful relationship. As a result, this provides you the vital fruits and energies that will foster positive changes in your life as well as in your daily business. Therefore, it's important to immediately recognize and accept the basic truths that prove the fact that the power of thinking and acting in terms of abundance is the ultimate potential source of inspiration, motivation, and passion. It's the substance of thought that brings you peace and happiness in your home as well as in your business environment. As a result, it produces real, positive, and lasting effects that inspire actions of great hope with great anticipation of the future. The spirit of success begins here and encourages voluntary efforts that enable you to stay ahead and take advantage of opportunities when they knock.

There is abundance of ideas that make life worth living, and they lie in your creative mind, patiently waiting for you to tap into their potential value. I'm sure you have abundance of life that you don't properly enjoy because you don't truly realize the fact that everything has been created to be used and peacefully enjoyed. Let this be the sum and substance of your knowledge and understanding, and let it be the sum and substance of your thinking and acting that determines your real life. The spirit of abundance emanates from a well-heightened intelligence and sense of awareness, a prompt decision and a profound understanding that lie deep inside you and are patiently waiting to be discovered. The most significant fact to know is that the future doesn't lie ahead of you waiting for something to happen; it lies deep inside of you waiting for something to be discovered. Positive thinking starts here and produces the best, clearest pictures that will communicate the meaning of life and a clear purpose of business endeavors.

It's critical to know the value of your thinking and feeling of abundance because when you're feeling abundance, you are appreciating nature's value, which draws multiple blessings. This is a useful knowledge that exists in your mind and actively materializes itself into power, a unified energy, and absolute purpose. Thinking in terms of abundance gives you a ceaseless energy and the power to consistently pursue greatness and excellence. As a result, it motivates and inspires optimistic spirits to render quality services that will draw more potential, spark positive actions, and germinate bountiful results.

The spirit of abundance is governed by principles and ruled by living in harmony with others. It eventually becomes a cooperative association of senses that fosters and enhances all of our creative innovations, connects all positive energies, and solidifies all of our productive actions.

To create and attract an abundance of good, we must appreciate Mother Nature. Nature is the creator of success and the fountainhead of all progress. Nature holds the clues that show us we can succeed if we think correctly and act wisely. It also holds substantial evidence of the abundance of intelligence, knowledge, and wisdom, including the sound principles of gradual growth and development, progress, and success. Basically, it produces the vital fruits needed to make smart choices and better decisions in life. It's a wonderful power that comes from a sound sense of creative vision, personal strength, mechanism of ideas, and logical actions. It reveals itself through practical ideas and the effective use of our knowledge, personal initiative, and strengths.

The basic question is this: How can we accumulate an abundance of values? We can achieve this if we can think constructively and act wisely. Then, little by little, we can develop and achieve all of our aims. Step by step we can accomplish all of our goals in life. Through a gradual process, we can add more and more value to our lives, and by compounding that value with interest, we can build enormous wealth.

Is that all it takes to build and achieve abundance? No, we also need a constructive mental direction, a reasonable self-confidence, and self-discipline that will help us sustain our lives. In addition, we need to embody useful knowledge that will make things happen. Finally, we need to use logical action and consistency to bring us multiple results, and we need persistence and determination to sustain our results.

Hard work is not enough; we must back it up with total commitment to grow and succeed. Most important, we must let all our struggles and efforts boil down to happiness and good health.

Every healing begins with a careful observation, self-confidence, a conscious awareness that arises from self-realization of abundance of truths. That will give us the best possible power, strength, and effort of mind. This requires synthetic imagination, logical consistency, and profound understanding. The spirit of abundance is the power that arises through harmonious reason, conscious awareness, and synthetic imagination and eventually comes from a coordinated attention and undivided interest. It's also a creative power that emanates from strength of character, moral discipline, and a constructive sense that ignites positive actions and produces positive results.

Everyone has elements of abundance, but only a few people use it. Abundance is the language of the intellect that brings us a richer sense of the language of the mind and heart. It's an explosive power that comes with a strong spirit of enthusiasm and an active spirit of passion, inspiration, and motivation. It provides us a real, powerful, and insightful knowledge that brings profitable changes to our lives. It's blessed with the power of attraction, self-motivation, and great ability. It's properly enriched with life surplus, power, and wealth that's fully equipped with great skills and strengths, passion and motivation, courage and faith, and finally with inner vitality, practical intelligence, and a pure sense of imagination.

There is an abundance of excellent resources that enrich our lives because nature has a long history of abundance of goodness. When it appears, power multiplies and progress and success will become notable. Then life grows, business profit increases and important relationship develops. The fear of poverty ends here because thinking in terms of abundance ends poverty, difficulty, misery, and suffering, just as light ends darkness. Remember, when light appears, darkness disappears into its natural oblivion of nothingness. The death of fear of poverty is certain because when light comes, darkness disappears, which means that when the abundance of goodness arises, poverty vanishes. An abundance of good will harness all of our creative powers and unite us with a divine intelligence that will actively enable us to seize favorable opportunities when they knock.

If we can totally shift our life focus to the spirit of abundance, we will become powerful individuals, and our behaviors will be ruled by principles that will grow in wisdom that enriches our hearts, inspires our lives, and brings us a well-heightened sense of value, purpose, and direction. This proactive approach to life can put us in a superior state, which can produce the ultimate good and a well-heightened sense of anticipation. That enables us to think properly, act effectively, grow in abundance, and actively live in wisdom.

Now that you know the importance of abundance, can you properly use it and benefit from it? To possess the spirit of abundance, you must own it, think it, live in it wisely, and practice it in consciousness. You should know by now that the spirit of abundance provides you the power to live a healthy life and take quality actions that bring you real change and make a huge impact in your life. Therefore, this is the power source to a greater life that gives you freedom of choice, inner joy, and long-lasting relationships.

Creating abundance is important in life and crucial to success because the spirit of abundance is equipped with goal-oriented mind, absolute purpose, and active life. It's a trusted power and a positive spirit that comes with the innate capacity and ability to take a consistent action to achieve a definite result. It's a well-loved and a well-blessed spirit that is endowed with heart. It's also a dynamic spirit that's endowed with useful knowledge and practical ideas, practical intelligence and creative wisdom. You should explore abundance of good because it enhances your spirit, and enriches your life. It's an influential power that comes from a functional mind, a representational wisdom, and from an excellent execution of intelligence that requires careful analysis, careful attention, and conscious awareness.

Maintaining and developing the spirit of abundance can help you gain a significantly better understanding of yourself and ultimately help you succeed in life. It will give you a constructive atmosphere of peace and the positive spirit of enthusiasm, which will greatly increase your receptive power and responsive mind to actively provide you the broadest sense of self-expression, self-reliance, self-determination, and self-confidence.

If you can keep your eyes widely open, you will understand why the spirit of abundance is the creator of profitable innovation, a passionate spirit of love that serves all your basic needs and supports your greatest desires because the spirit of success begins here. I guarantee you success because there is no other way to a worthy life than to create an abundance of good that lies at the very heart of life that supports all your purposes and enhances the courageous spirit that comes from creativity. This great attitude will give you lifelong happiness, peace, and courage that can bring you lifelong relationships. As a result, it will inspire the spirit of passion, unity, love, and oneness of mind and heart that represents the symbol of peace that brings you abundance of happiness and joy that arises from the spirit of all good. The spirit of abundance is measured not in the moments of time, but in the timeless moments of gratefulness. This is the power that sparks the light of awareness; generates the light of freedom; and ignites your hope, courage, and determination to win. It's also a transparent power that brings out all your inherent powers and inner strengths and therefore sharpens all your holistic perspective senses to eventually draw a collective interest, a collective attention, and a committed sense of awareness.

As we believe and abide in the consciousness of abundance, our willingness of heart and capacity of mind open the doors of abundance to actively lift us to a prosperity consciousness and spark our spirits of enthusiasm and passion for a lifelong, notable success. We should know that the feeling of abundance brings us a healthy life and deep comfort, which is the essence of our growth, motivation, and inspiration. As a result, it demands the spirit of passion.

When we use our minds to serve our purposes and achieve our goals in life, then the spirit of abundance will become an inescapable desire of the mind and an inestimable substance of the heart. Basically, it will be a well-balanced power that moves us in a unique way that balances our lives, aligns our values, and ultimately gives us a sound reason of the heart and a deeply rooted conviction of the mind that produces a classic sense of value.

In one sense, abundance leads the way to make success happen. This is a promising future, a turning point in our lives, and a new source of potential possibility in businesses. With this principal goal in mind, we can make it all better because the reason we don't believe is because we don't understand the profound meaning of abundance. Abundance lives in potentiality and wisdom that materializes through the potential possibilities that yield multiple results. It's a creative power that comes from undivided attention and an undivided mind, and it multiplies itself through logical consistency and clear action. Abundance is a creative wisdom that flows naturally from a positive mental revelation of a pure heart and open mind. Therefore, the feeling of abundance is something everyone longs for and that we typically work for and look forward to achieving.

So providing abundance is humanity's grandest challenge in life, and that's why active leaders, effective communicators, and efficient managers are enhancing the spirit of abundance and delivering abundance. The more they see abundance, the more they get abundance because they know that it is an open-minded expression of sound ideas based on practical insights that can be the fastest and clearest highway to attracting more value. They also know that the spirit of abundance provides them the fuel that ignites the fire of their desire, sparks their sensibilities, strengthens their power of imagination, and expands their consciousness.

Remember, the future is better than we think and greater than we see because abundance provides us all the basic ingredients for life and ultimately provides us the map for living and making the right decisions. As a result, it provides us a strong conviction and the strength of character that stimulate high powers and potential energies to bring us a blissful atmosphere of peace, a heavenly atmosphere of love, and an angelic spirit of enthusiasm.

As part of the solution and light of life, the feeling of abundance of goodness projects positive visual images in our minds and helps us sustain vibrant energies in our hearts to bring us delightful feelings. As a result, it provides us a spiritual unity of mind and reality of heart that sparks the light of wisdom, intelligence, and awareness and eventually expands the fields of understanding.

The more one grows in abundance of knowledge and wisdom, the fewer obstacles and hindrances one encounters. This is a profound truth because abundance of good covers our weaknesses, protects our goals, and gives us a sense of belonging, a feeling of adequacy, and a dedicated sense of purpose. It increases positive energy that blinds negative energy. It also increases the spirits of passion, progress, and enthusiasm, which blinds low self-esteem and feelings of inferiority, actively reforms our emotions, and refines our energy production to refresh our minds, restores our hope, redeems our hearts, and effectively germinate multiple outcomes.

The spirit of abundance comes from guidance of wisdom and intelligence that gives us a positive expression of our minds and then encourages empathy that comes from our hearts. As the light of life and part of a solution to a healthy and happy life, abundance produces a bliss-ful family of great hope, high expectation, and anticipation of a better life and greater future. All of this makes it the foundation of all success and development that provides us infinite energy and the anchor that guards us and guides our sensibilities. It increases our personal power and strength, which reinforces our minds and strengthens our hearts. As a result, it stimulates our interests to support a higher power of intel-ligence and eventually ignites a passion that propels action and provides us a visible or invisible goodness. As far as we choose to live our lives to the best of our abilities, it will continue to provide us a cheerful mental attitude of gratitude and awareness of thought that brings multiple suc-cesses, draws potentials, and produces prolific returns. Finally, it pro-vides us a new and better spirit to pursue excellence and helps us to set higher goals and seize profitable opportunities when they knock.

All you need is a reasonable self-confidence that enhances your spirit of abundance to be proud of yourself. This helps you use your mind to guard your body, use your body to enclose your mind, and keep aiming high and achieving great goals because your smart choices represent your best decisions. It's most important to remember that the feeling of abundance is the feeling of intellect, and the positive spirit of intellect comes with the passionate spirit of quality action. That's why positive feelings enable you to function from a superior state of consciousness that helps you perceive good energies and live in conscious awareness. This is the essence of your growth and development and the very es-sence of an intellectual intelligence, nobility, and wisdom. You should know that the spirit of abundance is a lifelong product of innovation and the lifelong property of the intellects. You should also know that it's a wonderful power that comes from an intellectual sense of purpose, an intellectual sense of adequacy, and integrity of the mind, which provides you a steady flow of profitable innovation that enables you to live in con-sciousness and helps you function in creative wisdom, active faith, and creative intelligence.

All that matters most in life is that the spirit of abundance gives you freedom of self-expression and a positive attitude of gratitude and ap-preciation that expresses the true meaning of life. As a result, it gives you a richer sense and a brighter point of view that enhances your consciousness, expands your creative sense of imagination, increases your creative wisdom, and draws active minds. In addition, it enables you to think healthier thoughts and live a more peaceful and happy life. Finally, it restores your hope and ignites your passion that sparks positive actions and eventually brings you positive changes in life. That's why you must keep your inspiring goals in sight, because the feeling of abundance of goodness shows that plenitude holds your innermost joy and your deepest comfort in life.

If you see a farmer work, watch carefully, and you will see that the feeling of abundance is a productive thought that comes from the heart, and productive thinking attracts whatever accepts its ruling and healing condition. It's a creative power that influences your pattern of thinking and acting and converts potential into material reality. It provides you a novel idea, a sound thought, and a clear feeling. It is an important component of all positive thoughts, a crucial component of all productive actions, and a major component of all growth and success in any creative field of calling.

CHAPTER 8

EFFECTIVE COMMUNICATION

> Wise men talk because they have something to
> say; fools, because they have to say something.
> —PLATO

E veryone talks, thinks, and acts, but not everyone talks clearly, thinks
equally well, or acts effectively. We all think differently and act differently because we all come from different environments that
shape different belief systems. We all have different training, upbringings, values, and beliefs. However, we also need to fulfill our dreams,
ambitions, and goals in life. The key to fulfilling all these needs must
come through effective communication. Effective communication is a
unique method of expression and a clear way to understand people,
and getting a particular message across. It provides us a solid connection among people. It's a concise and clear means of expression, the
best way of exchanging valuable information, useful ideas, and sound
thoughts among families, friends, and businesses. It's how we make a
positive impact in our societies, in our communities, and in our world.
It's the glue that holds our values together and guides our beliefs to better understand another person, resolve our differences, and build a real
and lasting relationship.

Effective communication is the essence of human interaction and
learning, it's part of human knowledge and intelligence, of human

progress and development, success and prosperity, and even health and happiness. Therefore, let me remind you that when it comes to a meaningful purpose and direction, effective communication guides your behavior, attitude, feelings, and actions; it even directs your thoughts to absoluteness of purpose.

The key to enhancing your life and enriching your purpose must come through effective communication by listening, observing, and noting facts. It's the driving force, the vital energy, and life force that enhances your life and enriches your well-being. It's the quality of your communication that distinguishes you and determines the value of your life. It enables you to make finer distinctions, finer selections, and better choices in life. It enables you to control and direct your behavior, feelings, and actions. It's the power that unlocks the door to success and eventually unlocks the door to a better life and future. It shapes your belief system, enables you to acquire new skills and better knowledge, and helps you gain useful experiences. It directs all your mental faculties toward a definite purpose and strengthens your mental vision to see the best possible pictures that will inspire your mind to enrich your life.

Feeling the purpose of effective communication and having the end in mind will help you in different ways. It will provide you the best possible ways of expression that will bring you the best practical solutions and spiritual strengths and bring you mental and emotional balance. This is the power that unites all creative insights, all functional minds, and all sound ideas into a unified field of energy, a unified field of purpose, and a unified field of knowledge. It's the power that stimulates your interests, crystallizes your energies, and ignites positive actions. It increases your cognitive understanding, improves your cognitive development, and enhances your emotional intelligence. Effective communication gives you a crystal-clear value, a transparent mind, and a pure spirit of enthusiasm. It will provide you all the positive energies to greatly increase your value and help you build a more productive life. In addition, it will bring you the finest quality of the mind and the best value of the heart, and eventually serve the best interests of your emotional well-being and physical health.

Effective communication brings you abundant resources that will provide you a bountiful, potential value that enhances your life and enriches your purposes. It gives you a real power and energy, reliable emotions, and accurate information that bring you success, happiness, joy, and inner peace and harmony, which support quality health and mental fitness. It also gives you the best of life and the most distinctive qualities of the mind and heart, which shows a clear expression of your unique intelligence, unique skills, and useful experiences that will provide you a wellspring of wisdom, hope, courage, knowledge, and understanding.

The essence of developing effective communication is to support all your meaningful purposes, sound ideas, and clear feelings to enhance positive actions and provide mental and emotional balance, physical stamina, emotional tranquility, and spiritual wisdom.

If you look at the world of business commerce clearly and logically, you will see that effective communication is a creative power that comes from a unique intelligence, unique skill, valuable information, and positive feedback that improve your intuitive wisdom and cognitive awareness. This in turn sharpens your sense of responsiveness, assertiveness, and imagination, leads you into the right direction, and clears the way to accomplishment. Eventually it becomes a marvelous power of creative thinking that makes you the master of the present and the director of the future. Effective communication is a unique skill that is endowed with the spirit of passion, enthusiasm, growth, and success that will provide you a unique knowledge that will bring you worthwhile value.

Effective communication enables you to become the change you're communicating and ultimately helps you become effective in action and productive in mind. It provides you a strong chain of positive events and profitable value that enhance and support your life. It also provides you emotional strength that gives you positive energy, which provides you positive feelings and enables you to actively live in the power of now. It enables you to adjust your attitude, behavior, and feelings and helps you control and direct your actions. It moves you in a balanced way that enables you to harness your power and keep you feeling positive energy that helps you truly nourish your life and well-being.

Understanding effective communication is the key to understanding people and enriching lives. Effective communication produces unlimited energy, unlimited life, and notable success. It fully benefits you and fully enables you to develop and increase your powers and strengths. It's the essence of your growth and development that will bring you steadily flowing creative innovation and continuous ascending ideas that will improve your daily life. It is the value that draws other values, the purpose that supports and enhances other purposes, and the quality that attracts other quality lives. It's an essential element of thought that adds more value to increase your self-esteem and self-worth. In fact, it's the fountain of life that provides you the best ingredients to transform your life and impact positive changes in humanity. It creates positive words, and positive words produce positive pictures that bring you a healing condition that will eventually enhance your life and support your well-being. In addition, it gives you the precise building blocks that will unite your life and enrich your purpose.

Creating a new life and producing more results begin with effective communication. It is the power that lies behind you, before you, and within you. It's also the power that contains all life-enhancing purposes that come with great benefits and multiple values, with sound ideas and profitable opportunities. In addition, it's the power that is blessed with educational values, skills, practical insights, self-training techniques, and a practice-based training. Remember, education itself is life-enhancing; it refines the wholeness of life that boosts your self-concept and enriches your self-worth. Effective communication guides you toward a spiritual evolution, mental growth, and emotional maturity and ultimately helps you connect with the divine power within you.

Understanding yourself and using your power to enrich your purpose will help you communicate effectively, and seeing what you don't normally see will shape your self-confidence and enhance your beliefs in effectiveness. Effective communication shapes your beliefs and enables you to acquire new knowledge, new skills, and new experiences that expand your consciousness. It stimulates positive energies and fulfills your needs, desires, and values that will greatly increase the values of your life and inspire positive actions. In turn this will help enrich other lives, which will help to create a real change in humanity by passing on intelligence, useful knowledge, and positive experiences that will shape strong beliefs and convictions in life. This shows that it's the power that drives values, enhances courageous spirits, and enriches your sense of sensibilities and wonder. It strengthens your energy fields, elevates your consciousness, and expands your mental vision. That increases the power that brings healing, positive energy, and enthusiasm into your life. It's the power that satisfies your deepest longings, as well as your deepest needs and most important desires in life.

The key to effective communication is mostly based on active listening, profound understanding, and keen observation. If you carefully observe through the mind, you will find out that effective communication comes from a sense of inner joy, inner peace, and inner harmony; happiness and self-discipline; and finally from your inner drive. It needs a reasonable self-confidence that supports a unique business intelligence, which requires a conscious awareness. This shows why it's an insightful knowledge that comes from your gut feelings and paying careful attention through a dedicated sense of purpose to win. It also shows why it's the inner expression of goodness and spirit of passion that you need to set a clear boundary of communication and clearly define what you're trying to achieve. This is an attitude of open-mindedness, a dynamic behavior, and an elegant spirit of enthusiasm that requires you to focus on a definite purpose, target a definite goal, and accomplish positive results.

All your aims in life must come through effective communication, which means using appropriate tools and effective strategies to explore new and better possibilities, new realities, and greater opportunities to increase awareness that helps you flow in wisdom and intelligence. To keep that end in mind is to deeply understand that effective communication is the means by which to reach a mutual agreement in the spirit of harmony, love, and passion. It's the power that comes with a life-enriching purpose, opportunity, and valuable experience that enables you to live a life of meaning and purpose that supports a logical direction. The essence of communication is to produce effective results; bring happiness; and improve your physical health, emotional strength, and psychological well-being to bring peace and joy into your life. This is a balancing power that brings you multiple blessings. That's why effective communication has life-enhancing ability to enrich more lives and foster progression. It's the essence of civilization and growth that comes with the best quality of life and the best profitable value.

You can't properly understand life if you don't have the ability and skill to communicate effectively. You can't achieve all your purposes and dreams in life if you don't have the power to communicate effectively. But when you have the end in mind, effective communication enables you to claim your full potential power and helps you enjoy full potential blessing. It's the power that generates abundance, draws positive energies within you and around you, and then becomes the blanket that protects you and enriches your life. It's the main root of your circle of connections, the frame of your circle of friends, and the guiding power of success. It enables you to actively live in a dynamic, prolific consciousness and inner sense of purpose. It's the essence of life energy, life-enhancing purpose, and a life-enriching mind. It's the envelope that contains your value that makes great things possible and increases the value of every other quality in your life, and then it enables you to share better insights and exchange valuable thoughts and useful information. It's the building block of all knowledge, purpose, and values. It's the principal source for acquiring unique skills and the key that opens the main door of success that leads you to many valuable rooms of progress and development.

If there is one vital element that makes life worthwhile, it is effective communication. Effective communication gives you a well-established energy, a well-established purpose, and a well-organized plan. Remember, your level of communication determines the quality of your results, and the quality of your results determines the quality of your life, which increases your awareness of the present moment. In every aspect of life, the benefit of effective communication rests on positive results that will provide you life-enhancing experiences that sharpen your awareness of the present and enables you to build an important relationship and trust that will further help you gain access to enter other minds and explore valuable information.. Effective communication shapes your experiences and brightens your future. It causes you to take quality action that produces quality results. Obviously, this is a power that has been well-trusted since the beginning of the world of business commerce, and the power remains with you and helps you succeed in business.

Effective communication enables you to map out your own little world, your own creative space, and your own desired life. It's a knowledge-based result, a result-oriented mind-set, and an action-driven intelligence. It's a unique knowledge that comes from an inner wisdom, inner sense of conviction, and inner power that provide you emotional support, mental strength, and spiritual awareness. It's useful knowledge and positive experiences that bring you an abundance of valuable returns, prolific returns, and multiple blessings. It inspires novel ideas and supports other inspiring and insightful knowledges. It's a language of the body, the mind, and the heart that comes with a pure enthusiasm, inspiration, motivation, and passion, which will bring you a richer, more refined language of an intellectual absoluteness of purpose and clear action.

Everyone knows that effective communication is a critical part of a successful life and very important in our daily efforts, but what is not clearly known to everyone is the degree of its importance and effectiveness. This is the unmistakable stamp of effective communication that represents a unique purpose and value, power and strength. This is also a critical part of a successful business, as well as successful relationships and a successful life, and can be so much more critical in marketing products and customer satisfaction. In addition, this gives us the power and strength to communicate our purpose, our vision, and needs in life. As a result, it makes valuable relationships, builds happy families, and produces brilliant children and great teachers. It also makes great workers and successful businesses that foster creative innovation. In the process, it gives us the key to expanding our areas of influence and building and developing better relationships, maintaining long-lasting success, and living healthy lives, which eventually boosts our spirits of enthusiasm and bridges gaps that prevent negative situations. This opens new and better opportunities that will flourish our minds and enrich our hearts. It also enables us to embrace and accept positive changes as an opportunity to advance into a better life and enjoy a greater future.

We must provide a higher standard value and quality service by enhancing effective communication techniques that will ensure success and make positive things happen. The essence of our communication is to improve our lives, enhance our experiences, and increase our levels of understanding in every aspect of life. In the most basic sense, quality life shows that effective communication is the single most vital element of success and a critical part of thinking and acting, or even learning and training. This is a unique skill that enhances positive attitude of gratitude that will always provide us the energy necessary to organize resources that will give us direction and purpose in life. This will shape our experiences that will brighten our futures and expand our creative visions, ultimately becoming our source of abundance, prosperity, and wealth. This is the most effective way to balance our careers, develop unique skills, and enhance our lives.

If you are seeking to balance your career and life, remember that your success will depend solely on useful information. The right information that creates a certainty of knowledge, an authenticity of word, and the dependability and reliability of the mind and the heart. That will enable you to expand your effectiveness and increase your inherent abilities, capacities, and strengths of character that come from your soundness of mind and absoluteness of purpose. Therefore, it's the substance of your thought and the solidity of your mind that brings you an abundance of health and happiness, peace, and harmony. Obviously, this shows that effective communication truly expresses your needs, feelings, and desires to help you open up to something new and better and take advantage of opportunities when they knock.

Managers and leaders will always need effective communication to advance in business and achieve better futures. Therefore, it's critically important that they implement effective communication strategies in their personal lives and professional careers. Effective communication is the power that influences other minds and brings us value. As a result, it gives us the ability to disseminate useful information and sustain the power that will further help us to actively listen, deeply understand, and effectively act in situations and get positive results. Our lives are endowed with power and strength to influence, grow, and succeed in life. That's why effective communication is powered by useful knowledge and blessed with the potential to build from the present existence and from future value. This becomes the faculty of willpower and mental strength that connects values and effectively enables us to relate with people from all walks of life. It also becomes the steam that powers our knowledge and strengthens our relationships. This means that it's the energy of life that fosters creative innovation, enriches our businesses, and enhances our purposes. This also means that it's a passionate spirit that brings us vitality and vigor into our lives. So it's the essence of our intelligence and the guidance of enthusiasm that controls our minds and hearts. It's also the vehicle that transports us to our destinations, and without it there can be no advancement into the future. But with it, we can make decisions to change our lives, and we can act with integrity and honesty. Most important, we can produce the desired results we all need because effective communication is the glue that holds together our blessings, guards our riches, and protects our lives, and a lack of it makes life unworthy and powerless. Effective communication is the tree of knowledge that produces an abundance of fruits, a unity of purpose, a distribution of values, and a diversification of riches. So let's build a long-term business plan by effectively communicating our emotional needs and getting the leverage that brings us great courage, great expectation, and great success.

The path to effective communication is the path to success, and it pays great rewards to start early. It's a necessary human resource that produces a psychological effect, which makes a great scientific impact in humanity, supports our well-being, and eventually brings us a civilized life.

This is the highest leverage, the best guidance of wisdom, and the source of your direction in life, which provides you the key that enables you to have the ability to effectively communicate your values. This is an infinite, potential reality that arises from creative thinking and power of reason; from a harmonious, intuitive power of awareness; and from a self-realization of truth. This is also a unique skill that requires a real and lasting patience, a great sense of humor, and a positive, distinctive, and powerful thought that can enhance your sense of balance and eventually support your emotions so you can make great decisions in life. It's a conscious, transformational thinking and acting, knowing and feeling good energy and achieving positive result that satisfies your daily needs. This is the main power that governs your life and an integral part of your success, health, and prosperity.

The use of effective communication as a source of power will always bring you good and bountiful returns. It's the battery that charges your emotional strength and brightens the light of your spirit of enthusiasm.

Without it, you're powerless. But with it, you can effectively synchronize the world of business commerce and make better things happen. Effective communication bridges gaps, covers your weaknesses, and reveals important qualities. In one sense, it's the power that guards your life, feeds your spirit and directs all your purposes. So it's a perspective sense of balancing all the value that gives you the power and ability to act and get positive results. It is also a powerful umbrella that protects you against any negative influence, undue influence, and abuse. Once again, this shows why effective communication is the vital energy that enables you to refine your behavior and helps you enhance the nobility of your purpose and well-being through a diligent practice and exercise.

So to believe in success is to believe in effective communication, and to believe in effective communication is to believe in success. Success is an integrated oneness of mind that shapes all positive lives and embraces all bankable resources, which can serve both the value of the mind and the heart and therefore must go hand in hand like twin brothers. Effective communication exists in the mind, heart, and body and actively materializes into power and absolute purpose. All of this boils down to success. For all personal growth and professional development, this is your internal frame of mind for a continuous growth, development and achievement. And it's at the heart of your wisdom, knowledge and understanding that comes with a material embodiment of truth, a spiritual acknowledgment of reality, and a mental recognition and realization of facts.

Effective communication requires specific, clear, and detailed information, careful attention, which eventually comes through conscious wisdom that emanates from a unique skill and a profound understanding of life that flows freely from a pure heart and an open mind and actively remains in the heart of an integral man or woman who thinks positive thoughts. This is the substance of thought and life; therefore, any man or woman who actively lives in effective communication, in creative intelligence, and in deep understanding becomes an integral being. He or she becomes invaluable in any creative discipline, an inseparable value, and an indispensable reality in any calling. He or she brings an immeasurable intelligence in his or her personal life and in the lives of others.

This has been recognized and confirmed by successful people who use effective communication to achieve multiple results. Effective communication strategies are the instruments of sound thought that brings you success, health, and happiness. This gives you a long, successful life. Life begins with inspiring action and ends with inspiring results. When creating and using effective communication strategies, there are significant facts to know. To begin with, you must know that all weaknesses are hidden in your mental ignorance because of a lack of effectiveness. You must also understand that effective communication is the "doctor" that diagnoses all your problems, leads you to find the best solutions, and heals you. It's the agency of thought that covers all your contingency plans and fulfills all your basic needs. It's also important to know that effective communication conditions the mind and directs the brain to act in a certain way to produce effective results. This means that effective communication improves your emotional well-being, sharpens your mental faculties, and shapes your belief systems. It also means that it shines the light of conscious awareness, brightens the light of wisdom and intelligence, and puts you in a state of mental readiness for a possible future event with great expectations.

But lack of effective communication reveals your weaknesses, can generate abuse, and makes you vulnerable. It creates anxiety, self-doubt, and procrastination that support poverty. It also promotes unreasonable fear that kills your goals and ambitions in life. Therefore, you should know that a lack of effective communication is a lack of inspiration and motivation, interest, and enthusiasm. The best part is that you can change your life by enhancing any effective communication strategy that gives you inspiration, motivation, and passion to support your goals and dreams in life.

Remember, inspiration shines the light of effective communication, expands your consciousness, and provides you a steady flow of motivation, passion, and positive energy that brightens the light of consciousness. So when it comes to knowledge, effective communication comes with inspiration, and inspiration increases your energy levels and helps you function so much better in any creative calling. As a result, it draws optimism, courage, and enthusiasm into your life. That's why inspiration is a system of communication that keeps your mental faculties lively and in the process maintains your emotional wisdom and sharpens your mental vision. It's also a system of belief that has been tested for instant results as well as for real and lasting transformational change. It's the substance of your knowledge and the vital elements of understanding that will eventually bring you all the fruits that determine your growth and success. This is the science behind an extraordinary life. It's the single most important factor that proudly supports and determines a quality life, a worthwhile life, and mental superiority and greatness.

Effective communication enables you to acquire, understand, and use knowledge. This provides you the pathways to success and development, health, happiness, and joy, which gives you a lifelong pattern of thought and a lifelong energy of enthusiasm that provides you inner vitality, inner power and wisdom, and inner peace and joy.

Life is beautiful, and you must communicate it effectively and live wisely in effectiveness because effective communication strategy has been successfully tested in good faith to improve profitable innovations in businesses. As a result, it boosts business profits, improves your emotional well-being, and gives you all the essential elements of success that will help you make quality decisions and finer distinctions in life. It enables you to take quality action, and eventually help you live a better life. In addition, it gives you the power and ability to accept your challenges in life and take responsibility and direct your life. This gives you the opportunity to win, the opportunity to acquire and progress, and the ultimate opportunity to succeed and advance your purpose. And the best part is that it opens the door to a better life and a greater future that provides you a larger window of profitable opportunities that will bring you multiple blessings.

This is the science behind an extraordinary life, which shows why creative people are the innovators of today and why they all believe in the potentiality of the future. This is one of the basic reasons they all believe in success and eventually produce quality results, because effective communication strategies gives them all the tools to achieve their goals. They have learned from their experiences and have used their positive experiences to advance into the future and accomplish great results. They're the ones who are using effective communication strategies to advance their goals and dreams in life. They're the ones who set realistic and attainable goals, and follow through on them. Through effective communication, they all have achieved great results and received multiple blessings. Remember, it's a great thing to set a realistic goal, and it's another great thing to achieve a real and lasting result.

Effective communication produces instant results and brings a lasting transformation based on constructive thinking and effective action. And it has been properly tested and proven by entrepreneurs; managers, leaders, and successful people from all walks of life have used effective communication countless times to produce countless results. So it has been proven that we can achieve our goals if we can communicate effectively. Almost everyone sets goals and has dreams, but not everyone possesses the skills and abilities to communicate their goals effectively. There are only few individuals who discipline their goals and have the guts to follow through on them until they achieve success.

Those unique individuals who have achieved success are worthy and noble because their effective communication strategies have provided them all the necessary tools they need to advance their skills as well as their careers in life, helping them have a positive view of life that enhances their future goals. Therefore, I encourage every wise man and woman seeking real and lasting success to know that effective communication keeps their mental faculties alive and active. It enables them to see realities through their own eyes, through their own visual minds, and through their own imaginative faculties. As a result, it further helps them to perceive the truth and feel reality, think realistically, and act on reality. It's the power that shapes truths, connects facts, forms reality, and in the process designs a meaningful destination that leads them to the desired end.

Leading the way and guiding your purpose is based on effective communication, because effective communication helps you refine your behavior and action, growing the meaning and purpose in life and building energy. You can elevate the moment of awesomeness because effective communication is a real power that comes with inspiration and spirit of enthusiasm. It requires patience so that it can be acquired by patient cultivation, by diligent exercise, and by consistent use. It also requires useful knowledge because it's a positive experience that arises from critical enquiry, from deep probing, and from thorough investigation. It's the real power that is perceived in the absence of ignorance just as light is perceived in the absence of darkness.

Every logical rule of reason has shown us that effective communication is a component of success, a major tool in all walks of life, and the key ingredient to enhancing effective actions that bring us more profitable results. This greatly turns up the power and becomes more productive and more useful for both knowledge and action. This will empower any wise man or woman to believe in his or her personal powers and initiatives because it's a real power that produces multiple outcomes, expands human consciousness, and enriches positive lives. As a result, it accelerates success and propels progress and development. It also gives us the real power and strength to project into a better future and live better lives.

So let's share the truths to building a better life because the more we communicate effectively, the more positive results we get, and the more positive results we get, the more positive energy we draw into our lives. Everyone deserves a better life and equality, without exception. Remember, there's no excuse for fear of poverty, which explains why effective communication needs courage and mental strength to enjoy more blessings with less stress, enjoy more life with no fear, and live life with no worry, without pain. Effective communication gives you passion to work, passion to live wisely, and the ultimate passion to grow healthy and wealthy. In addition, it enables you to work with love, love what you do, and do what you love. It also enables you to work to live wisely, work to gain pleasure from life, and to be happier and healthier. It works best in a pleasant and desirable atmosphere. This is a magical power that produces positive results out of deep listening, careful attention, and deep understanding.

Effective communication requires formal education, extensive training, and unique skill. It also requires a unique method of approach and skillful observation, a unique pattern of thinking and acting, and a profound understanding. So whatever the reasons for communication, you'd better understand and make it real and congruent with action because it needs a constructive mental direction, careful attention, and a diligent and effective use of the mind and heart.

Knowing your purpose in life can be as important as moving it forward. Effective communication enables you to carry the truths you know and helps you believe in those truths. That's why at the very end of life, effective communication produces the most desirable individuals, the most promising minds, the most creative people, and the most favorable and profitable brains that can make life so much better and continue to enhance and enrich other people's lives. They share inspiration, motivation, and values, which certainly come from an act of logic, sensibility, and reality.

I believe you can now perceive reality from a scientific perspective. Effective communication grows from a perceptive analysis, logical observation, and careful attention, and it can help you enhance value through conscious awareness. It enables you to think accurately, act effectively, and receive productively. It's a skillful knowledge that requires flexibility, subtleness, a congruity of ideas, and integrity of purpose and imaginative vision in connection with the body, mind, and heart. When this occurs, it provides you a collective attention, a collective interest, and a coordinated purpose that all serve to enhance your mind and enrich your life.

You can trust and believe in effective communication because it provides you the power to make finer distinctions, better discriminations, and quality connections. As a result, it imparts effectiveness and rejuvenates the body and mind. In the process, it stimulates your creative mind, creative sense, and energy of enthusiasm, which produces a creative, conscious spirit that balances your life and serves your greatest good. It's an energetic life force that empowers the spirit of self-expression, flowing energy of self-inspiration, and flooding power of self-motivation. It enhances the courageous spirit of passion that gives you physical power and strength of character, soundness of mind, and moral and ethical principles of effective action.

Maintaining and developing effective communication is a great way to enhance and enrich more lives and feel a sense of empowerment that will dramatically impact your life. Effective communication is the connection of truths and facts that will help you achieve that. It's a creative power that increases efficiency, enhances value, and impacts the future. As a result, it increases positive energy and supports the spirit of passion and enthusiasm. It's a creative thinking that cuts across the edges of knowledge and an art of inspiration that balances your emotions, feelings, words, and actions and brings you multiple results. Remember also that effective communication is a unique skill no one can ever take away from you because it's a creative energy that comes from inspiration, and inspiration comes from a sense of humor that sparks positive actions in your home and business environment. It enables you to feel more authentic, be more artistic, and act more congruently. As a result, it enriches your senses and enhances your creative understanding that supports all your purposes. It gives you the conventional wisdom to act consistently and produce consistent results. Effective communication actively flushes toxins of animosity out of your system and replaces them with positive vibes that will support your overall well-being. This converts negative attitudes into positive ones, complexity into simplicity, intention into action, and eventually transmutes all your difficulties into multiple blessings.

Without effective communication, all power fades, business loses control and direction, and then expectation dies from lack of proper feeding. Basically, you deserve to be in good hands, and you deserve a better life, so you should know that effective communication absorbs mental ignorance and internal conflicts, just as light absorbs darkness.

By using this communication strategy effectively, you can better connect with people and enrich your life. You can balance your energy levels, heal your sicknesses, and rejuvenate your mind and body. You can revive your spirit of enthusiasm to move with clarity, courage, and passion to work your way into a better future and greater life. You can now inspire and motivate yourself and others to do greater things in life.

The road to effective communication is a knowledge-based course, and it needs the ability to respond to stimuli and the strength to deal with substantial facts. So if you can make this course to represent your daily efforts, it will provide you with unlimited possibility, capacity, and ability. It will also provide you a symbolic wisdom and an intelligent disposition. As a result, it will give you a transparent personality and a crystal-clear idea of what you truly want and need in life. This will represent your best life, which will provide you the true embodiment of knowledge, the true meaning of wisdom, the true representation of facts, and possibly the true manifestation of a notable success.

The key to enhancing your life and enriching your purpose comes through effective communication, which will enable you to live a positive and meaningful life and help you better understand others. Effective communication is what you need and want to advance your purposes in life, and you can use it to start your day with the power of motivation that inspires positive words, motivates a positive spirit of enthusiasm, and sparks positive actions in the workplace. In the process, you can produce the best possible mental pictures that will greatly express the best meaning and communicate the best possible action that gets the best results. And then you can believe in it because it's the power that provides you a bundle of opportunities, hope, and courage to act consistently and live wisely. Even as you believe in it, it will continue to guide your mind, which rules your body, and direct your body, which controls your mind, and then inspire positive actions that bring you multiple results.

Basically, it sparks creativity in all profitable innovation and inspires the mood that supports your life. Therefore, remember that effective communication is a comforting reminder of the present as well as the past that helps you build useful experiences for a better future and have greater anticipation for what is ahead. This can arise in the most surprising and unexpected ways possible, building more and more value from a keen heart and highly effective mind, which bring you the best possible action and results. In addition, it enlightens your spirit, enhances your power, calms your mind, and redeems your heart. As a result, it fortifies your mental powers, strengthens your knowledge, and makes you more effective in life. In the process, it releases your tension, enables you to resolve your internal conflicts, and eventually helps you mobilize your greatest powers and strengths. It also allows you to deeply feel the stillness in silence and eventually sense the stillness in the present and the richness in now. In one sense, it gives you emotional enlightenment that solidifies your imagination and releases your energy of enthusiasm, which brings you good and quality reasons to take action.

Effective communication flows within and around inspiration, and inspiration radiates from the mind and attracts positive energies, building creative powers and life forces that will brighten the light within you and around you. When you think creatively and act effectively, certainly it comes with vibrant energy, with life force, and with a positive spirit that consciously expresses the wholeness of the mind and heart. You will definitely perceive the positive spirit of enthusiasm and its passion and vitality. That's why it's a necessary bridge to success, progress, and development. It embodies necessary thinking and acting that leads to prosperity, health, happiness, and joy. For all real purposes, it's a creative, energy-based inspiration and motivation, a love and a passion that proudly support and provide you with a positive light that sparks your sense of sensibility and wonder and strengthen your sense of imagination. It's also a knowledge-based inspiration that comes from a positive perspective and a creative vision. Most important, your effective communication comes from a real knowledge, and real knowledge goes hand in hand with effective communication. It's a necessary way to construct power, a necessary design to achieve wealth, and a necessary avenue to fame. As a gateway to a positive life, it converts potential into material blessings and translates visions into physical reality. In the process, it becomes the legend of creativity that stimulates passionate actions, enhances the spirit of enthusiasm, and sparks more positive, productive actions that bring you multiple results.

Remember, every positive action lies in sound judgment, so effective communication depends on positive thinking, a constructive mental direction, a realistic self-confidence, and congruent action. It also depends on active faith and sound sense. Another thing to note is that all success begins with effective communication and finally rests there.

So if you are struggling and striving to achieve real and lasting success, it's important to remember that effective communication is a critical component of success. It is an important tool that serves all aspects of life, all areas of growth, and all fields of development.

CHAPTER 9

USEFUL KNOWLEDGE

The essence of knowledge is, having it, to use it.
— CONFUCIUS

There are people who know everything. They listen to everything; therefore, they accept everything that comes their way, eventually believe in everything, and at last they know nothing. As a result of loose living, they get uninspiring results, become unhappy, and finally turn their frustration, misery, and suffering into blaming their father, mother, teacher, or even their Creator. These are the people we all know as common people who have no useful knowledge. But at the other end of the spectrum, there are particular individuals who don't have to listen to everything because they know what they're looking for; therefore, they focus on what matters most, take what they need, and hear what they want to hear. These are the wise people who are emboldening useful knowledge that serves and supports their well-being. They know that useful knowledge enhances and enriches their lives.

As we focus on what matters most, we will certainly understand why useful knowledge is the main source of our power and strength that draws growth and success and enriches our lives.

When it comes to peace, useful knowledge is the power that guides lovable families; encourages well-behaved children; and brings us peace, happiness, and harmony in our homes and in our different environments.

As we believe and abide in it, we will greatly benefit from it because useful knowledge gives us the power to act and get quality results. That's why when it comes to freedom of choice, or independent action, security, and guidance, useful knowledge becomes mental equipment, a necessary human resource that produces positive psychological effects, supports our emotional well-being, and enables us to live civilized lives. This is the material embodiment of all reality, a spiritual acknowledgment of all facts, and a mental recognition and realization of all the truths that can make life worthwhile. Useful knowledge is an integral part of all successful life and brings us a collective attention and interest that enhances our minds and enriches our hearts. It's a faithful truth, a unity of spirit, and an energy of enthusiasm that brings us a self-confident disposition and an attitude of gratitude.

In the most basic sense, useful knowledge serves as the connection of truths that can get you real results and give you a strong emotional dependence. So if your emotional awareness and intelligence, spiritual strength, and mental power primarily come from useful knowledge, that means you're educated. It also means that you can achieve your goals in life.

But before achieving these goals, it's critical that you become highly aware of the power of useful knowledge because useful knowledge comes with creative power, and creative power is the language of the mind that brings you a more refined language of the heart and the body, eventually enhancing the goodness of the heart, mind, and body. It's connected with everything in real nature that defines everything in life, which explains why useful knowledge is a practical sense or a positive feeling that supports rational movement and logical action and eventually helps you get positive results.

As good as this may sound, useful knowledge is the mother of desire and the father of all necessity. In the most basic sense, it shows that most of us are where we are today because we either have useful knowledge or lack it. That's why emboldening useful knowledge is important in life, as well as in business. This is the real power that synchronizes the world of business commerce and brings better results. It's the best possible knowledge that provides us the greatest opportunities for advancement. As a result, it communicates the best insights, expresses the most logical solutions, and gives us workable plans that make great business successes happen. This is an appreciable value that enables us to make a huge, discernible impact on human development. Successful people often see the value of useful knowledge because it's a clear, observable substance of thoughts, ideas, feelings, and actions. Therefore, it's a harmonious association of senses that fosters creative innovation. It's an indispensable substance of the mind and heart. It's the strength that enables us to convert potentials into realities. It's also the power that lifts us from the level of positive thinking to the level of actualization. It yields valuable, prolific returns and abundance.

Basically, useful knowledge is the vehicle that enables great minds to climb the mountains of the unknown and even helps them see the uncharted future. Useful knowledge is clearly leading profitable lives, profitable businesses, and maintaining successful relationships. So to continue to grow, we must believe in it, and we must sense its inherent values because it's a perceivable reality, an inheritable value that comes with a legacy of passion and truth with a sustainable purpose and a memorable desire. As this happens, we will often experience the intuitive reasoning of the mind, heart, and body, because useful knowledge fosters a functional mind, a representational wisdom, and an excellent execution of intelligence that shows the noble reasons that ultimately turn real and useful knowledge into a unique skill. This is one of the most important reasons why insightful knowledge keeps both mind and body prepared for adequate, effective action.

This is the most significant value that is perceived in the absence of ignorance, just as light is perceived in the absence of darkness. That's why it's a creative sense, a perceptible reality, an undeniable truth, and a fact that proudly rules in your home as well as your business. It's also the driving force of motivation that enables you to produce multiple results so you can add more juice into an important relationship and get real results in business so you can work less and enjoy more life with less stress. Useful knowledge is a logical expression of the mind and the main intrinsic value of life that ensures success. It's the power behind your sense of security, self-worth, and confidence. It's also a transformational reality that comes from a synthetic understanding, a synthetic awareness, and a coordinated attention, which gives you real and lasting satisfaction because it's a continuously flowing movement, a steadily flowing innovation, and a source of effectively ascending ideas of the mind and heart.

These are significantly great ideas born from power because useful knowledge is a real power that comes from mental clarity, a sound mind, and a clear sense. It's also one of the most dependable sources of business success because it arises from a systematic development and exercise that provides you unlimited possibility, capacity, and potentiality. As a result, it gives you bundles of opportunities and hope and the courage to think correctly and act effectively to live wisely. Useful knowledge enables you to use your body to guide your mind. Additionally, it keeps your mental faculties alive and active. In the process, it enables you to see reality through your own eyes and helps you perceive truth through your own visual mind imaginative faculty. Useful knowledge provides you a symbolic wisdom and intelligence and a crystal-clear idea of what you want. It shapes truths, forms reality, and helps you design a meaningful destination that determines your desired results. In the process, it enables you to perceive truth, feel reality, and act on reality. In addition, it gives you a conventional wisdom to act consistently and produce consistent results.

Of course, this can be one of the enduring ironies of success and the key to acquiring useful knowledge, which mostly depends on your keen observation, conscious awareness, and profound understanding. Another basic fact is that useful knowledge guides your body, mind, and heart, and in the process, it motivates and inspires your creative spirit, your creative energy, and your imagination, which eventually supports other inspiring knowledge and makes new, insightful knowledge possible. Useful knowledge produces a strong spirit of enthusiasm and an active spirit of passion, inspiration, and motivation. As a result, it provides you a highly refined skill, positive energy, and the spirit of excellent performance. It also provides you with intellectual interest, integrity, and transparency.

Useful knowledge stimulates the mind and eventually enhances a creative imagination innovation, and a creative interest that brings you multiple results. And one by one, it opens the doors of opportunity to lead you to many favorable rooms of success and progress, health, and happiness. And moment by moment, you can see that useful knowledge is enhanced with power that's filled with passion, which is created by increasing value, formed to attract value, and eventually endowed with strength. So it provides you the power to make finer distinctions and quality choices and eventually becomes the principal source of power that yields multiple results through a diligent practice and profitable use. It's acquired by patient cultivation, diligent exercise, and consistent use. It's also acquired through perceptive analysis, logical observation, synthetic intelligence, and profound understanding.

The science and the art of useful knowledge lie in your mind and depend on your brain. Art enhances your mental faculties and increases your emotional awareness, which sharpens your unique skills and power of observation. The science of useful knowledge tunes you into your sensibilities and gives you the spirit of passion. Useful knowledge enables you to think more accurately, efficiently, and productively. As a result, it enables you to refine your sense of perception through diligent practice and exercise and through a diligent use of your mind and heart.

I believe in useful knowledge because as I experience life today and look back on my past, it enables me to see through my mind's eye and mental vision. It gives me the power and ability to control my mind and direct my perception. As a result, it keeps my mental faculties lively, maintains my emotional wisdom, and sharpens my mental vision. In addition, it improves my power of observation and awareness and helps me perceive reality in a new, better, and more productive way. As good as this might sound, useful knowledge exists in the mind and actively materializes into power, unified energy, and absolute purpose.

This means that any man or woman who actively lives in useful knowledge, conscious wisdom, and deep understanding will become an integral being. He or she becomes invaluable in any creative discipline. He or she brings an immeasurable intelligence to his or her personal life and to the life of others. Useful knowledge produces the most desirable individuals, the most promising and favorable minds, and the most profitable and successful people.

The high road to useful knowledge comes through a constructive application of your mind. It also comes through a practical reason, a practical idea, and diligent use of your mind. This is one of the most favorable means of achieving success, and I believe in it because it's the power that arises from conscious transformational thinking and acting. It's the power that needs active intelligence, an effective mind, and keen observation. It requires a conscious, synthetic wisdom and intelligence, a unified understanding, and a deep well of sound thoughts. It's a powerful knowledge that comes from a profound understanding, flows freely from a pure and open mind, and actively remains in the heart of an integral person, eventually resting on diligent use, careful application, and peaceful enjoyment.

As you learn step by step, you should know that useful knowledge arises from the visual systems in the most surprising and unexpected ways and builds value from the keenest minds through harmonious, intuitive reason; intuitive, creative awareness; and a self-realization of truth.

This is the birth of power that comes through conscious alertness, careful observation and consistent practice. This is also the principal source of power and the means through which divine power can be channeled into your life; therefore, this makes it a creative power that arises through conscious awareness, connection, transformation, or conscious observation and deep understanding. This further justifies the reason of the heart, mind, and body, which can make useful knowledge exist when your visual mind and material mind coincide and agree. This is the best possible way to move forward to accept the basic facts and believe in the truth, which can prove that useful knowledge is the power that exists within your mind, your heart, and your body in agreement with your thoughts, feelings, and actions. Basically, this is a profound truth that shows you why useful knowledge must be tested and practiced to determine its basic facts, powers, and strengths. This explains why it's a skillful power that emanates from an articulate style of knowing, an artistic pattern of understanding, and a skillful method of application. It also explains why it gives you the articulate possibilities of the mind, heart, and body.

The more you acquire useful knowledge, the more powerful you will become because useful knowledge serves as a prerequisite to intelligence. Therefore, it's invaluable to business success, progress, and development. In the most basic sense, it's a self-awareness of spirit and an inward reality of heart and an outward sensibility of mind, which represents a symbolic, logical expression, and a symbolic, rational disposition. Certainly, this is a power that comes from a transformational thinking, knowing, and understanding of life, which means that to acquire specific information that determines useful knowledge, you must sharpen your mind through practical expression and enhance your sensory stimuli through a well-heightened sense of awareness and keen observation.

Look closely at the many things that may influence your life. If you pay close attention to success, eventually you will realize that a negative word acts like a snake that bites and destroys its own tail and its own kind. On the other hand, you will realize that a positive word supports and enhances your life. Useful knowledge is the sum and substance of all positive words; it attracts success and enhances lives. As a result, it further inspires more positive words, realistic goals, and productive thoughts. It becomes a motivating factor that inspires positive thinking, which fosters innovation.

Most of us are not successful today because we lack useful knowledge. Of course, many people are poor today due to lack of skills as well. We should know that useful knowledge provides us with novel ideas, sound thoughts, and clear feelings. It also provides us valuable insights and new opportunities that bring us profitable changes in our lives as well as in our homes, businesses, and relationships. Useful knowledge absorbs mental ignorance and inner conflict, just as light absorbs darkness. Remember, when light comes, darkness disappears, so when useful knowledge arises, poverty vanishes.

Obviously, you need useful knowledge to accumulate wealth. Useful knowledge gives you a sense of balance, a mindful spirit, and the desire to achieve success. It also gives you a sense of receptivity, a sense of commitment, and a dedicated sense of purpose, which eventually gives you the conventional wisdom to act consistently and produce consistent results. In the process, it provides you a blueprint of the future that reflects the positive, visual images of your action, which opens the door of success and enables you to design your own life in your own way. In addition to a greater future, it gives you solutions to problems and an insightful awareness of future needs. So it actively enables you to understand, to experience, and to face situations. Most important, it leads you to a better understanding, to better future, and greater success.

To acquire useful knowledge, you must experience it, practice it, own it, manage it properly, and use it wisely. As you believe and abide in it, it will further provide you realistic goals, sound plans, proper strategies, and effective action. Your dramatically improved patterns of thinking and systems of judgment will support concrete and clear action. Useful knowledge will enable you to build and develop new and better ideas and receive positive feedback and useful experiences that will yield valuable returns, multiple rewards, and bountiful outcomes. In addition, it creates valuable friendships that will greatly enhance all of your business purposes, support your goals, and enrich your life.

Most people have general knowledge, but only a few individuals acquire useful knowledge that brings profitable changes and fruitful results. Basically, the solution to life rests on useful knowledge and is enhanced by acquiring useful experiences, increasing and contributing value, generating superior investments, and bringing multiple returns. Useful knowledge produces unique individuals with personal power and strength of character who purposely lead valuable lives, manage profitable businesses, and build successful relationships. These unique individuals have provided us useful knowledge about how we should be acting and the meaning for living. These people have embodied useful knowledge because it brings them real power, which brings them useful knowledge that serves and supports their well-being. Therefore, it's important to remember that when useful knowledge improves, life grows, inspiration sparks motivation, and passion increases. Fear of poverty vanishes, worry disappears, and success rises.

The logical question is, where does useful knowledge come from? In the most basic sense, useful knowledge comes through sound reason, rational thinking, and positive feeling; it also comes through intuition and gut feelings, keen observation and conscious awareness, and learning and understanding how to distinguish sounds and voices. In addition, useful knowledge arises from sound thoughts, from the roundtable of meaningful discussions that bring us wisdom, valuable experiences, and insights. The best possible way to a better future comes through useful skill. We should also know that the best possible means of enriching the positive tendencies of life is through a continuous pursuit of useful knowledge. Seeing reason as a means to an end will ultimately help us deeply understand that useful knowledge is the power that arises from a cognitive awareness and conscious observation, from careful attention, and from a sound mind, which shows why it's the creative power that reveals itself through empathic listening and careful probing. As we believe and abide in useful knowledge, we will certainly succeed because when we are well informed, it sparks creativity in any calling. As a result, it unfolds itself through polite and patient observation and eventually through logical interest and dedicated attention.

In the most profound sense, useful knowledge means actual power that represents uniqueness of purpose. It's our main source of power and the distribution solution in our lives. It helps us plant the seeds for a healthier and better future. Perhaps this is the best approach to life, which comes by emboldening useful knowledge that is enhanced with power and designed to attract value. This shows that we can succeed if we endeavor to succeed. Useful knowledge holds the power of all life-supporting factors, the power that unfolds truths that eventually reveals them through prompt decisions, positive feedback, sensory experiences, and careful observation.

The more one believes in useful knowledge, the more confident one becomes. It is a vital ingredient for a healthy body, a positive mind, and a healthy heart. Useful knowledge is the most effective vehicle through which divine inspiration can be channeled into productive use—and it comes through realization of truth.

The vital force that creates the path to success comes through useful knowledge because useful knowledge is useful experience, and useful experience is useful knowledge. We all have experienced different things in life. But do we have the power and strength to hold the train of thought that conveys useful knowledge? Basically, we should consider the fact that useful knowledge is the very essence of the power that holds the secrets of a meaningful life, a healthy life, and peace of mind. Of course, we should know that it's the power that reveals its treasures through visual observation, conscious awareness, and mental alertness.

Leading the way and guiding your purpose is the real function of useful knowledge because it arises through keen observation and self-awareness and rests on paying careful attention to detailed information. You can choose your decisions based on your knowledge because it gives you a well-concentrated attention, a properly concentrated effort, and a diligent mind. You can also choose your actions based on knowledge because it's the power that comes from acquiring a unique skill through self-training and self-development. You can finally choose your direction in life because it's the power that comes from patience, endurance, persistence, and determination to get the end results.

Useful knowledge is an important component of success in all creative disciplines. It's a vital ingredient of the mind and body. It's the power that unites all creative insights, all functional minds, and all practical ideas into a crystallized whole, into a unified field of power and energy. This also means that it's the power that stimulates your interest, crystallizes all your energies, and sparks positive actions. The very good thing about useful knowledge is that you can use it to improve your life because it's the best possible knowledge that communicates the best insights, expresses logical solutions, and brings you the most workable plans. As a result, it provides you a unified field of understanding and spiritual awareness. You can believe in useful knowledge because it enables you to plan your work and work your plan. It also enables you to love your work and work with love. Most important, you can live in wisdom and grow in useful knowledge because it provides you the meaning and purpose of living, working, and gathering more useful experiences, which bring you more success. It also brings you the most prolific life and the most effective mind through which you can greatly increase the value of your life and enables you to produce the best possible results.

Transforming your potential into wealth requires useful knowledge because useful knowledge produces sound ideas and a passionate spirit that enhances positive action. It also produces a strong chain of positive events and profitable values that serve your meaningful purposes and support your life, which communicates a real action and pronounces actual results. Therefore, you can now change your life because useful knowledge is the power that rests on the essential rules of success and constructive application, which are basically giving you the best possible power, strength, and efforts of mind and heart to transform your potential into wealth. Obviously, useful knowledge gives you real power and supports your emotional well-being so you can take real action that spells actual results. It also gives you a uniqueness of mind, precise feeling, and accurate thinking.

Here you can clearly see that the purpose of living and working is to acquire a unique skill and in the process gain positive experiences that will expand useful knowledge that offers you the chance to invest in yourself. The more you invest and believe in useful knowledge, the greater your chances of success. Because useful knowledge is endowed with the spirit of enthusiasm and enhanced with the spirit of passion, this increases your creative efforts, harmonizes a logical plan, enables reasonable action, and finally brings you success. As a result, it brings you a lifelong pattern of thought, learning experience, energy of enthusiasm, and inner vitality. Now you can experience a steady power supply because useful knowledge is the power that comes from a self-trained mind, a self-designed action, a self-developed knowledge, and a constructive mental disposition. You can better understand people because useful knowledge arises from unique skills and from a lifelong habit of thought and feeling of success. It's a creative power that comes from a system of development and accomplishment. It provides you material goodness and spiritual blessings and carefully delivers you to your destination. It frees you to choose your destination in life based on positive experience because it produces functional minds and successful individuals who are willing and able to climb to a greater mountain of success, development, and accomplishment. That's why it's a power that requires painstaking effort, patience, perseverance, tolerance, and flexibility.

Obviously, useful knowledge comes from the public libraries, the marketplace, positive environments, our places of worship, our homes, our schools, and our intuitive wisdom. It is the awareness of the presence of our true power that arises from our experimental verification of facts, sound ideas, and feelings. It is also awareness of wisdom and understanding of useful knowledge that comes from a well-coordinated system of observation, a synthetic understanding, and from the most comprehensive value. Basically, it's the power that comes from intensive study, with extra value added through intensive training and from careful observation and diligent practice.

Useful knowledge requires a careful, systematic analysis; good observational skills; and careful attention. It also requires practical experiences, emotional wisdom, and due diligence. You can overcome all your difficulties through useful knowledge because it conquers all the complexities of fear of poverty through one simple, positive move. That's why it's the power that closes the gap of ignorance, feelings of inferiority, fear of failure, fear of poverty, worry, and anxiety. Instead, it builds reliable bridges of self-confidence, self-trust, self-assurance, and self-reliance. Useful knowledge moves energy just as energy moves life. Remember, where life goes, energy flows, and where attention goes, life flows too. Where useful knowledge goes, power flows, and where power flows, attention goes. Let us all remember that useful knowledge is the power that delivers value and makes success happen. Of course, it's the main key that guides your life and the energy that draws positive attention into your life.

Every logical rule of reason has shown that you will succeed if you acquire a unique skill that makes better things happen. That's why useful knowledge is an important ingredient of success and the major tool you need to advance your skills, goals, and career. In the process, it helps you have an optimistic view of life. This shows why it serves as an important component of success in all creative efforts. This also explains why useful knowledge is the sum and substance of your smart decisions and the most comprehensive value you can use to advance your profession as well as your goals and dreams in life.

CHAPTER 10

A REASONABLE SELF-CONFIDENCE

Optimism is the faith that leads to achievement.
Nothing can be done without hope and confidence.
— HELEN KELLER

Life will bear whatever fruit you demand of it. It will reward you according to your ability to think and to reason and according to your beliefs. Everything I have experienced in life teaches me that truly knowing and believing in yourself is the essence of self-confidence, and self-confidence gives you the ability and power to make clear, sound judgments that enable you to achieve your aims and live a prosperous and peaceful life. It's a faith in yourself and in your ability to control, manage, and direct your own life in your own way.

A reasonable self-confidence arises from a positive self-image, positive thinking, and logical action. It's an attitude of self-reliance, a sense of self-assurance, and a feeling of self-trust. It's the belief in your personal strengths and power to perform. It's also a mental outlook on your talents and mental strengths to perform to win. Positive thinking, clear judgment, and sound feelings allow you to believe in your personal strengths and live your life in way that serves your best and highest interests. This means you're prepared and are ready, willing, and able to act. It also means that you have a sense of direction and control in your life.

However, to constantly grow in self-confidence, you must know the limit of your powers and be aware of your weaknesses. You must be prepared to bury your weaknesses and focus on your strengths so you can set realistic goals and have great expectations that express congruity in the purpose of all your desires. In addition, you must design effective ways to handle rejection and criticism.

Not only does reasonable self-confidence exist, but so does a low self-confidence. Low self-confidence is an unreasonable feeling that can trigger fear and self-doubt and even cause you to have a low self-image or low self-esteem, which can spark self-sabotaging behavior, loose living, self-doubt, and procrastination that leads to poverty. Believing and trusting in yourself and in your abilities is what you truly need to succeed in life.

The key to having reasonable self-confidence is mostly based on your type of knowledge, on your positive feedback and useful experiences, and it strictly relies on your clear perception and deep understanding. But you can't succeed in life without action, so knowledge is not enough; you must believe in your knowledge to use it, and you must practice your knowledge to feel its realities and powers.

Remember, the genesis of knowledge is perception. Perception is the way you feel about yourself and the way you see yourself. The way you think and see yourself will determine your level of self-esteem and confidence. The most significant fact to bear in mind about self-confidence is that it means seeing yourself in a positive way, regardless of any situation or negative circumstance surrounding you. Self-confidence makes you a hero and a warrior and requires you to know what you want in advance. It requires you to have a realistic plan for how to achieve your goals. Self-confidence is the guiding force that provides you meaning and direction in life. It's the passion that drives your goals, which rule your destiny. It governs your thoughts and influences your emotions to action. In spite of any difficult situation, self-confidence is driven by a passion to succeed and a desire to win. It's an internal attitude that manifests itself and naturally inspires and motivates you to action. This is the distinguishing factor between those who can succeed in life and those who may fail. Those who succeed feed on self-confidence because they know it serves and supports their unique purposes. They know that every business is guided and controlled by self-confidence. They also know that every relationship is ruled and determined by self-confidence, so they believe and abide in it, and it serves their unique purposes.

So what do you have to lose by having reasonable self-confidence? Absolutely nothing, but without reasonable self-confidence, you stand the chance to lose your privileges, ending important relationships and losing your properties, your right of ownership, your natural rights, and most important, your right to own your life and live in peace. This explains why some people are poor and others are rich. It further explains why some people are healthy and happy while others are sick and depressed. Having reasonable self-confidence is extremely important in almost every aspect of your life and is a critical part of your effective action. Almost everything you want and need in life requires realistic, reasonable self-confidence to enhance and support your overall well-being. Self-confidence provides you the greatest power and the best possible action that brings the best quality results.

By enhancing and developing your spirit of self-confidence, you can do wonders. You can change your life and improve your overall well-being. Specific factors are involved in developing a reasonable self-confidence. Here are twelve:

1. Your pattern of thinking and your body language must deliver the same message to your nervous system.
2. You must accept and affirm yourself in a positive way, regardless of what people might have previously thought about you.
3. You must maintain a positive attitude and surround yourself with positive people.
4. You must focus on your strengths and bury your weaknesses.
5. You must know yourself and be aware of your environment.
6. You must focus on what you want and concentrate on what matters most.
7. You must focus on what you want to hear.
8. You must know what you're looking for and where to find it.
9. You must define the boundary lines of acceptable or unacceptable behavior.
10. You must know your natural rights and also know how to communicate them respectfully.

11. You must have ability to say no.
12. You must focus on what matters most and what is most important to you.

Building a reasonable self-confidence takes daily practice and consistent action, and it requires patience. When you eventually build and maintain your self-confidence and take proper control of your emotions, self-confidence will certainly serve your utmost good. As a result, it will become an integral part of your mental attitude that calms your mind, consoles your spirit, absorbs your fear, relieves your worries, and pleases your soul. It will provide you bundles of hope that will enable you to charge your inner strength and inspire a passionate spirit of success. Most important, it will help you overcome procrastination that causes indecision, self-doubt, and fear of poverty, eventually helping you build a strong bridge to a greater life and better future.

Self-confidence allows you to enjoy more life with less stress. If you can't resolve your internal conflicts, it's because you lack self-confidence to handle situations. Self-confidence is a symbol of an authentic personhood, giving you strength and courage and enabling you to test your knowledge and faith in yourself. This will eventually help you check your congruity and encourage you to examine your faith in life, which will empower you to test your beliefs in the creative wisdom of eternity, which determines your future endeavors. Self-confidence is created in wisdom because it illuminates your mind and lights up your heart, which helps you build positive experiences to dissolve your mental ignorance and internal conflict. When your internal conflict dies due to lack of feeding and maintenance, self-confidence grows in power and strength. When your feelings of guilt fade like the darkness of nothingness, then your integrated wholeness will emanate like a light that shines from the universe.

Is that not what you truly need and want? We all need a reasonable self-confidence that stimulates our senses, empowers our minds, inspires our spirits of enthusiasm, and propels us into action. You need an indisputable self-confidence so you can value your potential and possibilities. Are these benefits not the best and highest value you can feel and the best quality you can taste in good faith? Self-confidence gives you the unwavering support you need to enhance the value of your life that supports the absoluteness of your purpose and helps you live in an active state and function from a dedicated sense of active purpose. As a result, it provides you the exact foundational blocks that clearly spell out success and the degree of your happiness. And that helps you connect strongly and link effectively with all positive, delightful emotions and joyful experiences that will enable you to act effectively and get more prolific results.

Because self-confidence is a source of power, it enables you to be more selective, communicate with the right words, and get the right answers. It further helps you ask useful questions and get valuable information. This useful information will provide you a common point of view, a centralized idea, and a similarity of purpose that draws a collective interest and committed attention that supports your overall well-being.

No wonder emboldening useful information is the most powerful factor and the strongest fusion of life—it gives you the key to self-confidence and provides you in-depth knowledge of what you truly want and a profound understanding of yourself. This is one way of learning and a clear way of understanding that provides you a consistent way to practice the right thinking that supports quality action. This is one good way to transport yourself from one level of thinking to another that supports your ability to bring positive changes into your life that come from the unwavering support of self-confidence. Because self-confidence is a pure spirit that allows you to know, understand, and recognize yourself. It clearly defines and identifies a person more than mere words. It enables you to push the right buttons at the right time, in the right place, and in the right direction to produce the right results, which fuels your desire and expands your consciousness. So you can achieve your purpose because the purpose of self-confidence is to support and enhance useful knowledge and promote your overall well-being. Remember that knowledge without self-confidence is an idle wish, and it will always result in nothingness and will always bring you down. This means that knowledge alone is not enough—using it to produce results is what makes a worthwhile life.

Feeling the purpose of self-confidence and having the end in mind will help you improve your life in different ways. In one sense, it will help you climb the uncharted mountain, explore new realities, and get new ideas that will bring you better understanding and greater opportunities. As a result, it will give you the power and strength to make prompt and concrete decisions that will help you embrace and effect positive change as an opportunity to advance your purposes. This is so because the use of self-confidence as a source of power will always bring you good that will enhance your overall well-being that will inspire the spirit of passion, enthusiasm, and courage to move forward for a better future and a greater life.

This is a central idea of a progressive tendency of the spirit of success because self-confidence motivates the positive spirit of enthusiasm. The more you trust yourself, the greater your self-confidence will be and the better you can understand and trust your gut feelings and inherent powers. This shows that self-confidence lies in your mental power and rests on your quality of mind, which makes your life more desirable and more valuable and yields more bountiful returns.

This explains the reasons for the endless creativity of self-confidence. It's the critical part of knowing that self-confidence provides you a steady flow of innovation and even enables you to function from a superior state of consciousness that expresses meaningful action and indicates a positive outcome. So you can achieve your goals because the more you live in harmony with yourself, the greater your power to act wisely will be. Self-confidence will be ignited by a sense of purpose and a strong conviction to win. This is one of the best ways to build a stable business and can be an effective way to build important relationships that serve profitable businesses. So once again, the more you believe in your ability, the more you will be motivated by passion to win and the more you will be propelled by inspiration to achieve a definite course.

There is no other way to greatness than building a reasonable self-confidence. A reasonable self-confidence provides you an inexhaustible ocean of power that can help you think correctly, perceive positive energies, and enable you to live in conscious awareness. As a result, it helps your mind focus on a definite direction and act constructively. It helps you sharpen your emotions that will greatly prepare your mind for mental readiness, for inner awareness and alertness of the present moment, and for physical actions.

In fact, all human excellence in any organization is properly guided by self-confidence, which enables us to control our emotions and direct the intensity of our actions. As a result, it gives us a clear and sound feeling that enables us to perceive the world through our own mental minds, which virtually grows and diversifies value and eventually becomes the vital force that creates a path to a constructive life and a personal power that comes from a constructive application of useful knowledge. It's the power that facilitates and supports our desirable condition and our emotional well-being that guides our daily lives.

Remember that all human collective functioning, which is marked by useful knowledge, is controlled and directed by the power of self-confidence because when the train of self-confidence arrives, power arrives, positive energy flows in our hearts, and happiness and peace naturally flood our minds. Therefore, self-confidence is a necessary human resource and development tool that gives us good mental and emotional health and promotes a general healthy condition in our homes, businesses, and environments.

Raising your self-confidence level will improve your life because self-confidence is the tool you need to advance your skills, your profession, and career and even can help you have a positive, optimistic view of life that serves your future goals. As you live in harmony with yourself, self-confidence becomes the sum and substance of your life. In the process, it enables you to make prompt decisions that will greatly improve the nobility of your purpose with consistent practice. As you focus on your definite purpose, you will certainly increase your level of self-confidence. You will even improve your self-esteem by rewarding and praising yourself for good efforts and success. As a result, you will increase your self-worth by recognizing that your past failures and negative experiences do not control your future. They can be altered and eventually transformed into success. In addition, you can also increase your self-confidence by controlling your intense emotions and by thinking logically and constructively. You can challenge yourself by making something you have previously thought to be impossible to be possible. So you must learn how to say no to any irrational request. Even if you stumble upon a difficult situation, don't be afraid, and don't even whine about it—use your brain to resolve the problem or ask someone for help. You must learn how to express your feelings, desires, and beliefs constructively.

In the most basic sense, self-confidence refers to how you feel about yourself and how you use your abilities. Therefore, it's a power of self-awareness that produces an empowering thought that governs your attitude and actions. As a result, it gives you the key to achieve great goals in life.

Everyone knows that self-confidence is essential in life and very important in your daily endeavors, but what is not clearly known is the degree of its importance and its inherent power. Self-confidence enables you to clearly see where you want to go and how to get there. It gives you self-discipline and self-control and helps you believe in yourself and in your abilities. Having success in life lies in self-confidence because it enhances your emotional and spiritual well-being. It increases the value of your life so you feel the positive visual images in your mind, and then gives you a self-expression of gratitude and appreciation that validates your life and improves your overall well-being. In addition, it gives you a cheerful disposition of mind that supports your well-being. Self-confidence enables you to properly use your environment as a field of opportunity, the place you can explore something new and rewarding.

Learning depends on self-confidence because you can't properly achieve your purpose in life if you don't have the strength and courage to move forward. You can't properly understand life if you don't have the ability to ask questions that will reveal the mysteries of life. A reasonable self-confidence determines the amount of space you will occupy in your small world, how well you will live there, and how well you will enjoy your life and be happy. The purposes of self-confidence are to synthesize useful knowledge and positive experiences, get reasonable feedback, and gain valuable skills that will promote your overall well-being and proudly support your purposes and actions.

Some people don't have self-confidence because their environments condition them to feel bad about themselves. Friends and associates condition them negatively and make them feel inferior and unworthy, or their parents are mentally blind and don't possess self-confidence of their own; therefore, these people are forced to grow up with negative beliefs and eventually end up with low self-confidence. They believed that was the way of life, so they learned to live with it, and as a result, it became part of their personalities. Now it's an innate pattern of thought that they constantly feed, resulting in a low self-confidence that denies them inner peace and happiness.

But any man or woman who recognizes the truth and is willing to change can live a much better life. The eyes, or the windows of the person's soul, will open wide and become brighter, enabling that person to breathe more active and dynamic oxygen that comes from the inner heart and inner mind.

Seeing the truth can be as important as believing in it, and believing the truth about self-confidence is what you need to set you free. Therefore, if you believe and abide in the consciousness of it, you will succeed in life because self-confidence gives you what you want, when you want it, and how you want it. It gives you a substantial evidence of truth, emotional intelligence, and mental strength. You can better understand others because self-confidence enables you to gather vital information that fosters creative understanding that brings you a desirable life. This is a personal power that comes from within consciousness because it's the oxygen for the breath of life. It's the essence of creative wisdom and intelligence and the nobility that serves and supports your mind and heart. So if you live in harmony with yourself, self-confidence will strongly connect all your delightful emotions and joyful experiences and empower you to live wisely. In addition, it will enable you to fully use all your mental faculties for greater purposes. It will help you properly adjust your attitude and balance your mind to perform so much better and produce much more effective results. This means that a reasonable self-confidence will enable you to gather and organize all the specific, useful information to make prompt and quality decisions that will support all of your meaningful purposes.

No wonder self-confidence is the property of the intellect and a major tool for people in all walks of life! You can think and believe in good faith because self-confidence is a mental power and a diligent expression of the mind and heart that determines the value of your life and the quality of your outcome.

Self-confidence plays a critical role in all creative endeavors and in all successful lives. It's an indispensable quality and inherent power that serves and supports our purposes, and in the process it enhances our lives. It enables us to pay undivided attention and give unwavering support to our unique purposes and goals in life. Self-confidence enables us to make diligent effort and be effective in the face of difficulty. As a result, it provides us a strong reason for action, an inner conviction to stay active, and a motivation for consistent action. It's an exchangeable value and leads to a mindful, respectful disposition.

Acknowledging that there are things you don't know will help you advance your knowledge, and seeing what you don't normally see will further help you expand and advance your ideas about yourself. So when it comes to learning and developing your ideas, self-confidence gives you the key to build useful knowledge that will advance your life. Believing in the power of self-confidence allows you to use your mind to direct your purpose and keep your brain on the course of action.

Having a reasonable self-confidence is the key to understanding people and achieving success. Self-confidence is the stronghold of the future that determines healthy behaviors that drive your destiny. It's the source of power and energy that supports your mind and guides your heart on the course of action to bring about the kinds of change that will help you live a healthier life. Self-confidence comes with a creative wisdom and guidance that rules the minds of valuable people. As a result, it opens a major gateway to perfection of skills that support and serve their purposes and enable them to use their indispensable power to enhance their goals, which reinforces their sense of self-confidence, willingness of the spirit, capability of the mind, and integrity of the heart. This is a reasonable self-confidence that guides a unique business purpose. So if you can think properly, you will realize that self-confidence is the power and oxygen of the mind that enhances your sensory systems and enriches a favorable condition of the mind and a desirable state of well-being that gives you a pleasant mental gratitude and appreciation of life.

This is the difference between those who have achieved success and those who have failed to accomplish their goals in life. Self-confidence enables reasonable individuals to build value, and therefore supports success. In the process, it gives them the power to escape undesirable and unpleasant conditions. So what is the difference between the winners and the losers? Self-confidence, of course. Winners believe they can perform. They also believe they were born to win, born to succeed, and born to be happy. But losers don't believe in their abilities and strength, so they allow negativity to dictate their future and therefore allow others to rule and control their destinies. They don't have the power to control their destinies because they don't have the spirit of self-confidence to rule their lives. They don't have enough strength to face reality. This is why I'm providing them the tools to help them build enough strength to believe in the power of self-confidence, which will greatly enrich their lives.

The key to enhancing your life and enriching your purpose comes through a reasonable self-confidence because self-confidence is the underlying power of purpose and a great way to enhance your business and improve the quality of your life. This explains why reasonable self-confidence plays a critical role in business success—it's the most important factor that clearly spells out success in advance and adequately represents a certainty of the mind and congruity of action. This basically means that a reasonable self-confidence provides you a supportive emotion that guides a spontaneous action. The sureness of the nervous system is what promotes your emotional well-being and serves a dependable and desirable condition that ignites effective action and brings you quality results. As a means of developing and supporting value, it gives you sound judgment that ultimately gives you the key to growth and success. This means that a reasonable self-confidence is the power that accelerates progressive development in any calling, and in the process, it provides you an active spirit of enthusiasm, a good element of heart, and a quality frame of mind. This can be achieved if you can develop a positive mental disposition and reflection of the mind and heart, which eventually enhances the power of purpose and guides a real, positive, and powerful attractive force that begins with the right thinking and depends on a logical consistency. Self-confidence is a creative thinking that is born out of a keen observation, or a thorough analysis, which of course is the root of all meaningful knowledge, all sound thought, all effective communication, and all the freedom of self-expression of the spirit of enthusiasm. This is the key that holds all businesses together and opens all doors to business opportunities. This is also a potential source for building a solid rapport and enhancing long-lasting relationships that allow you to gain access into other people's minds. Self-confidence is a strong, positive spirit that bonds, motivates, and empowers you to live a better life, which eventually enhances your future, because it's a product of ingenuity and congruity of the mind and a positive self-contemplation of the spirit of passion that helps you achieve all of your burning desires.

Self-confidence is extremely useful when it comes to growing your business and reaching your goals and dreams in life. As benefits in business motivate you to take action, self-confidence inspires and empowers you to take quality actions that will feed your purse and enrich your meaningful purposes. In addition, it provides you the ways and means of aligning your life and eventually achieving your goals and supporting your purposes. It also provides you a higher and a richer level of operation of the mind that will enable you to use your powers and strengths in the most active, productive ways possible. This helps you follow the right road that enriches your well-being and supports your life.

So whether you are seeking to succeed in business or planning to enhance your important relationships, self-confidence is the vehicle that drives all your emotional needs and delivers positive results based on useful knowledge. A sound mind and a reasonable heart come with a strong sense of conviction and realization of truths that will enable you to exercise your powers of thought and the freedom to choose your actions based on useful knowledge and profound understanding. Certainly, it will help you design and direct your life in positive ways because it's a life-enhancing purpose and a life-enriching thought that helps you maintain a positive personality. In the process, it enables you to live wisely and achieve great results.

By doing something you previously thought to be impossible, you can develop a new way of seeing reality. As a result, you can develop a clearer perception and a better vision. Most important, your belief will grow, your consciousness will expand, and your self-confidence will take its position. When a reasonable self-confidence takes its rightful position, you will become more specific and accurate, you will become more effective and efficient in business, and eventually you will become more productive in life. If you can take absolute control of your life, you can have outstanding positive results that will satisfy all of your heart's desires. However, before you can rightfully control and direct your life, you must first understand and believe in yourself and your ability to produce the results you need. This is why self-confidence enables you to live in self-discipline and a resourceful state of mind. In one sense, this shows that there is no permanent result without a permanent self-confidence, and there is no permanent success without a steady result. That's why self-confidence allows you to create a permanent success and ultimately enables you to have a permanent positive image and enjoy a much more desirable life.

Every careful thinker and doer has observed that self-confidence is an indispensable tool that unlocks potential powers of the mind. As a result, it naturally helps you fully use your potential. In addition, it helps you acquire full power and enjoy the complete blessings of the heart because self-confidence provides you the power of concentrated attention, undivided mind, and spontaneous action. This shows that self-confidence is the power that expresses soundness of mind, congruity of spirit, and integrity of heart and body.

The quality of your self-confidence will determine the quality of your life, and the quality of your life will determine the quality of your self-confidence. Self-confidence regulates your life, and in the process, it gives you the flexibility of mind that you need to handle business in daily life. It also gives you the freedom of choice you deserve to have to make better decisions that will serve your life. That's why a reasonable self-confidence puts you in an enabling state of mind, or in an empowering state that will help you make more quality decisions and take quality actions that will bring you more quality results. When your self-confidence is growing, you're growing, but when your self-confidence is fading, you're fading, too. This is the main reason self-confidence is a cooperative channel of blessings that provides you a useful life and a better future. As a result, it provides you all the vital fruits that will support your progressive life. In the process, it will help you control and direct your emotions to clear the way for a better future. In addition, self-confidence will give you the spirit of devotion and commitment in business success to foster your goals, give you the opportunity for future advancement, and ultimately give you the spirit of passion that provides your mind the oxygen of action, a dedicated sense of loyalty, and a pleasant disposition in all your profitable businesses and important relationships.

So keep all these facts in mind, and keep moving with self-confidence. You will see that self-confidence comes from a profound sense of understanding, and you will eventually realize that you are guided by a reasonable self-confidence that has a deep mental effect that enables you to see clearly where you're going and how you will get there. But before you get there, remember that your self-confidence is based on useful knowledge and eventually becomes a coordinated system of positive experiences, useful feedback, and sound ideas that enhance your life and enrich your purposes. The only way you can clearly see everything that happens within you and around you is through the filter of reasonable self-confidence that comes from mental harmony that passes through a dedicated sense of purpose, wisdom, and spontaneous action.

You will clearly seek and look, think and observe, and feel good and happy because self-confidence has a mystic charm and powerful magic. It will never fail to work, and if you think constructively and act wisely, self-confidence will be a unique refinery station that produces a miraculous outcome and draws an abundance of good that inspires creative efforts that motivate the mind, empowers the heart, and mobilizes optimistic spirits to render quality services. This eventually increases receptivity in the marketplace and ultimately increases sales in businesses because it's the power of a purposeful business that enhances your responsive mind and supplies energy to your inner drive.

Without self-confidence, all power fades, the center loses control, and expectation dies from lack of feeding. Today, if you look closely, you will find that many people are poor or have health issues because they lack the ability to ask useful questions that will enhance their well-being. As a result, they lack the ability to understand things from different levels and prevent negative situations. They lack self-confidence because they lack useful knowledge.

When you have self-confidence, you feel great pride and respect. As a result, self-confidence empowers you to see positive change as an exciting journey and a profitable opportunity to make great impact in life. That's what you need to grow in life. If you know how to make smart choices and better decisions, you will realize that self-confidence grows your mind, expands your knowledge, increases your wisdom, and enriches your heart. You will also know that self-confidence provides you a constructive atmosphere of peace, happiness, inner harmony, and success. This shows that it gives you the inner joy of justice and the freedom of self-expression of mind and heart. It also shows that it gives you the greatest desire and the broadest sense of expression of self-reliance, self-control, self-direction, and self-discipline.

Through an exciting experience and knowledge of self-confidence, you can now change your life through the ultimate power of self-reliance. In fact, every known principle of reason and logical sense clearly tells me that your major responsibility right now is to decide what you truly want in life. So if you can make a diligent effort to love with the passion to win, you will eventually conquer unreasonable, persistent fear and eliminate worry, anxiety, stress, and pain. Finally you will subdue the fear of failure that kills your goals, dreams, and ambitions in life.

Once again, remember that the road to self-confidence is a knowledge-based course, and it needs the ability to respond to stimuli and produce constant results that bring you positive changes in your life. Therefore, when it comes to making smart decisions and taking effective actions, a reasonable self-confidence provides you a constructive channel of expression that brings you constructive results, eternal peace, and inner joy. It's the power that comes from a pleasant mental attitude of gratitude and appreciation and the power that opens the windows of opportunity in your everyday endeavors.

In every situation you consciously encounter, you will stay connected as long as you continue to feed, maintain, and strengthen your self-confidence. Thus, it will continue to exist, and in that way you will never live in lack. As long as you continue to feed and empower your self-confidence, success will continue to exist, and progress will become a stream of prosperity consciousness. Self-confidence is what your mind truly wants, your heart really needs, and your body rightfully desires and deserves. Just as water is an inescapable need, self-confidence is an indispensable substance of the mind, heart, and body. It determines the best alternative plans and the best possible actions because it's the power that opens the trunk of knowledge that will lead you to succeed in life.

So your ability to act and succeed in life depends on self-confidence. When a reasonable self-confidence is born, success arises, progress comes, and power multiplies. Then poverty, pain, and suffering will disappear because self-confidence dissolves all your difficulties, just as light absorbs darkness. Remember, when light appears, darkness disappears into its native nothingness. Therefore, when self-confidence appears, ignorance disappears, and fear vanishes into oblivion.

If you truly want to succeed in life, you must hold the power of self-confidence and maintain your self-esteem, which increases your self-image. You must be well-guided by a reasonable logic. If you're not properly guided, someone may play mind games with you, which will eventually lower your self-confidence and allow that person to get what he or she wants. The most important thing to remember is that a reasonable self-confidence will always serve you well, but an unreasonable one will always lead you to fail. A reasonable self-confidence is what you need because it will always help you gain something beneficial.

Wise men and women are always the people pioneering the progressive tendency of self-confidence. They're the ones who enhance and enrich the positive spirit of self-confidence. They're also the ones praising and praying and thus believing in self-confidence. They live with the spirit of self-confidence, and the positive image lives within them and follows them around like a guard. Always they perceive and feel the invisible substance of the positive spirit of self-confidence, so they see the good pictures of certainty and assurance that enable them to live a proper life, stay strong in mind, and be effective in spirit. This shows that self-confidence is synchronizing the minds of successful people, helping them attract a steady flow of good that strengthens their faith and empowers their moral values and unique characters. This also shows that self-confidence provides them a protective ground for effectiveness and efficiency and prepares their minds for unexpected circumstances. It makes them more aware and knowledgeable individuals who can exploit new opportunities, create better customer service, and expand their economic resources.

Self-confidence is synchronizing the world of business commerce and guiding personal lives. It enables you to separate your business life from your personal life and gives you an outstanding quality of character and moral values that will increase your potential power and strength. In addition, it gives you the ultimate ability to enhance your mental and emotional strengths. You can clearly see the world through the eyes of the soul of self-confidence because it represents a unique value that produces a mechanism of ideas and actions that will greatly support the world of business commerce and make better things happen. You can also see the world through a logical method of approach and through a scientific method of a continuous growth, development, and accomplishment. This shows that a reasonable self-confidence is a rational conclusion that controls your destiny and determines your destiny from the beginning of your action. This means that a reasonable self-confidence is the creator and the mover of action. It is born of power and a spirit of self-confidence and grows in wisdom and understanding, becoming much stronger in power and capacity through consistent practice.

Of course, it requires consistent practice and a constant energy to sustain positive feelings that will enhance and enrich your business life as well as your personal life. So if you can adopt an effective method of approach, self-confidence will enable you to manage your feelings, thoughts, and ideas and greatly enhance your knowledge and wisdom. As you continue to adopt an efficient and effective pattern of approach, self-confidence will continue to produce effective results, and in the process, it will continue to produce people of outstanding values who will never give up and never fail. As a result, it encourages people of outstanding qualities to see failure as a learning experience and an opportunity to grow stronger, bigger, and better. As a measurement of self-improvement, self-confidence controls your behavior, directs your actions, and enables you to seek the best ways and means to produce better results. It improves and expands your beliefs and solidifies your convictions to drive your values and accomplish positive results. It will also enable you to take full advantage of your knowledge, thereby increasing your wisdom and understanding and effectively helping you practice your knowledge to determine its powers and values. In addition, it gives you the willingness of heart and the strength of mind that opens the doors of abundance of goodness that lifts you to a success consciousness and sparks your spirit of enthusiasm.

Seeing the reason can be as important as acting on it; people don't act if they lack self-confidence. To change your life, you must be able to act on your reasons for living. This can be your main source of security because self-confidence is the lever and the fulcrum that aligns your life and supports your daily actions. It's the power that balances your daily needs, and in the process, it supports all of your meaningful purposes. It's also a powerful camera that watches your mind and heart and enables you to clearly see the truth by looking into other people's eyes and to hear and understand the truth through your own ears and mind. In one sense, this provides you a roundtable of wisdom and understanding of life that enables you to exchange sound thoughts that will foster all your business purposes. In addition, it provides you solid and sound ideas that deal with substantial facts and authentic realities that arise from your inner revelation of truths, which will help you understand and use your mental powers and emotional strengths to generate positive results. Basically, self-confidence is an indisputable reality and an unmistakable power of a useful knowledge and conscious action that will produce multiple results.

Feeling the power of self-confidence and understanding the reason for thinking and acting can be one of the most valuable investments in your life. Self-confidence creates meaning and pronounces results, and in the process, it helps develop your self-image and support the best self within you that attracts the best things to you. When you take proper care of yourself, the certainty of your best self will automatically continue to serve your best needs, and your life will increase in value. Therefore, remember that your active belief is the main source from which your feelings of self-confidence flow. Without it, your best self is limited in power and could become a source of abuse.

So knowing your purpose in life can be as important as moving it forward. If you can carry the truths you know, hold on to your active beliefs, and have the end in mind, then self-confidence will become your best friend and the source of your personal power and strength. Self-confidence gives you unlimited potential energy that serves and supports your meaningful purposes, which represents your personal strength that guides your power of thought, thereby controlling your feelings and actions. As a result, it attracts your inflow of blessings, draws your inpouring riches of good, and brings you notable results. Life can be guided and controlled by self-confidence; therefore, it demands a better life, calls for a greater future, and expects positive results. This mind-set eventually increases your mental strength and enhances your emotional intelligence, which draws an abundance of good returns. So if you're actively seeking a better future and clearly looking for a better life, self-confidence will provide it because a growing self-knowledge inspires the spirit of enthusiasm that enriches your life.

So many people use self-confidence to advance their goals in all walks of life. Self-confidence is not something new; it's the creative power that was born in the beginning with the first positive words. Self-confidence unfolds our hidden powers and the potential possibilities of the future that will grow naturally with a positive attitude, constant practice, and self-discipline. It is the power source of all creative efforts that will eventually bring us highly refined intelligence.

Self-confidence enables our mental faculties to direct all positive energies into singleness of purpose to accomplish positive results. In the process, it empowers our mind, ignites our spirits of success, and gives us the spirit of passion to accomplish more and more desirable results. It becomes the light of life that brings courage and healing into our minds and hearts, which eventually enhances a positive mental condition that calms our minds, frees our hearts, and inspires our actions because it's a favorable state that sparks our hearts, inspires our goals, and motivates our spirits. This eventually gives rise to so much more because self-confidence provides us richness of mind and passion of heart, and it serves as an excellent guide for our souls. This is the magnetic power of knowledge that brings us a unified field of understanding. It's also the power that provides us a roundtable of wisdom and unified purpose, which produces a unified energy that sparks positive actions. As a result, it encourages active discipline that draws progressive efforts and germinates great minds. In the process, it helps us achieve great results. It's the power that enriches our minds, supports our emotional well-being, enhances our spiritual awareness, and serves our meaningful purposes. Eventually, it promotes our self-image, increases our self-worth, and expands our self-concepts.

When self-confidence naturally becomes an integral part of our spirits of success, we become magnets of positivity because self-confidence gives us a dedicated sense of purpose and commitment and the superiority of the mind that enables us to mobilize our greatest potentials and continuously think and act in conscious awareness. It also enables us to form an exact picture of what we truly want. In the process, it provides us well-disciplined minds and properly controlled spirits of enthusiasm, which allows us to reach our goals in a reasonable time frame. As a result, it enables us to experience the past, exploit the present circumstances, and advance into the future. That helps us gain a higher and broader point of view and gives us the inspiration to continue learning and growing in business.

Self-confidence produces capable minds that will consistently hum the melody of truths and produce high-quality thinking that leads us to ask penetrating questions, which can bring us higher-priority values and eventually support our unique skills and qualities. As we are working and striving to succeed, self-confidence gives us a strong sense of purpose and provides us a positive spirit of persistence and the determination to achieve our goals. It also provides us a unique mental disposition that enables us to build enough strength and courage to take the bull by the horns until we achieve our purposes. As a result, it enables us to live wisely, helps us act constructively, and rapidly helps us build more value and get enough power and strength to transform our lives for a better future and a greater purpose. So whether we want to build a business relationship or personal relationship, self-confidence greatly increases our value and provides us a unified field of knowledge that can give us the power that proves the fact of sameness, likeliness, and equality.

Every known rule of reason and logical sense will empower any wise person to accept these facts as true. When self-confidence gives us life, we must hold it with active faith because a reasonable self-confidence stays alive through creative intelligence, active faith, and consistent practice. This provides us a well-heightened sense of anticipation of greater good. Therefore, it serves as a mental enterprise that produces a supreme value and brings us a heightened sense of purpose and direction that enables us to cultivate and harvest prolific returns.

Once again, remember that self-confidence gives us the power that unfolds the mysteries of life, which gives us the ultimate strength to hold our secrets for a greater purpose. It's the power that arises from a practical mind, from a practical intelligence and wisdom, and ultimately from practical ideas. Furthermore, it's a sacrificial power of purpose that unites us with the divine intelligence and actively enables us to stay alive and breed more good. That's why a reasonable self-confidence demands diligent effort, quality frame of mind, and strength of character. Therefore, it's critical to know that self-confidence encourages self-reliance and supports positive action that reinforces our skills and strengthens our positive beliefs and strong convictions.

Self-confidence is a sensible reality and a perceptible fact that spells out our strong convictions and beliefs in life, which help us build stronger bridges to connect with others. It also enables us to burn the negative bridges that lead us to self-doubt, procrastination, fear, and poverty. If we can think constructively and act wisely, self-confidence will permanently enable us to eliminate all procrastination that kills our ambitions and goals in life and ultimately help us build the strong bridges that support our dreams and purposes in life. Here we can now see why self-confidence brings us the strong army of clear purpose and the guiding spirit of passion that makes all positive things happen.

As we think and act, let us all remember that we are questioned by life, and one way to respond is by developing a reasonable self-confidence that enriches our lives and boosts our purposes. Even as we continue to think and act constructively on our economic journeys, self-confidence will help us grow effectively in business because it plays a critical role in guiding the direction of our business endeavors. Just as procrastination kills our ambitions that foster creative innovations, self-confidence supports our goals and brings us the strongest armies of clarity of purpose, which changes situations, reduces complexity into simplicity, converts difficulties into blessings, and channels our ideas into sound thoughts and meaningful purposes. As we believe and abide in the consciousness of it, self-confidence strives to develop and augment our superior thoughts; it also strives to blind inferior ones, absorbing their negative powers and weakening all their negative purposes, thereby eliminating irrational fear. But the more one grows in useful knowledge and self-confidence, the fewer obstacles and hindrances one encounters. Let this serve as a valuable lesson, and most important, let us all know that we can succeed if we believe and abide in self-confidence. As a result, self-confidence will help us succeed because it's the power that refreshes our minds, redeems our hearts, and restores our hope. As an additional result, it transmutes our potential futures into physical realities, making positive things happen.

It has been scientifically proven that the more one accumulates useful knowledge, the more one grows in power, which ironically means that the more one looks at people's eyes, the more self-confident one becomes. In the most definite sense, we all know that to think positively is to feel positive energy, and to think negatively is to feel negative energy. This is the single most important factor that distinguishes a winner from a loser. A winner thinks positively and acts effectively to win, while a loser thinks negatively, feels inadequate, and acts unreasonably to lose. Therefore, what makes a winner win is that he or she thinks positively and acts with self-confidence.

So I believe, and you may believe too, that a reasonable self-confidence needs useful knowledge, positive affirmation, and useful expression that provide us a protective ground for solid action. It also needs a specific and thorough expression that opens more windows of opportunity for success and progress. That's why understanding yourself is so important in life. A reasonable self-confidence calls for a passionate spirit of enthusiasm, a courageous spirit, and conscious awareness. It also calls for a sense of humility and tolerance in business and a great sense of humor in business relationships.

In the most profound sense, this shows that everything in life balances through a business relationship, personal relationship, and deep understanding. Self-confidence provides us inner power and strength that influences our environments and helps us build valuable rapport with others so we can have access to enter and explore any valuable mind. The best part is that it fosters creative changes in our businesses, our relationships, and our homes and environments, and then it opens the doors of business opportunity one by one for a better life and a greater future. That's why self-confidence satisfies our hearts and helps us fully accept our responsibilities and properly face our challenges in life.

When the courage of self-confidence grows in our hearts, fear of failure disappears, poverty vanishes, and eventually we become naturally successful individuals. If we continue to maintain our lives, success will continue to grow in our minds, enrich our hearts, and inspire our lives.

Our lives will become perfect channels for riches and a high road to advance into the future of awesomeness and enrich others' lives.

Every healing in life begins with a reasonable self-confidence that comes from a self-realization of truth that consoles our hearts and enhances our minds to give us the best possible solutions. It shows us that everything is possible if we believe in the power of self-confidence, which becomes the power that draws personal values and blessings and brings us great benefits. Furthermore, it also shows us that it's the power that attracts great rewards and high incentives that foster creative innovations, which can kill fear of poverty, indecision, and procrastination that gets us into self-doubt, ignorance, and neglect. Self-confidence absorbs incongruity that kills our goals and ambitions, which may likely bring failure, poverty, and suffering into our lives. Obviously, all this shows us that self-confidence is a mental power that covers our deficiencies and weaknesses in life and enables us to feel better, more energetic, and more adequate in life. This also shows us that self-confidence is a mental disposition of perfect intelligence that brings us excellent passion and strong convictions. This further shows us that mental action, constructive behavior, accurate thinking, and a proper spirit of enthusiasm bring us perfect harmony in all our creative endeavors.

Therefore, consider the fact that there has been only one true mind, one true heart, one true body, and one true life, and all of this boils down to one realistic life that can be enhanced by a reasonable self-confidence. It holds our secrets, guides our minds, and carefully delivers us to our various destinations, helping us share useful information that fosters our businesses. As a result, it clears the road for good spirits and active energies to live and breed more quality results. In the process, it sharpens our awareness and observation and eventually helps us live in a delightful state in the present moment and get the best out of today. As we go deeply within ourselves, we should understand that self-confidence is a mind-set that produces a logical perfection and provides us an excellent use of our skills and talents. It also provides us a constructive mental energy that supports our emotions, inspires our minds, and produces multiple results. That's why it permits flexibility of mind that brings worthwhile changes in our businesses. Then it gives us the ability to move with clarity, intensity, and certainty and even helps us probe deeply into other minds, which typically produces powers that will strongly connect us like a strong chain of active force. As we continue to believe in the power, it will continue to provide us a reliable emotion and a sustainable channel of development, progress, and success. At some point, it will obviously show us that we need to think constructively and act responsibly to really create our best selves because a reasonable self-confidence is the principal source of all our blessings, the stream of all our happiness, the flood of all our peace, and the triumphant joy of our souls.

But before we can build on the momentum, let us remember that self-confidence comes from the soundness of mind and a crystal-clear idea that drives us toward absoluteness of purpose. It's the power that produces a logical excellence and a mental superiority that clearly defines our values and explicitly expresses our beliefs, our self-worth, and our self-concepts. It provides us the best reservoir of wisdom and the greatest preservation of intelligence that frees our minds from the limitation of worry and anxiety, fear and failure, indecision and self-doubt, and finally from procrastination that leads to poverty.

Seeing the reason for living and guiding the value is what matters most in life because self-confidence will provide us a protective ground that constitutes a solid foundation for a future action that will bring us better rewards and higher incentives. As a result, it will help us increase the degree of our interests in the marketplace. In addition, it will provide us the trust that builds up a higher degree of hope and excitement, thus providing us the trust that increases the degree of our interests in any harmonious business relationship. This is one striking aspect of realistic business success because self-confidence enhances a positive, optimistic spirit of success that provides us the trust that builds loyalty in our businesses and encourages voluntary actions when we strongly depend on self-confidence. It will continue to provide us a positive affirmation that inspires and motivates our minds and empowers our actions. As a result, it will convert positive energy into effective results that will enable us to stay ahead and use the advantage to seize any opportunity when it knocks. This will also help us convert our intentions into positive actions and eventually transform positive actions into productive results.

Once again, remember that lack of self-confidence kills trust and promotes fear that kills our goals and ambitions in life. Self-confidence is the key that holds our power that supports our innermost values and guides our direction in life. It's the power that is born with the self-realization of truth that shapes circumstances in our environments and then satisfies our daily needs and wants. It's the glue that binds our values, enables us to communicate our values, and hopefully enables us to receive all the benefits that will support our lives and growing businesses. Self-confidence is the birthplace of all meaningful purpose and the main power source of all actions that can effectively communicate value and faithfully represent value. It's a mental mechanism of sound thought that shapes situations and then conditions the mind to act in a certain way to bring certain results.

As a prerequisite to success in every arena of life, self-confidence requires a careful attention, persistent determination, and a ceaseless energy that produces a supreme quality and eventually generates positive outcomes and supports the creative drive in our personal and cooperative endeavors. As a result, it stimulates our interests and then provides us powerful insights that will support our well-being, create our beliefs, and then provide us the potential power that ignites positive actions and produces effective results. This shows that self-confidence is a personal belief that originated from the beginning and eventually became our pattern of thought, which crystallized into a habitual pattern of expression and then became the principal source of our energy production. This also shows that it's an effective channel of expression that provides us active emotions and the powers of reason. It supplies us the inflow of power and inner strength that enables us to stay calm and listen to the inner voice that comes from within. It ultimately helps us use that unique knowledge to pursue greatness and excellence. As important as this may sound, we should remember that self-confidence is a functional wisdom, an intuitive awareness of the present moment, and a magical evolution of a mindful action that comes from within our consciousness. It calls for a diligent application and therefore demands effective practice, practical ideas, internal freedom, and willingness to face reality and firmly fix the mind to accomplish a sound and clear purpose. Truly, it's a mental maturity that reveals our physical realities and leads us to a triumphant evolution of the mind.

Self-confidence is a powerful tool that you can use to enhance your own life as well as the lives of others. It's also a tool you can use to develop your own skill as well as the skills of others. Self-confidence has been used for years by people who have achieved success and by the people who are admired by others and inspire confidence in others. Every successful individual knows that all these facts are true. Every great person knows that self-confidence holds the key to a successful life. This is one of the main reasons so many people are rich, and as a result, they have healthy lives. But lack of self-confidence can also be part of the reason many people are poor, and as a result, they have health issues because they lack a sense of self-confidence to move forward in life. Most important, they don't have the ability and power to direct their lives or the inner drive to push their talents into a productive use because their traditional upbringing didn't permit them to enhance their self-confidence, so they ended up in poverty due to lack of enthusiasm and spirit of enterprise.

These are the people still undermining their own capabilities, potentialities, and inherent powers, thus leading to low self-confidence. To achieve success, they must do something quickly to restore their self-confidence. Once they're radiant with self-confidence, they can become more useful to themselves and much more valuable to the community at large.

The introduction of this subject at schools will have a direct impact on people from all walks of life. It will improve personal stability and self-assurance and instill a sense of self-reliance. In addition, it will enable students to make an extra effort to develop a reasonable self-confidence and a passionate spirit of enthusiasm in their curriculum. As a result, they will use reasonable self-confidence to breed useful knowledge and further use useful knowledge to breed self-confidence in the workforce. Most important, it will enable students to regain hope and integrate into society and make a greater commitment to excellence, honesty, integrity, and transparency. Their positive outlook and appearance will express a sense of self-confidence, self-worth, congruity, determination, active faith, and perseverance.

So if you believe in nobility, then you must admire, respect, and value a sense of self-confidence because it plays a vital role in the success of every professional career as well as in every personal relationship. In addition, it's a critical ingredient that serves your life and supports your purposes. This means that you must believe in self-confidence, think constructively, and act effectively. You must know yourself and believe in yourself to have the strength and courage to trust your abilities and inherent powers. So remember, the more self-confident you are, the more effective you will be. And for every organized sense of self-confidence, there is a multiple return. So if you trust yourself, then move yourself effectively to achieve your ultimate goals and purposes in life.

ABOUT THE AUTHOR

Charles Ajero is a professional real estate agent and author who has dedicated his life to helping others find their true purpose. He is a prolific thinker and doer and a social media guru of our time who is inspiring bright minds and desirable hearts and enriching valuable lives.

As a result, he has helped change people, inspired and transformed both young and old, and effectively used a powerful, positive, and lasting charisma to change many families and businesses.

As a man of transcendental reality and meaningful purpose, as well as a sought-after speaker, he has helped change people's belief systems, shifting their paradigms and helping them build new and better values.

Ajero is a man who was born to change the course of history that started during the Nigerian/Biafran civil war, when he lost his compassionate father, Dr. Stephen Ajero, who was killed by soldiers while treating sick and injured people.

He was born in the midst of war and in the midst of agony, pain, misery, and suffering. With the help of God, he survived and was inspired by pain and suffering to find a lasting solution to eradicate poverty.

www.ingramcontent.com/pod-product-compliance
Lightning Source LLC
Chambersburg PA
CBHW060843280326
41934CB00007B/904